Remembrance of Repasts

Remembrance of Repasts

An Anthropology of Food and Memory

DAVID E. SUTTON

Oxford • New York

First published in 2001 by
Berg
Editorial offices:
150 Cowley Road, Oxford, OX4 1JJ, UK
838 Broadway, Third Floor, New York, NY 10003-4812, USA

© Daivd E. Sutton 2001
Paperback edition reprinted 2006

Berg is the imprint of Oxford International Publishers Ltd.

Library of Congress Cataloging-in-Publication Data

A catalogue record for this book is available from the Library of Congress.

British Library Cataloguing-in-Publication Data

A catalogue record for this book is available from the British Library.

ISBN 1 85973 469 3 (Cloth)
      1 85973 474 X (Paper)

Typeset by JS Typesetting, Wellingborough, Northants.
Printed in the United Kingdom by 4edge Ltd, Hockley, Essex.
www.4edge.co.uk

To Max, the future cooker

Contents

Preface

This book is a study of the relationship between food and memory on the island of Kalymnos, Greece. It is an extension of my original research on Kalymnian historical consciousness, or the felt relevance of the past to the present (Sutton 1998). Although ethnographically focused, this book is not meant as an ethnography of food and social life on Kalymnos. Rather I hope to use grounded ethnography to consider issues of current theoretical concern. I believe that such a grounded and simultaneous consideration of the topics of food and memory will shed light on current diverse theoretical approaches, ranging from structure and history, to "embodiment," to consumption. This book will be successful if it casts some light on these issues while at the same time suggesting new and important questions for future ethnographic research.

It has been said that anthropologists often choose their fieldsites based on gustatory preferences, or more generally that the anthropologist and the community find each other, in the sense of a mutual attraction of interests and personality traits. This certainly proved the case in my own experience of the Greek islanders of Kalymnos in the Eastern Aegean. As a child I had been infected by my father's passion for cooking. The kitchen in our 9-room rent-controlled apartment in the Washington Heights neighborhood of New York City was for the most part not functionally discreet. Rather, it was spacious enough to house a large butcher block counter for chopping, and an old round oak table, where the vast majority of our meals were served even when friends and guests were present. This meant that the kitchen was a gathering place in the evening. It was where my father brought his colleagues/friends/students home on a regular basis to continue the day's work at the kitchen table. And work imperceptibly shifted to drinks and hors d'oeuvres as my mother returned home from teaching, and my parents and their friends discussed and argued about work and politics and shared jokes, while my father, sometimes my mother, and increasingly I myself, helped prepare the meal. After the meal discussion continued in the kitchen, as guests were usually assigned the task of dishes. It was only then, for coffee and dessert, that we sometimes moved to the living-room to listen to music on our old phonograph. The oversized living-room was also the place for special events: New Year's parties, where I would assist once again in the cooking and take pride in offering hors d'oeuvres to friends, even a humble blue cheese on crackers. Thus there was no question for me that eating was a pre-eminently social, as well as a pleasurable sensual activity, firmly integrated in, and perhaps even the center of, home life. But food also became my own peculiar mnemonic, as visits to my parent's friends always provided the hope for me of some new and interesting culinary treat. Thus when my parents would ask me, "Do you remember So-and-So?" whom we had met two years ago, my stock response was "What did we have for dinner?"

My own experience of learning to cook partook of both oral and written approaches. My main teacher was my father, a self-taught cook, (and experimental scientist by day) who would joke about the difficulty of getting the Syrian-Jewish recipes he remembered from childhood from his sister, who had learned cooking through a more traditional apprenticeship to her mother.

"When I ask her how much flour to put in, she says 'enough.' When I ask her how long it should bake, she says 'till it's done.'" Although he had a scientist's faith in trial-and-error and exact measurement, he also retained an "embodied" sensibility, perhaps from his own family background. I remember his recounting to me, in Talmudic fashion one night while we were getting dinner on, how he had once heard a noted chef asking his student what was his most important cooking implement. After due consideration, the student replied, "the whisk." The chef shook his head, and, eyes twinkling, said it was first, the nose, and then the tongue. Other influences included my maternal grandmother, Vera Woloshin, and later my adopted "aunt" Edith Low, a neighbor, Ruth Hamlin, and my wife, Bethany Rowe, who has joined me and often led me on new culinary adventures in recent years. In different ways they all taught me an embodied apprenticeship in cooking rather than the abstractions of recipes and precision, one of the issues I will be addressing in what follows.

From my first trip to Kalymnos, as a high school senior on a study-abroad program run by Nick Germanacos, I found Kalymnians who held a shared passion for discussing and sharing matters culinary. But it was the taste of Katerina Kardoulia's cooking above all that provided a small solace and a reminder of home that cemented our relationship early on. And I have her and her husband Yiorgos Kardoulias, their daughter and son-in-law Katina and Nikolas Mixas to thank for their long-lasting friendship and the many insights they have provided me into Kalymnian food practices, through their stories and recipes. Ageliki and Yiannis Roditis and their son Dimitris are also present on these pages, as the memories of the many meals Ageliki prepared in her kitchen for me (her "co-faster"). Special thanks to Yiannis for the use of his paintings. Nina and Manolis Papamikhalis and Nina's mother Irini also contributed greatly their time, insight and friendship. Nina and Ageliki deserve special thanks for keeping food diaries for me, and answering my many badgering questions. Julia and Michalis Koulias were gracious hosts during this project, and I had a number of enlightening discussions of food around their table.

Too many cooks rarely spoil the soup of ideas, and many people have influenced my writing through discussion, words of encouragement, and reading over various pieces of this manuscript. In England, Renée "Nona" Hirschon was a critical influence in helping me think this into a book. Much of the genesis of this book came during a post-doctoral fellowship (Democracy 2500) at St Peter's College, for which I gratefully thank the donor of the fellowship, the Master of St Peter's, John Barron, as well as the fellows at St Peter's College.

In Carbondale, the department of anthropology has been an unusually congenial setting in the world of academic tempests, and I thank my colleagues for the supportive atmosphere they have provided. Thanks to Andrew Hofling (who helped me ford linguistic waters) and Jonathan Hill, both of whom read and commented on drafts of this manuscript. Thanks to Ted Weeks, who invited me to present this project at the European Studies workshop at SIU. I also benefited from stimulating and rigorous discussion at the University of Illinois - Urbana/Champaign anthropology workshop. Thanks to Andy Orta, Matti Bunzl, Alma Gottlieb and in particular to Janet Dixon-Keller, who provided important leads and stimulating discussion of issues in cognitive/embodied anthropology.

My colleagues in Greek studies have stimulated me through their work and their comments, including Jane Cowan, Nick "Wiseguy" Doumanis, Yiannis Hamilakis, Laurie Hart, Michael Herzfeld (who remains unmatched among anthropological cooks), Susannah Hoffman, Margaret Kenna, Elia Petridou, Charles Stewart, and Vassiliki Yiakoumaki. Special thanks here to Dimitris Theodosopoulos and Elizabeth Kirtsoglou for going well beyond the call of ethnographic duty in sharing their stories of food-in-exile, and to Neni Panourgia for entertaining my long late-night phone calls over the details of *kolliva* and other questions of food theory and practice. Thanks to Vassiliki and Neni for their gracious help with pictures. I also gratefully acknowledge the technical assistance with pictures provided by Tony and Gregory Barrow and Jason Gonzalez.

A number of other people have read and commented on various drafts of this project. Thanks go to: Debbora Battaglia, Carol Counihan, Antonio Lauria and Steve Reyna, and to my Godmother, Paule Marshall, for helping me face my fear of "the blank screen." And of course to two mentors, Jim and Renate Fernandez, who have provided nourishing models of an anthropological thinking not lost in airy abstraction, but finding inspiration (and stimulating good taste) in a rich and tangy bowl of soup. Special thanks go to two people who overcame their inherent skepticism over my subject matter in order to dig in and read this manuscript with their usual critical care: Peter "food as fuel" Wogan, and my mother, Constance Sutton. Convincing them that food could be theoretically interesting set the bar high, and I am grateful for their challenge.

Kathryn Earle taught me that publishers are people too, and she and her staff at Berg have made the putting-together stage a fun, rather than just a necessary task. Finally, thanks to Erica Hill for her indexing.

My initial research on Kalymnos (1992–1993) was supported by the following granting agencies: The Fulbright–Hays Doctoral Dissertation Research Abroad Fellowship, The Dissertation Fellowship of the Joint Committee on Western Europe of the Social Science Research Council and the American Council of Learned Societies, and the Sigma-Xi Grants-in-aid-of-Research Program.

A part of chapter three was previously published in *Anthropology and Humanism Quarterly*, 25(2) under the title "Whole Foods: Revitalization Through Everyday Synesthetic Experience."

"A Proustian Moment" by Renate L. Fernandez

Introduction: A Proustian Anthropology?

The Remembered Octopus

"Food and memory? Why would anyone want to remember anything they had eaten?" This sardonic comment, made by an Oxford don, seemed to sum up the response when I presented a paper on the topic in 1996 at the department of anthropology at Oxford. Indeed, as I sat with my fellow gowned colleagues surrounded by all manner of forks and spoons, and experienced for myself the extreme emphasis on form over substance at Oxford High Table, where a profusion of potatoes and overboiled vegetables was presented and just as quickly whisked away, I realized that this comment was not at all out of place. And although my topic did not receive such derogation when I presented it to US anthropological audiences, neither was there the normal buzz of suggestions: "Oh, if you are studying that, you must read . . ." Instead, when I consulted with the person who was most focused on the issue of memory in the department of anthropology at the University of Chicago on possible sources on food and memory, the response was a hardly less sardonic "Try Proust!" My only encouragement came from colleagues working in Greece or other Mediterranean contexts, who would share with me their own anecdotes about tales of long-remembered meals.

And then there were the Kalymnians themselves . . . From the first time I visited Kalymnos as a high school senior on a study-abroad program, clues abounded to the connection that existed on the island between food and strategies of remembering. Kalymnian friends noted and continually mentioned my dislikes (my complaints about the predominance of eggs in our daily meals), as well as my penchant for their Kalymnian version of beef stew. But they not only noted, they remembered these likes and dislikes, and brought them up again on my return trips two and eight years later. So it was not a total surprise when I began fieldwork to hear the frequently phrased injunction: "Eat, in order to remember Kalymnos." I had my own ideas of what this meant, and had collected fieldwork stories in the exotic mode for the folks back home: from the sea urchins that I watched Kalymnians collect with their bare hands, open with a fork and eat live, to the octopus, pounded on the rocks and eaten fresh off the grill, to the roasted goat, whose severed head was dangled over mine when someone decided "playfully" to wake me from an afternoon nap. But there was a difference here, because my Kalymnian friends did not have such, from my perspective, "exotic" foods in mind. Any meal could potentially be the object of this injunction. And as the comment was repeated, I began to realize that this was not simply a suggestion made to a foreigner to take back culinary souvenirs of his stay along with the photographs, postcards, and in the case of Kalymnos, the ubiquitous sponges that are the more common objects of tourist expropriation from the island. *In telling me to use the transitory and repetitive act of eating as a medium for the more enduring act of remembering, they were, in fact, telling me to act like a Kalymnian.* As I listened to their own stories about the past, as part of my research project, which focused on the topic of historical consciousness, I began to realize the extent to which ordinary foods permeated their memories. This was evident in fifty-year-old tales of plump purple figs served to a fiancé return-migrant from the United States, as well as in more mundane stories that began "It was during the German occupation on Rhodes. I was eating a bag of apricots, when my friend Yiorgos came by and suggested we investigate the abandoned Jewish synagogue . . ." Did Kalymnians really remember such far-off incidental details of their lives as a bag of apricots? If not, what were the apricots doing in the story? As I thought about these issues, other questions began to swirl in my mind: concerning stories people would tell about their own food-related generosity, as well as the reverse, people claiming to steal fruit in memory of dead neighbors. And what about the memorials for the dead that center around the sharing of special foods? Was it the ordinary or the extraordinary meals that people claimed to remember, or perhaps something in between? As I began to think back over my fieldwork a whole battery of questions centering on food and memory posed themselves. But how could I contextualize these questions? Was there relevant theory to be consulted, or could I only "try Proust"?

"Scholarship-lite"?

Food itself seems to be a topic in ongoing search of legitimacy, as evidenced by a 1999 *Chronicle of Higher Education* article entitled "A Place at the Table," which refers to food studies as "a hot new field." This article, in fact, prompted an internet-sponsored discussion over whether food studies was a legitimate academic pursuit or "scholarship-lite." At least for anthropology, this may reflect the fact that, unlike other cultural domains, such as kinship, ritual and religion, exchange or politics, food does not have its own well-developed specialist terminology and tools of analysis. The uses and meanings of food can on the one hand seem trivial to those who live by the maxim "food as fuel," while on the other hand it seems a topic where "native exegesis" can be as perceptive as specialist knowledge, as indicated in the following quotation from a British father on the meaning of meals:

> I try to eat the evening meal with the household. My daughter doesn't comply. It's part of her attitude to food, her attitude to freedom. Generally she likes to please herself, eat what she likes. I've tried to persuade her eating isn't just about eating, it's a social situation (cited in Bell and Valentine 1997:83).

But perhaps the obviousness and taken-for-grantedness of food can provide focus for research in itself: the fact that the Oxford don found my topic absurd, while Greek and Italian colleagues instantly related to it, is in itself ethnographically interesting. Yet this obviousness can be deceptive as well, because food can hide powerful meanings and structures under the cloak of the mundane and the quotidian. Something as seemingly innocuous and salutary as the rise of micro-brewed beers and Starbucks in the United States in the 1990s, for example, can open a window on to shifting American economic and class structures. Beer and coffee, two of the most democratizing beverages in American society because of their cheapness, ubiquity, and homogeneity, have been transformed into badges of class distinction, as well as icons of the end of mass production and mass marketing. Drinking beer no longer need be an identification with "Joe six-pack," as urban professionals sip beer from wine glasses (the change in glassware is itself a symbol of the transformation in the status of beer; it used to be necessary to switch from beer to wine to mark your class distinction) at $9.00/six-pack. And the most humble act of American gift-giving, the offer of a cup of coffee ("Joe" once again), must now be prefaced by a discussion of preparation methods and bean origins.[1] The power of food here is to mask these class issues under the guise of "personal preference" and "matters of taste," the unquestioned baseline of our American economistic view of the world. Many other such examples of food's symbolic power can be adduced. Feeley-Harnik, in her study of biblical transformations of Passover, notes that the power of linking religion to dietary rules was in the simplicity of its message as contrasted to the arcana of scriptural interpretation: "Food seems to have been regarded as the most accessible, the best way of introducing ordinary mortals to the ineffable wisdom of God" (1994:166). Food, then, can carry hegemonic identities through its very ability to connect the mundane with the pleasurable and the necessary.[2]

Perhaps there is another reason that the topic of food is met with such raised eyebrows. That is that it seems for many in our culture to involve the baser senses, instincts and bodily functions, not suited for scholarly or "mental" pursuits. As anthropologists have argued (see below), there is a hierarchy of the senses in the dominant cultures of the West that ascribes vision to the more evolved cultures and taste and smell to "the primitive." Food is not generally seen as conducive to thought. It always has the potential, in our puritan-derived culture, to be labelled as a giving in to our "primitive" nature, the line between the gourmet and the glutton being seen as quite thin; and the injunction "don't eat like a pig" can be found on the lips of many a parent socializing their children into proper manners. Or as Jeanneret (1991:1) puts it aptly:

> All sorts of ideological barriers exist between sense and the senses, between intellectual activity and the consumption of natural produce. The head and the stomach are at odds . . . We have to choose whether to speak or to eat: we must not speak with our mouth full.

Food Memories

These very associations of food with "the primitive," as well as anthropologists' longstanding commitment to documenting the quotidian, the everyday, suggest some of the reasons that anthropology

---

1. On micro-breweries, see Bertsch 1997; on the rise of speciality coffee, see Frenkel 1998; Roseberry 1996.

2. For examples, see Allison 1991; Cowan 1991; Rasmussen 1996.

has traditionally been in the very forefront of food studies. Anthropological study of food can be traced back to the origins of the
discipline, witness the perceptive writings of Robertson-Smith on
commensality (see Meigs 1988, for a discussion). Since then, food has
appeared as a theme in diverse classics such as Morgan's (1950 [1876])
depiction of "Montezuma's dinner" as an example of primitive com-
munism, Boas's salmon recipes,[3] Radcliffe-Brown's discussion of food
and social sentiments among the Andaman Islanders (1948), Evans-
Pritchard's (1940) analysis of cow-time among the Nuer, Richards's
(1939) ethnography of nutrition, agriculture and social life among the
Bemba, and Lévi-Strauss's (1970) voluminous musings on things raw,
cooked and rotten. Anthropological work has produced a broad
consensus that food is about commensality – eating to make friends –
and competition – eating to make enemies. Food, in the view of both
Mary Douglas and those working on ethnicity, is a particularly good
"boundary marker," perhaps because it provides a potent symbol of
the ability to transform the outside into the inside. In more current
terminology food is about identity creation and maintenance, whether
that identity be national, ethnic, class or gender-based.[4] In the US
context food has also been shown to be about assimilation, and, for
the majority population, about "tasting the other." As Kalcik (1984:37)

3. That Boas was on the road to an anthropology of diverse sensory experience is
indicated in his broad treatment of aesthetics in *Primitive Art* (1927). For a discussion,
see Forrest (1988: 22ff.)

4. On food and ethnicity see Brown and Mussell 1984; on class see Bourdieu 1982;
Goody 1982; Rasmussen 1996; Sahlins 1976. On gender see Counihan 1999; Meigs 1992,
Allison 1991; Caplan 1994. Food has also been examined as a potent source of kinship
symbolism, because of its ability to create "shared substance." As Meigs puts it,
"Underlying the Hua understanding of food and food rules is a world view that
emphasizes relatedness. All organisms are linked in chains of mutual influence; borders
between bodies are permeable; . . . Through his or her continual acts of food exchange,
both as producer and as consumer, the individual is constituted as part of a physically
commingled and communal whole" (1988:354–5). Similarly, Carsten notes that for
Malays, "Food creates both persons in a physical sense and the substance – blood – by
which they are related to each other" (1995:224), thus echoing a point made in
Robertson-Smith's classic work on the *Religion of the Semites*: ". . . after the child is weaned,
his flesh and blood continue to be nourished and renewed by the food which he shares
with his commensals, so that commensality can be thought of (1) as confirming or
even (2) as constituting kinship in a very real sense" (cited in Meigs 1988:353).

wittily puts it, "The formula here seems to be 'not-so-strange food equals not-so-strange people' or perhaps, 'strange people but they sure can cook!'"[5]

Recent studies have focused on issues of power and hegemony. For example, Cowan notes how women are taught, in the Greek context, to consume sweet things as part of learning their "sweet" gendered disposition. She registers the difficulty of challenging the association of sweets with women, where to resist this formula is both to go against one's desire, and to make something out of what is perceived as "nothing": "The very triviality of many of the things people do . . . not only blocks them from consciousness, since they constitute acts of utter common sense, but also serves to trivialize any protest" (Cowan 1991:181). In other words, food must not be seen as providing meaning *only* through structure, through providing categories of clean and polluted, edible and inedible, as Mary Douglas has well illustrated, but also through the everyday practices that have increasingly come to our attention as part of anthropological interest in "hidden histories," the "practice of everyday life" and the "history of the present," to fold recent theoretical developments into a batter of catchphrases.

This ability of food to both generate subjective commentary and encode powerful meanings would seemingly make it ideal to wed to the topic of memory. Memory and its oft forgotten alter-ego "forgetting" generate popular interest and commentary while simultaneously encoding hidden meanings. Like food, memory is clearly linked to issues of identity: gender, class and other. Yet one roams far and wide in scholarly studies of food to find discussions of the perception of foods past. Feeley-Harnik (1994:xv) offers the following complaint:

> Across major differences, from *yada* to *gnosis*, the biblical writers emphatically insist on the mutuality of eating-speaking and remembering . . . Yet despite the prominence of this theme in the arts, the hints of similar

---

5. An earlier generation of food studies engaged in debates over material vs. symbolic approaches, "good to think" or "good to eat," while most people recognized the truth in both positions. Another version of this debate was between synchronic structural approaches (represented by Mary Douglas) and historico-materialist approaches (represented by Sidney Mintz, Jack Goody and Stephen Mennell in various forms). Once again, each position has its strengths and weaknesses, a fact attested to by Mintz's recent collection of essays (1996), which attempts to inject more "meaning" into his earlier approaches. But these debates, which stimulated the field earlier, seem to have run their course (for a review of the positions, see Wood 1994).

connections in ethnographic monographs (Trobriand Islanders locate memory in the stomach), and some attention to the memory-enhancing effects of acetylcholine and glucose in rats and elderly humans, there is surprisingly little research on this topic.

This in spite of the fact that it is evident to many that if "we are what we eat," then "we are what we ate" as well.[6] Recent concern with transnational identities has put the issue of nostalgia on the theoretical table.[7] Yet the obvious link of food and nostalgia has produced only some intriguing descriptive material (Bahloul 1996), and Hannerz's (1996:27) suggestive anecdote that the first thing a Swedish couple did after a trip to Borneo was to drink a glass of cold milk at their kitchen table: "Home is where that glass of cold milk is." And while Mennell, Mintz, and Goody have together injected a renewed interest in history into food studies, none of them has shown an interest in historical *consciousness*, or the understanding of people's subjective perceptions of foods past.[8]

The one writer who brings us close to a consideration of these issues is Mary Douglas, particularly in her work on "Deciphering the meal" (1971). While this work is known for its famous structuralist analysis of the meal as made up of A + 2B (meat and 2 vegetables), and the many algebraic elaborations that she cooks up on that basic formula, a second key insight she provides concerns not the structure within meals, but the relations between meals. She sees these relations as a system of repeated analogies. Each meal, to be a meal, must recall the

---

6. "We are What we Ate" is the title of a recent collection of short stories by various authors working in a Proustian vein (Winegardner 1997).

7. See for example, Appadurai (1996:66–85).

8. Mennell (1995) looks at changes in food practices and table manners in France and England over several centuries, arguing for a shift in manners in line with Norbert Elias's work on "the civilizing process" (Elias 1978). Mintz (1979, 1985) traces the production and consumption of sugar as a key site for examining the links between expanding capitalism and industrialization in Europe and colonialism in the New World. Goody uses a cross-cultural examination of food practices in Europe, Asia and Africa over time to argue for the relationship between production, social hierarchy and the differentiation of eating practices. Mennell has discussed the subject of perception of time in relation to food, using Elias's scheme to argue for a historical trend toward rationalization and quantification of time (1996). But this leads him to a consideration of changing time-allocation and "foresight" in relation to food, i.e. growing recognition of the after-effects of gluttony, rather than a focus on memory.

basic structure of other meals: "A meal stays in the category of meal only insofar as it carries this structure which allows the part to recall the whole" (1971:67). At the same time, ordinary quotidian meals "metonymically figure" the structure of celebratory or holiday meals, so that these meals simply elaborate the basic structure: A + 2B becomes 2A + 4B. There are significant patternings of meals as well: daily, weekly, and yearly cycles are the most obvious, but they can stretch out over the life-course as well. Because of this, Douglas argues that linguistic analysis is in fact often inappropriate to understanding meals: a sentence can be said in a minute, but a "food sentence" takes a lifetime to complete.

In her earlier work on Hebrew food taboos, Douglas argues that food is used to state repeatedly the message of purity, of the perfection of separated categories, which can be applied to religion, politics, or territorial boundaries (1971:76–7), much like Feeley-Harnik's argument about identity above. But this argument partakes of a more static structuralism current in the early–mid-1970s: thus its resonance with Sahlins's (1976) discussion of US food taboos and class eating practices. But in later work, Douglas develops this other, more temporal perspective: she sees the message of meals to be in their power to represent experiences of time, development or evolution: "To treat food in its ritual aspect is to take account of its long spun out temporal processes. It is an evolving system that can be a metaphor for any other evolution, great or small, the evolution of just one marriage, and even of the whole human species" (1982:115). Further, in her discussion of meals as metaphor and metonymy she seems to prefigure some of the tools used to infuse structuralist approaches with history: history as "paradigmatic" repetitions of key themes ("History repeats itself") or as "syntagmatic" chains of events ("One damned thing after another").[9] It seems a shame, indeed, that these different structuralisms, of food and of the past, were not brought into conjuncture, even in recent explorations of the seemingly fateful voyages of Captain Cook on his ship the *Endeavour*. One only has to wonder how history would have been different if Captain Cook had not insisted on including sauerkraut among his provisions: his voyage might have been prematurely cut short by a bout of scurvy (see Lust 1998). Perhaps this theoretical omission is soon to be rectified: it is encouraging that the revisionist Obeyesekere refers to his own recent endeavor as his "cook book" (1995:169).

9. See for example, Sahlins 1981; Hanson 1983, and the collected essays in Ohnuki-Tierney 1990 for illustrative examples of this type of anthropological approach to history.

Among anthropologists of food, then, Douglas seems to take us the furthest into issues of memory. And yet what tends to be neglected in her argument is a remembering subject. Thus we are presented with meals as metonyms, "recalling" other meals, "carrying the meaning" of other meals, rather than people remembering what they have eaten. Yet elsewhere she praises Maurice Halbwach's view of memory as working by drawing on external stimuli which helps us to renew past experiences: "We remember when some new memory helps us to piece together small, scattered, and indistinct bits of the past" (1982: 258). This seems a perfect description of the parts that Douglas sees as recalling the whole of other meals. But if Douglas did not make the connection fully explicit, her work still provides the best guidepost in the literature on food to experiences of temporality, and we will return to these insights into parts and wholes, patterns and structures, metaphors and metonyms and missing structuralist approaches to history, in considering the work of remembering meals on Kalymnos.

If we approach things from the other direction, and turn to the literature on memory in anthropology for discussions of food, we find suggestive paths leading to similar surprising silences. Memory is a much more recent anthropological topic than food. By and large, anthropologists have been interested in the active, rather than the passive nature of memory. That is, in the fact that memories are not simply stored images drawn out of the brain at appropriate intervals, but are very much formed as an interaction between the past and the present, a point made by those working on memory in a number of different disciplines.[10] To quote Lambek and Antze (1998:xxix): "Identity is not composed of a fixed set of memories but lies in the dialectical, ceaseless activity of remembering and forgetting, assimilating and discarding."

Anthropological interest in memory develops concurrently with anthropological interest in nationalism, since the mid-1980s. Anthropologists have been attentive to questions of what is publicly memorialized in writing and other official sources, as part of state projects of

10. See for example, Murphy 1986 and Comaroff and Comaroff 1992 on the way memory uses tropes to condense and recontextualize experiences and meanings; see also Carr 1986 for a philosophical discussion of the relation between group existence and a group story; see also Sacks's (1995:172ff.) discussion of the work of Bartlett and others in cognitive psychology. As he cites Bartlett: "Remembering is not the re-excitation of innumerable fixed, lifeless and fragmentary traces. It is an imaginative reconstruction, or construction, built out of the relation of our attitude towards a whole active mass of organized past reactions or experience."

constructing national identities. They have also been attentive to counter-memories, that is, what is left out of official histories and can be reclaimed through the traditional anthropological recourse to oral sources. As Lambek and Antze (1998:xvi) phrase the issue: "the past and its retrieval in memory hold a curious place in our identities, one that simultaneously stabilizes those identities in continuity and threatens to disrupt them."

Thus there has been considerable attention paid to the *content* of memories, especially in political contexts. Somewhat less attention has been paid to the *form* of memories, and how these forms might be culturally shaped.[11] This is what makes Paul Connerton's book *How Societies Remember* (1989) such a touchstone for recent studies of memory. Connerton's slim volume is indeed often the *only* reference provided by anthropologists in their discussions of memory (see, for example, Stoller 1995; A. Strathern 1996). It is because he focuses attention on the question of *How*, rather than *What*, that he has proved so useful to those approaching these latter questions. Indeed, one could say that Paul Connerton's book *How Societies Remember* stands to memory as Anderson's *Imagined Communities* stands to nationalism in anthropology (interesting that both books are written by non-anthropologists). Connerton revives Halbwachs's concern with the group spaces and places of memory, that is, certain culturally determined foci for memorial practices, such as religious ceremonies. As he argues, Halbwachs focuses attention on the social spaces of memory and the "mental landmarks" of the group. Anthropologists have taken off from this, and from the work of Pierre Nora,[12] to examine culturally constructed

11. See Stoler and Strassler (2000) for a critique of the focus on "event-centered memory" in post-colonial studies that assume that "subaltern" memories that will challenge colonial histories are there waiting to be tapped. Stoler and Strassler suggest that an attention to the form of memories – often non-narrative and focused on sensory experience – provides a more complex picture.

12. Nora has edited several volumes on history and memory in France. The English translation of the introduction to these works provides a useful entry point (Nora 1989). While he has worked with the concept of spaces of memory (*lieux de memoire*), he has also been criticized for his evolutionary perspective on traditional and modern societies (i.e., the idea that modern societies have marked out spaces of memory because they no longer inhabit landscapes of memory (*milieux de memoire*).) While Nora's phrases are evocative, they make a too radical break between worlds of tradition and modernity. As Lambek and Antze (1998:xv) note: "It is unlikely that there ever were untroubled, homogeneous *milieux de memoire*, worlds of pure habit . . . or that such *milieux* were not characterized by specific formulations of memory in their own right."

memory sites such as landscapes (Kuchler 1993), boundary markers (Rappaport 1994) or particular ceremonial or personal objects (Parmentier 1987; Hoskins 1998). Food, we could posit, might be such an object or place for memory practices in certain societies and not others, and ethnographic work is beginning to describe the contours of such sites of food memories (Bahloul 1996; Battaglia 1990), though this work remains part of larger works on "the architecture of memory" or "memory and personhood" rather than the foci of studies in their own right.

But Connerton further argues that Halbwachs is less clear concerning the "actual acts of transfer that make remembering in common possible" (Connerton 1989:39). Or as Tonkin puts it, Halbwachs becomes vague on the question of socialization itself, seeing it as a passive process of reception of cultural materials rather than an active appropriation, a problem that has long bedevilled social theory more generally.[13] Lambek makes a similar point in arguing that we must pay more attention to different societies' "cultural means of inscription, storage and access" (1998:238). Lambek notes the more objectifying storage mechanisms in the West, based on the technology of film and photography, which go along with our passive and individualized view of memory (1998:238–9). One thinks, for example, of soap operas, in which memory is depicted as scenes replayed from previous episodes with echoey music in the background. This is an example of what Lambek sees as characteristic of Western memory production, which "freeze[s] words and images, . . . put[s] frames around them; and . . . render[s] remembering mechanical and impersonal" (1998:238). Contrast this to other cultural memory production that stresses the way memory is created "between people."

A less visualist approach to memory also means following Connerton in moving us away from understanding memory, and culture itself, in terms of written, or textual models. He notes that such "inscribing practices" exist, but argues that hermeneutics has given too much attention to them at the expense of what he calls "incorporating practices." Thus he is much closer to Turner's view of culture as performance than Geertz's culture as text. In focusing on performance, he wants to see a different type of memory at work than that which we call "semantic," i.e., knowledge of how to do something. Thus he

---

13. See Tonkin 1992:105ff. Recent work on socialization and cultural theory includes Gottlieb 1998; Pallson 1994; Schieffelin 1990 and Toren 1993.

coins the term "habit memory" for this more embodied view of ritual performance:

> An image of the past, even in the form of a master narrative, is conveyed and sustained by ritual performances. And this means that what is remembered in commemorative ceremonies is something in addition to a collectively organized variant of personal or cognitive memory. For if ceremonies are to work for their participants, if they are to be persuasive to them, then those participants must not be simply cognitively competent to execute the performance; they must be habituated to those performances. This habituation is to be found . . . in the bodily substrate of the performance (1989:70–1).

Connerton does not want to dismiss narrative or textual memories, and neither will I do so in my subsequent analysis. However, he draws our attention to the importance of these other types of memories that can be found "sedimented in the body," in a way similar to what Bourdieu, always cryptically, refers to as "bodily hexis" or the work of culture through time on posture, gesture and other bodily practices.[14] The corset, for example, does not simply symbolize female constriction, but actually "moulds" the female body to produce certain behaviors and to associate certain habits as being natural and proper (1989:34–5). Strathern notes that manners at High Table act similarly to symbolize class differences and to resocialize the body through ceremony into the naturalness of these proprieties and the difference that they symbolize (1996:33). Thus we are close to Cowan's analysis of gender and sweetness here, but with the added component of memory made explicit. Once again, it would seem profitable to draw out how food might play into these types of memories, which are more embodied than verbal or textual. In other words, in exploring the question of why Kalymnians insist that I "eat in order to remember" I am drawn to issues of how this process of ingestion takes place, how sensory experience and cognitive processes can be analyzed in understanding the evocative power of Yiannis's apricots.

In framing collective memory in this way Connerton contributes to current anthropological concerns with "embodiment" and a related literature concerning "the anthropology of the senses." These writers wish to overcome the "visualist bias" in anthropology and Western

---

14. For a comparison of Connerton and Bourdieu in relation to embodiment and habit memory, see Strathern 1996: Chapter 3.

culture more generally by avoiding Cartesian dualisms of mind and body, expressed in symbolic approaches that reduce varied behavior to "texts" that contain or symbolize linguistic meanings. Thus in the view of Csordas (1994:10 ff.) much work focused on "the body" such as that of Douglas (1966) simply reads the body "semiotically" rather than attempting to get at "embodied experience." Such an experiential approach would not privilege mental constructions, but would see the interrelation of cognition and bodily experiences, a "mindful body" as Strathern (1996) calls it. Parallel work by Fernandez (1986) and Lakoff and Johnson (1999) has looked at the way language itself, through the use of metaphor, is deeply shaped by basic bodily experiences such as balancing, and cultural experiences such as farming or forestry. These insights lead to an attempt to recover and evoke such experience ethnographically. Once again, note that they do not lead to a rejection of symbolic or textual approaches *in toto*, but rather constitute an attempt to supplement such approaches: "The point of elaborating a paradigm of embodiment is . . . not to supplant textuality but to offer it a dialectical partner" (Csordas 1994:12). Similarly Jackson's phenomenological approach still gives centrality to narrative, but "acknowledge[s] that discourse always belongs to a context of worldly interests and influences" grounded in "the sentient life of individuals interacting with objects and with others in the quotidian world" (1989:18). Jackson exhorts us as ethnographers to "not forget the taste of Proust's *petite madeleine*, nor music, nor dance, nor the sharing of food, the smell of bodies, the touch of hands" (1989:11). Here phenomenology joins with the "anthropology of the senses," and the work of Howes, Classen and Synnott among others, which redirects our attention to "the shifting sensorium," i.e., to the ways that societies divide up the work of the senses differently to "make sense of the world," again criticizing the visualist bias that they see as dominant in Western societies.[15] As Classen (1997:401) summarizes: "It is the task of the scholar to uncover the distinctions and interrelationships of sensory meaning and practice particular to a culture." This task is seen as political as well as intellectual, since, as Classen argues, Western focus on the visual involved a hierarchy of the senses, whereby the "lower" senses of taste and smell

---

15. To cite Howes (1991:4): "The anthropology of the senses is primarily concerned with how the patterning of sense experience varies from one culture to the next in accordance with the meaning and emphasis attached to each of the senses . . . only by developing a rigorous awareness of the visual and textual biases of the Western episteme [can we] hope to make sense of how life is lived in other cultural settings."

were assigned in evolutionary fashion to the "lower races" of mankind. In revaluing other sensory modes, anthropologists challenge this hierarchy.[16]

As yet those who see themselves working on the anthropology of the senses have focused mainly on smell, hearing, and to a lesser extent movement, with least attention given to taste.[17] This literature also has not yet given much attention to memory, despite its popular status as "sixth sense" in Western culture.[18] Stoller and Seremetakis provide exceptions here. Stoller's title *Embodying Colonial Memories* captures his project of describing non-textualized counter-memories among the Songhay of Niger. Once again, he cautions against transforming the body into a text: "For in its textualization the body is robbed of its movements, odors, tastes, sounds – its sensibilities, all of which are potent conveyors of meaning and memory" (1995:30).[19] Stoller's focus is on spirit possession and dance, and unfortunately he does not touch on food, despite an earlier interest in sauce as social action (1989).

16. Relevant here also is recent work on "materiality" from a Marxist perspective, such as Stallybrass's account of the development of the concept of fetishism in the West to describe non-Westerners' fixation on "trifles," or other objects seen as valueless to the Western mind inculcated into the ultimate values of market profit: "What was demonized in the concept of the fetish was the possibility that history, memory, and desire might be materialized in objects that are touched and loved and worn" (Stallybrass 1998:186). Pels (1998) also argues for a re-evaluation of fetishism and "materiality" in terms of a less symbolic and representational approach to objects. As he puts it: "the 'material' is not necessarily on the receiving end of plastic power, a *tabula rasa* on which signification is conferred by humans: Not only are humans as material as the material that they mold, but humans themselves are molded, through their sensuousness, by the 'dead' matter with which they are surrounded" (1998:100–1). On fetishism and materiality, see also Cohen (1997).

17. On smell see Bubant 1998; Classen, Howes and Synnott 1994; Corbin 1986; Rasmussen 1999; and for a harbinger of this approach see Gell 1977. On hearing see Feld 1982, and on movement Farnell 1994. An exception on taste is the work of Howes and Lalonde (1991), which plays on the double meanings of taste in Western society, and suggests historical reasons for its development, without however examining the actual experience of taste ethnographically.

18. Indeed, memory is not mentioned in Classen's recent review of the field of sensory anthropology (1997), despite her discussion of the works of Stoller and Seremetakis.

19. Some oral historians have been sensitized to such concerns. Even in narrative accounts, Chamberlain (1995) argues that Barbadian men tend to tell their life stories in terms of facts and figures, whereas women focus more on textures and sensory qualities, which convey important information, at times "counter-memories."

Seremetakis, working in the Peloponnese region of Southern Greece – the place where her ancestors came from – captures counter-memories, but of a very specific kind: the 'sensory-perceptual dispositions' embedded in objects such as peaches and other agricultural products, and in gestures such as the drinking of the morning cup of coffee. They are counter-memories in part because they are, according to Seremetakis, under threat from the consumerization of Greek society, and also because they challenge Western epistemologies along the lines noted above by Jackson and Csordas: "sensory semantics in Greek culture . . . contain regional epistemologies, inbuilt theories, that provoke important cross-cultural methodological consequences" (1994:5). Seremetakis' short essay is a cross-sensory exploration of the materiality of Greek culture, captured in gestures such as picking greens in her fieldwork village (which also happened to be her home village), and suddenly recognizing the body memory involved in this gesture: "I had tasted them [growing up in New York City] . . . and I had heard all kinds of talks around them. When I went out to collect them, the sensory memory of taste, order, orality stored in the body was transferred to vision and tactility. My body involuntarily knew what I consciously did not" (1994:16). Thus her approach brings together themes of embodiment, habit memory, socialization, tradition and modernity, historical consciousness, the senses and memory around the collection, cooking and eating of food. As such she provides a guidepost for several of the kind of issues I wish to raise here, and I will have occasion to discuss her work again in subsequent chapters. For the moment I take what I imagine her response might have been to that Oxford don (or my own, if I had been quicker): Why food and memory? Because whole worlds of experience and interpretation are contained therein!

In summary, because the topic of food and memory is indeed unexplored in anthropology, I plan to be fairly eclectic in suggesting possible paths and theoretical approaches, illustrated primarily through my Kalymnian material, that might productively begin this exploration. My approach will be to use food to address some of the *formal* issues of memory processes that have been usefully raised by recent work on embodiment and the senses, while at the same time suggesting some other neglected avenues. At the same time I will be using memory to energize studies of 'food past,' by explicitly adding the question of historical consciousness to work that looks at food in terms of ritual and everyday uses, that looks at histories (of production and consumption) and identities (ethnic, gender and other). Food and memory, I argue, provide a space both for extending current theoretical approaches into new ethnographic contexts and for productively creating new theoretical tools and combinations.

Plan of the Book

In Chapter 1 I investigate the venerable anthropological topic of ritual, and the way that ritual and everyday contexts of eating echo and mutually reinforce each other. Thus I begin with a consideration of some of the everyday contexts in which food is bought, prepared and consumed on Kalymnos, giving a sense of how food structures both daily routines, and more long-term rhythms represented by seasonal harvests, feasts and fasts, and life-cycle markers, particularly death. Food structures temporal rhythms not just objectively, by placing constraints on people's lives, but also subjectively, as people actively look forward to meals while at the same time looking backward to past meals and "prospectively remembering" the special meals, the Easter feast in the midst of the Lenten fast. It is this dense web of food rhythms that provides the sense of food structuring days, weeks, months and years on Kalymnos. Food's role in life-cycle rhythms is also explored in the context of funeral and mortuary "memorials," and this is set in comparison and contrast to work in Melanesia and Amazonia on the role of mortuary feasting in processes of remembering and forgetting. Finally, certain foods become particularly significant because of their symbolic charge across everyday and ritual contexts. In the Orthodox Christian tradition one key food in this regard is bread. Thus the role of bread as memory food, passing between the sacred and the mundane, is examined.

In Chapter 2 I develop the theme of memory in the context of exchange: exchange itself as an attempt to create potential future memories through the destruction of material objects.[20] Acts of food exchange do not work to create memories on their own on Kalymnos. They must be reinforced by *narratives* of generosity past, of failed generosity or of the false generosity of others. Food generosity, then, can be seen as a *lieu de mémoire*, a *topos* on which Kalymnian ideas about name, reputation or honorable personhood are constructed. But food generosity is also a key site for elaborating notions of group

---

20. Cf. Kuchler (1987) on the production of memory through the destruction of carved "gifted" sculptures.

identity, in particular a "modern" identity that poses itself in contrast to a lost past in which generosity made up the shared substance of everyday life on Kalymnos. I explore these memories of community, or *gemeinschaft*, for what they can tell us about Kalymnian historical consciousness. I also examine some of the changing modes of food production and their implications for the generation of food-based memories.

In these first two chapters I essentially take traditional anthropological topics, ritual and exchange, and suggest the productivity provided by a re-examination of well-trod material through the lens of food and memory. I suggest that memory was implicit in these issues all the time, but has not been drawn out until recently, in particular in the work of a few Melanesian anthropologists. In Chapter 3 I turn to some of the more recent theoretical concerns discussed above. I take steps toward an ethnography of the sense of taste and the related sense of smell on Kalymnos, to see eating as "embodied practice." I argue that food's memory power derives in part from synesthesia, which I take to mean the synthesis or crossing of experiences from different sensory registers (i.e., taste, smell, hearing). Synesthesia, I argue, is a key aspect of eating practices on Kalymnos. I further suggest that synesthesia provides that experience of "returning to the whole" which Fernandez has analyzed in the context of religious revitalization, and which, I suggest, helps us to understand the significance of food in the maintenance of the identity of Kalymnians and other migrants who have left their "homeland" behind. I also look at taste and smell from the perspective of cognitive anthropology. Unlike vision, which is divided up into a developed categorical system such as named colors, taste and smell have relatively few verbalized categories associated with them. Because of this, I will argue, taking off from Dan Sperber's work, that they instead become evocative of social situations with which they are associated.

Chapter 4 marks a return to the meal taken as a whole. In it I shift from experience and embodiment to questions of structure and repetition to look at the play of sameness and difference, metaphor and metonymy. I argue that these types of relationships provide the key for one meal recalling another, or better put, for Kalymnians recalling past meals while collectively consuming present ones. Some have argued for the role of analogy and memory as the very basis of cultural processes (Shore 1996). Developing such a view I look at the way the meal is constructed as an "event" that fits within (without exactly replicating) a significant structure in ways parallel to how "history" itself is seen as a series of structure-full events on Kalymnos (a point developed in Sutton 1998:135ff.). Or alternatively one could say that culture and history are "cooked," prepared in ways similar to those of a proper Kalymnian meal.

A final chapter considers recipes, on the one hand in terms of the recent wave of "nostalgia cookbooks" that fight for space with offerings on "how to eat like a pig and lose 50 pounds" and other tomes on the shelves of Barnes and Noble's bookstores. But it also looks at the role of recipe transmission in a more active view of processes of enculturation, which is at the same time a key site for the transmission of certain types of memories and histories, both textual and embodied, that may challenge more official sources of knowledge concerning the past. And of course, I provide you the reader with a signature Kalymnian recipe, copiously annotated so that you can better ingest *and remember* my theoretical and ethnographic reflections through a more embodied experience, so that you too can *eat in order to remember!*

The Ritual and the Everyday

An obvious place to begin our study of food and memory is to turn to ritual and religious practice. Obvious, and yet only a few studies have given explicit consideration to the intersection of food, memory and religious ritual.[1] I will argue in this chapter that ritual is a key site where food and memory come together, but that this should not blind us to the importance of everyday contexts of memory. We must avoid the temptation to oppose ritual as the time for the symbolic and everyday activities as the time for the practical. Indeed, in many cases ritual and everyday memory are mutually reinforcing, especially in the context of one of the key concepts with which I will examine food memories: that of *prospective memory*, i.e., the idea that Kalymnians *plan in the present to remember food events in the future.*

Let me begin with a consideration of a few recent approaches to ritual. For my purposes, a key text is Paul Connerton's *How Societies Remember* (1989), in which he describes what he calls *incorporating memory*, involving ritual ceremonies whose mnemonic power rests on generating sensory and emotional experiences that sediment memory in the body. Connerton's approach to ritual is to see it as a fairly inflexible system of limited gestures that must be repeated with exactitude, like a spell. This means that rituals change quite slowly, and preserve much of their past form:

> To kneel in subordination is not to state subordination, nor is it just to communicate a message of submission. To kneel in subordination is to display it through the visible, present substance of one's body . . . Such performative doings are particularly effective, because unequivocal and materially substantial, ways of "saying"; and the elementariness of the

1. Battaglia (1990) and Munn (1986) provide exceptions; both of these are studies of Melanesian societies, where interest in memory has been particularly well developed in recent years.

repertoire from which such "sayings" are drawn makes possible at once their performative power and their effectiveness as mnemonic systems (1989:59).

Recent anthropological work on ritual would certainly question such a formulation, examining instead the improvisational and historical aspects of ritual (Comaroff and Comaroff 1993; Parkin 1992), without, perhaps, denying that in some cases ritual gesture does have a certain cultural staying power (see for example, Panourgia 1995; Seremetakis 1991). Many have also questioned the definition of ritual, and the distinction of ritual and everyday life, not satisfied with the view expressed by Parkin (1992) that ritual is "loud" and "announces" itself, but instead seeing ritual as the meaningful, or poetic, aspect of all experience (Comaroff and Comaroff 1993). Such a definition preserves the sense of "specialness," without the necessary sense of "loudness." In other words, it turns our attention to the meaningful aspects of everyday, as well as formal ritual activity. This is especially important for looking at memory, where, as Cole (1998:611) recently notes, anthropological studies remain silent on the modalities and sites of social memory in everyday contexts. Anthropological studies of food, on the other hand, have long recognized both poles, in showing how the functions and meanings of eating extend from the quotidian, yet meaningful, practices of daily provisioning to the extraordinary contexts of celebration and commemoration. And, as Mary Douglas has long argued, mundane and extraordinary eating are connected: mutually entailed in systems of meaning, metaphors of each other.

Thus a shifting focus on both formal and informal meaningful practices will serve me well in the three main contexts in which I will be examining food and memory in this chapter, first in the agricultural/ religious calendar, second in Eucharist practices, and third in formal and informal death-related practices. In the first section of this chapter I will begin to introduce some of my ethnographic materials from Kalymnos as background, to give a taste of the food system on Kalymnos, while providing some initial suggestions on the importance of food narratives to be developed in subsequent chapters. In a second section I will discuss the relationship of food, memory and different types of calendars, which introduces an idea of prospective memory, as well as providing a context to understand the interweaving of the mundane realities of material production with the sacred realities of religion. In a final section I will look at food in relation to the rites-of-passage associated with death, which will develop the theme of the ritual and the quotidian, as well as allowing me to engage with recent theoretical literature on food, death and memory in Melanesia, suggesting some of the overlaps and contrasts provided by the Greek material. In all, this chapter will serve to introduce the reader to the Kalymnian context while beginning to suggest some of the ways that a focus on food and memory can invigorate a traditional anthropological topic such as ritual.

Context: Food and Everyday Life on Kalymnos

The daily handling of food is an opportunity to shows one's intelligence and skill, for women in preparing food, and for both men and women in shopping for food and getting the best deals. Shopping, particularly for women, is a daily activity that breaks up the mundane routine of housework and family care. For some women, the fruit and fish trucks that pass through the neighborhood are the opportunity to run into neighbors and have a conversation about the day's events. There is much more opportunity for this for women (and men) who do their shopping downtown, along the main commercial strip of Kalymnos's harbor town. To paraphrase one woman, explaining her technique to me:

> you walk down the main street and you note prices without buying anything: how much Vangelio is selling her tomatoes for, how much are Yiorgos's grapes. Then once you reach the harbor you walk back up, and you buy your grapes here, your tomatoes there, your onions somewhere else. It takes intelligence to get the best deal.

Indeed, daily food prices were a constant topic of conversation in some families, who could also cite the prices of items going back 50 years into the past. Furthermore, Kalymnians claim that they are notorious for never buying anything in small quantities; to do so would be to announce economic ruin. In this regard, shopping has slightly different connotations for men than it does for women. While both men and women are expected to bargain to get the best deal, men also have the contradictory expectation that they will express their "honor" (εγωισμός) through performing their disregard for monetary concerns (see Herzfeld 1991). Thus one woman noted that store owners will take advantage of this by cutting larger portions of whatever item a man requests, assuming that he will "wave his hand" at the additional trifle. And while some Kalymnians noted that it was increasingly acceptable

Agonistic shopping from an itinerant vegetable seller Kalymnos, 1996

to buy things in limited quantities, one man admitted his embarrass-
ment over doing just that, saying that when his wife tells him to buy
two eggplants (to make a specific dish of stuffed vegetables) he self-
consciously tells the store-owner "I'm shopping touristically today"
(ψωνίζω τουιστικά). Indeed, fruit merchants told me they can always
spot as a foreigner someone who purchases two apples, three tomatoes,
or some other laughably small amount.

But it is not simply daily shopping that is a focus of attention and
comment for Kalymnian men and women. It is not unusual for
Kalymnian families to make special purchases: to buy a year's supply
of some food in order to get a better price. I have been witness to the
purchase of 50 pounds of cheese, 50 liters of olive oil and 40 pounds
of spaghetti, 50 pomegranates and 300 pounds of watermelon (stored
under beds) for a family of 4 adults and two children. Part of such
provisioning (κουμπάνια) is no doubt so that there is always food on
hand to be offered when a visitor shows up unexpectedly. It also can
mean that your neighbors come to rely on you. As one woman notes:
"my mother and aunt always taught me to keep a *koumbania*. That
way, while rich families in the neighborhood were always short a carrot,
some sugar, whatever, despite my modest means, I was the source for
the neighborhood." This class element is significant because others
told me that during the Italian Occupation (1912–42) the rich used to
keep a different sort of "provisioning," buying tax-free foodstuffs in
large quantities and keeping them in warehouses to sell when the prices
went up, an inversion of the ethic of generosity, part, rather, of the
ethic of "hunger" described below.

An equally important aspect of shopping is that one show oneself to
be a shrewd bargainer, not someone who can be taken advantage of.
One woman used to boast to me that through such purchases her
family, which was not rich, could enjoy good olive oil for half the
price of what most Kalymnians pay. Part of shopping, then, is building
up one's reputation for intelligence, as well as commenting on the
different practices of shop owners. Thus the daily rounds of shopping
by a Kalymnian man or women are only completed through a post-
shopping discussion among husband, wife, and perhaps mother- and
father-in-law, sisters or other relatives. Such discussions are always
comparative: what is Grigoris selling *feta* for today, and how does it
compare in price and quantity to the last time we bought from Grigoris?
In this way, a storehouse of knowledge is built up about price, shrewd-
ness (one's own) and honesty (the shop-owner's) that marks out such
small daily transactions as memorable.

Special shopping excursions can provide ideal opportunities for all these elements to come into play. Women would plan excursions to the neighboring island of Kos, for example, to pick and purchase a year's supply of grape leaves for the typical Kalymnian Sunday dish of *filla*, or *dolmadhes* (Kalymnos has almost no grape production, while Kos, with its much wetter climate, produces a considerable amount). Much planning would go into such an excursion. For one family the daughter had initially planned the excursion, but had decided against it when she learned she was pregnant. The mother went instead, accompanied by her sister-in-law as well as the daughter's best friend, who had been included in the daughter's initial plans. Last year they had bought their grape leaves from an older couple's vineyard at 800 drachmas/kilo. They called up the couple, hoping that the price had not gone up. The woman who owned the vineyard said, yes indeed, prices had gone up, but then quoted them 800/kilo, much to their satisfaction. When the three women (accompanied by the ethnographer) arrived on Kos, they stopped at the house of a Kalymnian friend who had moved to Kos. She told them that grape leaves were selling at the local market for 650 dr. a kilo. Two of the women went to investigate, and when they found this was the case, bought up all the grape leaves on sale – a scant 9 kilograms. Then they plotted to tell the woman at the vineyard that they had happened to pass the market on their way, and out of curiosity had checked the price. Couldn't she cut them 100 dr. to make it 700 a kilo? The woman assented to this when they arrived, with little debate. Grape leaves are on a pick-your-own basis, so the three women set to cutting the leaves, though with the help of the woman who owned the vineyard. While cutting and collecting the leaves, a process that took about 3 hours for a total of 60 kilos, there was time to reflect on traditional and modern agriculture, how much had been ruined by chemical fertilizers recently. As the vineyard owner told me, her son lives in the United States, and when he returned after 15 years he complained that things didn't taste the same any more. When the transaction was completed, the women noted with satisfaction that the vineyard owner had thrown in some extra leaves, so that their final cost had been closer to 650/kilo. On the way back there was some discussion as to how much should be charged to friends and neighbors who wanted to buy a few kilos. One woman (the youngest, the daughter's friend) wanted to tell people still that they had paid 800/kilo. The daughter's mother said that with taxi costs and boat costs, that was fair, to cover your expenses, though later she told me that she would charge people 700, the other woman was "hungry" and trying to turn a profit.

The point of this "excursion" was that intense concern for price was not purely an economic, but a social matter. Just as Miller (1998) has pointed us to the meaning of "thrift" among London shoppers as having a sacred rather than a simply utilitarian function, on Kalymnos one must look beyond monetary savings to the core values represented by the expedition described above. What was important was to show that you are intelligent, that you can drive a good bargain and not be taken advantage of (since much of your savings may in fact be spent on hospitality or gifts later).[2] It is also to show, in the case of the older woman, that she was not the type of person to try and turn a profit at the expense of family or neighbors. This type of memory creation, in the sense of building your reputation, is discussed further in the context of hospitality in Chapter 2.

Preparation is also an area where Kalymnians show off their skill and intelligence. They constantly watch and comment on their neighbors' cooking. Unlike shopping, engaged in by both men and women, preparation is primarily a female domain of expertise. While some men claim to be good cooks, they would certainly not exhibit such skills on a daily basis. Here it is significant to note that the standard Kalymnian dishes are just that, standard. Kalymnian cooking styles are, from my point of view, somewhat limited. Many main dishes such as meat, beans and fish are prepared using a basic "red sauce," containing onions, garlic, tomatoes, salt and sometimes parsley. Any variations from the standard recipe for lentil soup, for example, will be criticized by neighbors. After mentioning to one woman that my wife used carrots in her lentil soup I was told that this was wrong, carrots and lentils "did not go together." There is certainly an element of power going on here: of women policing each other. One woman, a Kalymnian who had grown up in Australia, came in for particular criticism by the neighborhood women who felt that her attempts to alter recipes were part of her more general claim to be better than they were.

From the preceding material one might get the impression that food is more significant in the daily lives of women than of men. Women's control of food has been claimed as a key source of female power in a number of different cultural contexts (for Greece, see Dubisch 1986; cf. Williams 1984; Beoku-Betts 1995; Counihan 1999), although some have argued that even when women prepare food, men may retain

2. Cf. Miller's (1997:275) discussion of Trinidadian women who compete against extended kin to show that they are the shrewdest bargainers. In the Kalymnian case the competition seems more to be directed toward neighborhood women rather than other family members, though there was some evidence of the latter as well.

primary control over food choices (see Murcott 1983; McIntosh and Zey 1989). On Kalymnos, while men do not take a primary role in the preparation of food, they take considerable interest and attempt to exert influence over their wives' food preparation, whether for guests or for themselves. Men will give their wives extremely specific directions about how they want their food prepared and seasoned. "Cut me some tomatoes, with a little salt and just a little oil." "Make sure you put enough oil on the fish, don't make it dry." Sometimes these comments were made by men self-consciously, and in cases where others were present, one husband felt the need to add "last time she made fish it was great!" (το κάτι άλλο, lit. "something else"). Men would admit to being "difficult" about their food. One man said he was no good at cleaning fish from the bone, and his wife responded by doing it for him while infantilizing him at the same time: "there, my little Dimitri (Dimitraki), now you can eat it." Women would also complain to each other and to me over how difficult it was to cook for their husbands, who demanded freshly cooked food at every meal and refused to eat leftovers. And women sometimes would throw their husbands out of the kitchen when they tried to direct the cooking too closely, or even for putting a bottle of cola in the freezer. While food exchanges were not necessarily hostile, they always seemed to involve negotiations:

Husband (discussing his evening meal):
Aren't there some eggs to fry up?
Wife: We finished the eggs. We'll get some more tomorrow.
Husband: Cut up a little cheese with tomatoes.
Wife: The cheese is finished too. What if I fry up some zucchini?
Husband: Whatever you feel like (όπως το καταλαβαίνεις) . . . Is there any canned ham?
Wife: Ham there is.
Husband: Cut a little ham and a tomato, one of the fresh ones, not those that have been sitting around. I'll eat it with these beet greens (leftover from lunch).

The point here is to suggest that, although women have primary control of certain aspects of the food provisioning process, this should not necessarily lead us to suspect that food is a more important source of memory for women than for men. As I have argued elsewhere (Sutton 1998:208ff.), the form of historical consciousness is largely shared by men and women, and unlike other areas of Greece, Kalymnos does not exhibit a distinct "poetics of womanhood."

Food also provides a key metaphor of social well-being. Those who are miserly or stingy are referred to as "hungry" (πειvασμένoι), with the idea here being that they are more interested in putting their money in a bank than in enjoying the pleasures of life encapsulated in eating. Indeed I was told numerous times by poorer families that the "rich" on Kalymnos eat worse than anyone else, always counting out the number of beans that they cook with a scale (με το ζύγι), a key metaphor for the fact that they do not enjoy life or know how to have proper social relations, which involve a performed disregard for measurement and counting of portions of food or of money (see, for example, Herzfeld 1991). Little respect is given to those who have saved money by scrimping in such a way. When Kalymnians travel to Athens or elsewhere they comment on the smallness of people's portions and the lack of interest in cooking. One woman told me that when she was in an Athens hospital caring for a relative she was constantly going down to the local shop to fill her pockets with food, while other Greeks looked at her incredulously. Kalymnian prodigious eating is a subject of comment by neighboring islanders as well, as the Dodecanese oral historian Nick Doumanis notes (1999 personal communication with author).

Always to have a full plate, then, and always to have enough to offer others, is seen as a sign of fulfilment by many. People scoffed at neighbors who, they claimed, ate only once a day to save money, or who used the Lent period as an excuse to starve their families. One woman in the neighborhood was especially ridiculed for this, as I was told that her husband was always dropping by to ask for a few olives or some cheese, whatever he wasn't getting at home. This woman's behavior was seen as the height of being "hungry." The word meaning "to eat" (τρώω), as is generally noted in the ethnographic literature, is a metaphor for betraying or taking from others (see Cowan 1990:65).[3] But it also is commonly used to mean "to enjoy," i.e., to get one's portion in life. A woman referring to the division of her parents land, asked "my brother ate his portion, when do I get to eat as well?" Or in referring to party politics a man noted, "All politicians steal, but when PASOK is in power, we ordinary people eat as well," with "eat" not being meant strictly in a literal sense, but in a more general sense of enjoying the goods of society. Herzfeld has also noted the common

---

3. To eat in Greek can also mean to waste something you didn't create, as in the expression "s/he ate an estate" (έφαγε μία περιουσία) especially referring to someone who comes from an affluent family and does not contribute to this affluence.

use of the rhetoric of hunger on the part of Cretan shepherds to justify their illegal practices in relation to those seen as powerful:

> Above all, they insist, they are hungry. They were hungry under the Turks, so they stole livestock in order to have something to eat. . . . Perhaps they are less hungry today; but a young shepherd may still plausibly cite hunger as his motive for stealing several sheep in a night's work (1985:21).

Food and Seasonal Cycles

A first approach to the food–ritual–memory complex is provided through a consideration of the role food plays as a mnemonic for the passing of time and the seasonal cycles. But mnemonic is perhaps not completely the right word, because food is equally important in creating *prospective memories*, that is, in orienting people toward future memories that will be created in the consumption of food. What is notable here as well is the interdependence of ritualized memory and everyday memory in relation to food. In other words, it is not simply at "loud" ritual occasions that food and memory come together, but in the pragmatic and the ritualized aspects of everyday life. This is seen most clearly in the interdependence of the different calendars through which Kalymnians organize their year. These include the agricultural cycle of ripening, harvest and availability, the cycle of male absence from and return to the island on fishing/sponge diving ventures, and the religious calendar, with its feasts and fasts, special foods associated with Saints' days and Easter, and ritual foods associated with life-cycle markers.

I was often told in great detail what kind of fish and fruit were available at what time of year. Red mullet with the sailboats in late February. Figs and prickly pears after the summer heat in August. Oranges and tangerines in late October. Interestingly, the reference to such foods has the effect of placing one in time: one knows that if certain foods are being planted or harvested it must be a specific time of year. Thus a man telling a story about the treatment of figs with a special Kalymnian tool (σικούρι) was interrupted by his wife, "When was that?" He responded, "You hear σικούρι and you don't know it's August?" Not all food associations are agricultural, especially on an island such as Kalymnos, oriented toward the sea. Thus until recently April was the time for preparing large quantities of καβουρμάς – sliced pork, half-fried with onions and covered with salt to preserve it, and then packed in metal cans to take along on the long summer sponge-diving expedition.

In many ways the cycle of production and consumption of food works hand in hand with the religious calendar. For example, one couple told me that figs ripen after the first moist day in August brought in by a westerly wind, while another man noted that the figs on my tree would be ripe just before St Anne's day (cf. Zonabend 1984:31ff.). Or as Fourlas notes for the region of Nafpaktias in Roumeli, "The first figs on lower ground come out around the feast of the Virgin (23 August).[4] And they hang on, if the weather is good, until St Dimitris's Day (26 October). But the month for figs is 'Grape-Harvest month,' September" (Fourlas 1985:421; my translation; see also du Boulay and Williams 1987:18). Hart has argued for a more significant role of such connections than purely mnemonic, seeing them as "a mechanism for linking the rhythms of 'natural' production to forms of social reproduction" (1992:256). In other words, religion and ritual are naturalized through the practices of everyday life, and vice versa. But equally important is the linking of past, present and future in such practices, in what I am calling prospective memory. When I spent several weeks on Kalymnos one June and July numerous people remarked that it was a shame I could not stay till August to enjoy the first figs and prickly pears. This is not simply solicitousness to the foreigner. Seasonal foods are looked forward to as a change in the normal routine much in the way that, as an American, I might look forward to going to an "ethnic" restaurant. As du Boulay and Williams (1987:17) note, the harvesting of fruit has an air of festival and overabundance, when, owing to lack of preservative technology, all produce must be consumed: "'Come and see us in September,' is a frequent comment to the stranger. 'Then whatever you want you'll find – figs, apples, pears, grapes. . . .'"

This idea of prospective abundance is most clearly expressed in people's attitudes toward fasting periods, and the feasts that follow them (Easter, the Feast of the Dormition, Christmas). As Megas notes for Greece generally, the pre-Lenten period all the way through to Easter is marked by specified food practices: ". . . the Carnival spirit begins to make itself really felt . . . on Tsiknopefti, the Thursday of the second week. On this day, even the poorest man will cook some meat over his fire and inhale the good smell of grilled fat" (Megas 1982:60). Once into Lent, Cheese Sunday marks the last day one can eat dairy products, and the last food consumed is an egg, which is accompanied by the

---

4. The feast of the Virgin is celebrated on 15 August. I assume that this reference is an Old Calendrist dating.

significant phrase marking out the period of the fast: "with an egg I close my mouth, with an egg I will open it again" (1982:71). This refers to the breaking of the fast with red-dyed Easter eggs. Similarly, on Palm Sunday one refers both to current and prospective food consumption with the expression: vaya, vaya! ["palm fronds"]. On Palm Sunday – we eat fish and mackerel – and next Sunday – we shall eat red eggs'" (1982:91). People also looked forward to Lent as a time to "lighten" their diet from its typical heaviness, not simply in terms of the amount of food consumed, but the avoidance of meat and dairy products, and the substitution of foods not normally consumed during the year, such as *tahini*. During Lent itself people constantly queried me on whether I would be on Kalymnos for Easter, and when I affirmed this, I was told in great detail about the upcoming Easter feast, how good the lamb and all the foods would taste.

Saints' days and feast days are also a time for ritual exchanges of food to take place (for a full description of the structure of different meal offerings as well as material/nutritional implications see Gavrielides 1974). Such exchanges may have been more formalized in the past. The Kalymnian folklorist Kapella (1987:33) describes the obligations in former times of a married woman to her mother-in-law: "[to bring her] various gifts of food at all the major holidays (γιορτές) of the year, which had to be done according to the rules, not any which way. . . ." In my research on Kalymnos in 1992–3 some evidence of these practices remained. But more significantly, holidays seemed to be an opportunity for women to prepare out-of-the ordinary foods and to have reasons to socialize with neighbors that they might normally lack. They were thus looked forward to as variations in an otherwise grinding routine (cf. Hart 1992:247). On St Andreas's day (29 November) we were presented with a plate of donuts by a neighbor who had never had occasion to offer us hospitality before, and this thus gave us a chance to talk. These donuts were offered in memory of the souls of the dead (see discussion below). Food is only one element of the sensory experience of calendar customs, which may also include drink, music and dance, parades, and other such activities. As Noyes and Abrahams (1999:79) note: "Calendar customs are powerful sensory experiences undergone in common, consensual in both the usual sense and the etymological one: felt together." Connerton sees calendrical feasts in terms of ritual repetition: "The same feasts are celebrated on the same dates . . . the participants thus find themselves as it were in the same time: the same that had been manifested in the festival of the previous year, or in that of a century, or five centuries earlier" (1989:66). And

Noyes and Abrahams similarly see such calendrical repetitions as "out of ordinary time" and thus a chance for people to reflect on the passing of time: how their lives have changed while the rituals presumably have not (1999:82). While I would agree with these formulations, two other points need to be made. First, as argued above, there are everyday habits that can evoke similar reflection. Seremetakis sees the daily cup of coffee as a chance to achieve "stillness," or "expressions of non-synchronicity": "Each sip [of coffee] and sigh signalling a deepening in thought, returning . . . thought to distant times" (1994:13). Thus once again we must not oppose the everyday as practical activity and the ritual as the time for memory. Secondly, the point of my examples is that food production and consumption not only structures time through providing repetitive markers annually *across* the years. It is equally important that these food-related events are looked forward to from the point of view of the experience of the passing of the year (intra-annually).

These food-events provide possibilities for future "prospective" memories. That is what people meant when they directed me to eat "so that it remains unforgettable for you!" (να σου μείνει αξέχαστο), a phrase used equally in reference to a major event such as the Easter feast as it is to such small gestures as a woman pouring the oil and vinegar from her preserved anchovies on top of my salad. Food does provide calendrical structuring, but within this structuring human action has the potential to make particular food-events especially memorable, an idea I explore further in later chapters.

Bread and Death: Consumption or Rebirth of Memory?

I now turn to two other examples of the overlapping and mutually reinforcing uses of food in everyday and ritual contexts not directly tied to the yearly calendar: briefly, first, the significance of bread for memory, and second, a more extended discussion of the relationship of food to memories of the dead.

Bread is the basic staple in the Greek diet, and no meal would be complete without bread to accompany it. As "rice" means "food" in East Asian cultures (Ohnuki-Tierney 1992; Hendry 1990), so bread for Greeks. As the Greek folklorist Alki Kyriakidou-Nestoros (1975: 443) puts it, "The meaning of food is identified for the Greek with bread. 'Bread and food you eat with bread' (προσφάϊ) they say, and the curse of hunger is 'to call your bread dear'" (να πείς το ψωμί ψωμάκι). The

Coffee Shop Banter in Kalymnos Harbor, 1992

preceding phrase is especially difficult to translate, as it relies on the diminutive tag "-aki", which does not exist in English, and which means both something small or scarce and something adored (which is why I chose the ambiguous word 'dear'). It relies on the idea that there is no deprivation worse than having to treat bread as "dear." A Kalymnian woman used this phrase to refer to times when her family was poor while her husband was spending what little money they had at coffeeshops. And for one Athenian woman with whom I spoke about this phrase, bread evokes the image of children and desperate people during wartime crying out in desperation "psomaki" ("a little piece of bread").[5]

5. I owe insights into this phrase to Neni Panourgia. Mayol (1998) also notes that for the working class in France bread represents a baseline, so that if bread is available and abundant this signifies that all is well. Similarly bread has an evocative power as a symbol of past hunger: "Bread arouses the most archaic respect, nearly sacred, to throw it out, to trample over it is a matter of sacrilege; the scene of bread thrown in the trash arouses indignation; it cannot be separated from the working class condition: to throw bread in the trash means to forget the story of poverty. It is a *memorial*" (86–7; emphasis in original).

Fresh baguette-shaped bread is bought by Kalymnian women on a daily basis from the numerous bakeries in town, or, for the busy wife, from the bread trucks that pass through the neighborhood every morning plying fragrant loaves. Bread could be eaten as a snack during the day with a little cheese, olives, or tomatoes. Dried store-bought bread rusks made of wheat or barley flour were also a staple in most households. Sometimes people would also obtain *kouloures* (κουλούρες), still made and sold by some of the older women on the island out of wholemeal flour shaped into a donut and baked till dry. They would be soaked in water for several minutes and eaten with cheese and olives, or added to a special Kalymnian salad (μερμιζέλι), which I was told was the "authentic Kalymnian breakfast food." *Kouloures* provide the Kalymnian folklorist Themelina Kapella with a local version of Proust's *madeleine*:

> At least for us old folks we don't just long for them for their delicious taste but because they awaken in us, unconsciously, a series of rare scenes which are being constantly lost and remain only memories (Kapella 1981:26; my translation).[6]

Bread is also used as a mid-morning snack, dribbled with olive oil, rubbed with a juicy tomato and sprinkled with salt. This snack is considered by many to be a particularly Kalymnian food, and people recalled bringing it with them to school, along with a few dried figs. Workers still use this as a coffee-break snack. But most of all, bread is considered a must at Kalymnian meals (the main meal being eaten between 1 and 2 in the afternoon), where it will be used to sop up the pools of olive oil and sauce that accompany any Kalymnian main dish.

Bread, of course, has deep religious significance for Christian populations. On an everyday level, bread is constantly moving back and forth between home and church. As Hart describes:

> Bread baked at home is brought to the church for use as communion bread and as the andidoro (blessed bread taken home for non-church attenders) handed out to the congregation at the end of the service. Basil grown at home is brought to the church to be blessed, and carried back to the kitchen to convey this blessing to the starter used for bread, or to be placed before the icons (1992:148).

---

6. I will have more to say concerning *kouloures* in later chapters.

More specifically, special bread stamped with a religious seal is called offering bread (πρόσφορο). It is generally made on the feast days of the saint for whom someone in the family is named, or on the feast day of a protector saint (also on All Souls' Day, and sometimes on the major feast days as well). Women stamp the dough on the top with a special seal ("τύπος" on Kalymnos) that contains the words "Jesus Christ Conquers." They then bake it in their homes or in communal ovens and bring it to the priest, along with a list of names ("list of souls" (ψυχοχάρτι)) of living and dead family members.[7] The priest cuts the seal off the top of the bread and crumbles it into the communion wine to make Eucharist as he is reading the names on the list, thereby "memorializing the names to the saints" (Kapella 1981:50).[8] The rest of the bread is, as Hart notes, redistributed to the community, linking it to a sense of community defined by commensality. But the interesting point for our purposes is the reciprocal remembering that is explicit in this practice set up between families, ancestors and saints. Through providing bread on a saint's feast day, the community remembers the saint. As Kapella notes:

> Women don't only bring bread to the major churches in the town. They take them to the far off little chapels on the mountainsides which spend all year empty and silent waiting for the once-a-year feast day for their liturgy to fill with people. People don't even forget Saint Dimitris, off behind the castle of the "Golden-Hand," not even Saint Fanaris, nor Saint Athanassis or Saint Barbara. No saint is left to complain of being forgotten . . . (1987:65)[9]

One of the things that people are remembering is the stories of the specific saints and their martyrdom that are told in their feast-day liturgy and were retold to me by some of the older women of the community. People's remembrance of the saints by providing blessed bread for their feast is then reciprocated in the saints' remembering to

---

7. For a detailed description of all aspects of bread preparation see Panourgia 1995:99–100.

8. For a full description of the preparation of the "list of souls" see Kapella 1981:49–52.

9. Arnott (1975:298) notes an interesting mnemonic use of bread in the Maniat region of the Peloponnese. At Christmastime dough used for Christmas bread is moulded in the shape of all of the animals owned by a family, and the small figurines are boiled in oil and given to the children of the house, who keep them on a small table for several days before eating them sometime before the new year. Arnott notes that "it is believed that should one animal be forgotten it will sicken and die."

look after the living and to intercede on behalf of the souls of the dead (the names of both having been read by the priest while cutting the bread). The living at the same time remember their dead, and, as Kapella puts it: "[the dead] participate in life again because their names are heard again" (1981:51).[10] The final connection in this chain of bread and memory is the remembrance of Christ. Walker-Bynum (1992:142 ff.) has discussed the importance of the Eucharist in remembering Christ, as in the Last Supper, in which Christ offers bread "in remembrance of Me."[11] Walker-Bynum argues, however, for a different sense of "remembering" than we would think of today: an "imitatio" or actual reliving, much as Connerton takes the Communion liturgy as his ideal-type ritual, because it is a "re-enactment of actions that are considered prototypical" (1989:52–3). Thus Connerton points us to ritual actions that remember the past by celebrating a pattern, expressing "a wish to repeat the past consciously, to find significance in celebrated recurrence" (1989:63). In the Greek context a significant example is provided by Iossafides (1992:83), who describes the multisensory experience of nuns prior to receiving Easter communion:

> The boundaries of your body are secured through the fast; social interaction is minimized or absent. The divine is the only outside entity upon which you can focus. The incense is strong, overwhelming, aromatic. The lights flicker upon the icons gold and red. The voices of the nuns are raised in glorification of God. All your sentiments are focused on that glory and by contrast also on that which is considered weak and human: the grumbling of your stomach; your thirst; your cold feet and hands. You are made to feel acutely aware of the chasm dividing the divine and the human, the spiritual and the material. The preparation is over. The liturgy has begun.

10. The importance of "hearing" names in order to keep memories of the dead alive is tied to ideas of intergenerational connection through names, as well as the linking of "name" and reputation in the Greek context. For a full discussion, see Sutton 1998:181ff.).

11. Once again we can connect "ritual" and "everyday" practices, as du Boulay argues that the daily meal in the village of Ambeli is experienced as an act of communion, between family members, ancestors and the sacred: "In the presence of the family itself and the food which comes from family land, there is implied a sense of continuity from the 'grandfathers' . . . from whom the living family draws much of its identity; the power of God is implied in the very existence of the meal and the house at all; Christ the Saviour is invoked in the sign of the Cross which each person makes at the beginning and end of every meal; and very often the Mother of God is ritually invited in the words, 'All Holy Mother of God, come and eat with us'" (du Boulay 1974:55).

This describes the prototypical Turnerian ritual intensification that I also observed on Kalymnos among some of the older women who, after observing the strictness of the fast during Holy Week, would stay up all night in church on Good Friday following the liturgy and then late into the night on Saturday. A neighbor of mine, Kalliopi, who was in her early 90s, had done exactly this, and when I saw her on Easter Sunday she was running through the *plateia*, bringing food to a neighbor and shouting "Christ is Risen," in a manner suggestive of Connerton's "temporal immediacy" or Walker Bynum's "imitatio." But what is interesting again is that such "remembrance" is not only found in ritual contexts, but in everyday contexts tied to food as well. As Hirschon notes, when women in the neighborhood of Piraeus where she worked offered food it was often with the comment "as Christ did, so do we," (1998: 20).

The final context I wish to consider here is the role of other foods aside from bread both in mourning rituals and in everyday remembrances of the dead. Comparative material is provided by several Melanesian ethnographies that explicitly focus on the role of food in mortuary rituals. The stress in this literature is for the most part on food's role not in remembering the dead, but in their forgetting. As Munn argues for Gawa, mortuary rites serve the function of a "temporary memorialization," but, in fact, "when the mourning is over, the chief mourners will return to the activities of daily life and forget . . . the dead" (1986:170). Food exchanges between affines and matriclans in the context of mortuary feasts are interpreted by Munn as a way of *closing* paths of exchange (1986:177) and *finishing* social relationships that had been put in play during the dead person's lifetime (1986:171). As Battaglia (1990:184) argues, in one of a series of mortuary feasts among the Sabarl a spear is hurled by the affinal group over the heads of the maternal clanspeople as a way of "killing the 'memory' of the deceased . . . 'so that he [the deceased] cannot get up and give again.'" In her work in Amazonia, Conklin has taken a similar approach to past mortuary cannibalism among the Wari'. Here mortuary practices are a time for a last remembering of the dead person before the cutting, roasting and consuming that will sunder social bonds with the dead and "disassembl[e] . . . physical objectifications of social identity and social relations" (Conklin 1995: 86). Wari' contrast this positively-viewed forgetting to present-day burial practices, which mean that people's thoughts return to the sadness of the dead body lying in the cold earth.

Weiner, by contrast, is interested in how people fight against the loss represented by death by creating memories through "inalienable possessions." But she suggests that food makes a poor inalienable possession, because of its tendency to decay, and pays it scant attention (Weiner 1992:38). Foster affirms Weiner's view in focusing on the opposition between food and durable goods in New Guinean mortuary "force-feeding" rituals:

> I once asked a man to choose hypothetically among a pig, a shell disk, and cash. The man chose the shell disk on the grounds that cash would be 'eaten' or spent, and likewise the pig would be consumed. A shell, however, could be placed in his strongbox. It would not 'stink' or 'rot' (*mapu*) the following day. Although he would die . . . someone else would inherit the shell and someone else again ad infinitum. In short, the distinctive feature of shell disks is . . . their relative resistance to being consumed (Foster 1990:44).   *↳ Interesting*

Thus whether the dead are remembered or forgotten,[12] food is associated with the ephemeral rather than with remembrance. Battaglia is an exception in the regard, providing a more ambiguous picture of the food–memory–death nexus. On the one hand, much of her account confirms that of Munn, in which mortuary feasting provides a 'phased closure' (because feasting goes on over several months) that deconstructs earlier social relations in order to provide the space for new relationships. Mortuary feasting, then, "ossifies, petrifies and blocks further development of that memory *in the public domain*" (1990:194; emphasis in original). But the phrase "in the public domain" is significant for Battaglia, because she leaves room for individuals to nurture memories of the dead even after they have been "killed" by custom: "Simon will never use sugar, believing this was the cause of his small daughter's death" (1990:198). Battaglia also notes that new social relationships and new histories are produced not simply to fill an empty space left by deconstructed social relationships, but "over and around (in respect of, informed by, in spite of) their antecedents" (1990:196). Mortuary

---

12. Another position generally noted in the cross-cultural mortuary literature is the idea that the idiosyncratic individual must be forgotten so that the transcendent ancestor can take his place. This is why in many mortuary rituals personal property of the dead is ritually destroyed. For a review of this approach, see Jackson 1989:75–7. Suggestive comparative material on Ancient Greece is provided by Hamilakis 1998.

feasting, she concludes "sends new stories, like new shoots, out from the body of the dead" (1990:196).[13]

The image of new shoots is appropriate to begin our discussion of food and death in Greece. For in Greece, I will argue, there is no impetus to forget the dead, nor is food held in opposition to hard, perdurable objects. The food that is most important in terms of mortuary symbolism and practice is boiled, sugared winter wheat (*kolliva*, κόλλυβα).[14] *Kolliva* is part of the collective memorial ceremonies for dead relatives on All Souls' days discussed above,[15] and in individual memorial ceremonies (μνημόσυνα) held at prescribed periods after the death of a relative.[16] A plate of *kolliva* is also set out in individual houses, and the door left open for the dead to eat from on All Souls' days, thus stressing the ongoing communication, through commensality, between the living and the dead (just as we saw above with the use of the blessed bread). The ingredients of the *kolliva* have special symbolic significance. The wheat is prepared with such things as pomegranate seeds, nuts and raisins, giving women a chance to exhibit their skill and artistry in decorating the *kolliva* with fancy designs, within the limits of prescribed patterns and ingredients (for a fuller description see Kenna 1991). The religious symbolism of the *kolliva* is linked to the ability of grains and other seeds to regenerate life on their own (Panourgia 1995:130). As one Kalymnian religious scholar noted to me, "the grain rots in the ground then new life springs forth," thus suggesting a parallel to the

---

13. Maschio (1994) similarly describes a more enduring place for memory of dead kinspeople in another Melanesian context (New Britain). He describes the sense of emotional "plenitude" or nostalgia created by contact with objects associated with the dead person, often objects such as fruit trees, associated with that person as a provider of food (1994: 76–7; 204). Maschio also bridges the ritual/everyday distinction in arguing that ordinary objects are used in ceremonial contexts because they are experienced as carrying marks of the faces of the dead upon them. "Cultural creativity or invention seems to consist . . . in making the personal memory into an object of custom" (1994:77).

14. Unlike in Athens, on Kalymnos the word *kolliva* can be used in the singular or the plural interchangeably. It also can be used as a synonym for "memorial ceremony."

15. The Saturday before Clean Monday, and the Saturday before the feast of the Pentecost (see Zairi 1989).

16. According to the Kalymnian folklorist/historian Maria Zairi (1989:250) these periods are 3, 9 and 40 days after the death; then, 3 months, 6 months, 1 year and 3 years. After that memorial ceremonies can be repeated yearly on the anniversary of the death, or whenever relatives feel it to be appropriate. Panourgia, citing the original canonization of the practices, notes a slightly different chronology (1995:133).

potential human regeneration of life.[17] More than this connection, however, there is also the Christian symbolism that we die on earth but that our souls can be reborn in the Kingdom of Heaven, just as Christ died and was resurrected. We can contrast this to our Melanesian materials, where the main symbolism discussed was that of food's consumability and perishability. Here perishability is always followed by new life, a particular Christian symbolism, perhaps, but suggestively echoed in Battaglia's comment about "new shoots" coming from the dead. In fact, the association of food and rebirth can be found elsewhere: in New Caledonia, for example, where yams being buried in the ground and producing new tubers have similar connotations. Such symbolism has its own local inflections as well, as these yams are particularly male symbols, and in this context represent "the long line of men stretching back to the founding ancestor" in New Caledonia (Leenhardt, cited in J. Turner 1984:141).

Both as symbol and as social practice, then, the *kolliva* ceremonies are clearly about continuity. They are ceremonies for the remembrance of the dead, at the same time that the sharing out of *kolliva* reasserts the community of the living. As one couple pointed out to me, the fact that in Athens people buy prepared *kolliva*, and it is covered with flour rather than sugar and is thrown away after it has been blessed, indicates that the Athenians are "on the European system," where community no longer matters.

But what, specifically, is being suggested about the dead in *kolliva* ceremonies? This raises the question of how memory is not simply a passive capacity, but a culturally structured process of shaping the past. What is being attempted in these memory injunctions is the shaping of a specific culturally-valued image of the dead person: one of generosity, and specifically of food-based generosity. At the liturgy performed prior to the first memorial for a recently deceased, the bowl of *kolliva* is placed in front of a picture of the dead person, as if he or she were offering it to the attendant congregation. This is followed by the memorial itself, where people gather to drink coffee and eat a variety

17. See also Zairi 1989 for a clear statement of this idea. It should be noted, however, that the word used for rotting food (σαπίζω) is not the same as the word for a rotting corpse (λιώνω – the meaning of which is closer to the English "decompose"). On the symbolism of the decomposition of human bodies see Danforth 1982; Panourgia 1995:190–1. It would be interesting to know whether (noting the distinction in the verbs) the same adjectives are or are not used for both rotting food and rotting corpses.

of sweets and other items (such as cheese pies). People wrap up extra cakes in napkins, and place *kolliva* in bags to take home for those who did not attend the memorial service.

We can understand the significance of these memorials as formalized extensions of more everyday (though equally culturally-shaped) memory practices for the dead. One often offers food to strangers or neighbors with the injunction "so that you remember my dead mother or father." This can also be phrased "so that my father/mother/dead relative will be forgiven," which was explained to me as meaning that the soul of the dead person will be lightened of its sins by these acts of generosity by the living (see Hirschon 1998:216). More specifically, if a person has bad memories of someone who has died, they are asked to forgive any wrongs that have been done to them in this transaction of receiving food (cf. Kenna 1991:104–5). Kenna also suggests that the preparation and serving of the *kolliva* and other foods associated with memorial ceremonies is a statement to the community of the degree of its felt obligation to the dead relative (1991:106). In Athens, as Panourgia notes, one may substitute preparing a meal for the elderly at a senior citizens' center for the holding of a standard memorial ceremony, or even for the benefit of sick relatives:

> Dinners are . . . offered as supplications for the health and well-being of the family or the quick recovery of an ailing member. . . . the person who pays for the dinner has the exclusive rights to decide the names of the persons (dead or alive) who will be mentioned in conjunction with the dinner (Panourgia 1995:134).[18]

In all these examples a certain image is being shaped of the dead by the living. In effect, the community are being asked to edit their memories to retain an image of the dead person's past acts of generosity through similar acts of present generosity performed on their behalf. Thus we cannot claim that memorial acts are done on behalf of the living community (as a Durkheimian approach would suggest). Older people actively seek to ensure that their relatives will care for their memories, and the threat never to perform a memorial ceremony for

---

18. This sharing of meals can be once again seen as creating community with both the living and the dead. To cite Panourgia (1995:116): "the partaking of the meal further strengthens the sense of the imagined communion of the dead among them and with the living. Although as an affirmation of death, it is also an acceptance of the fact that human existence extends beyond itself."

an aged parent is a particularly potent one. These acts, formal and informal, of food generosity, are key elements of preserving one's good name within the community even after one has died.[19]

What is going on here is not an attempt to "finish" or "kill" the memory, or to secure a place for the individual dead among the collective ancestors. Unlike Melanesia, Greece is not a clan-based society, where social roles must be deconstructed in order to make space for new social relations.[20] Nor do Greeks associate the dead with "ancestors" (πρόγονοι), a term that is reserved for the ancient Greeks. Instead they use the term grandfathers (παππούδες) to refer to the dead of more recent historical times. Furthermore, memorial ceremonies can conceivably be carried out in perpetuity, just as people can continue to put people's names on the list-of-souls, and will in fact continue to do so as long as some felt connection is retained between the living and that dead person. Once again this emphasizes the importance of the specific symbolism of food and its association with rebirth in tying it to other symbolic practices such as naming children after grandparents or dead siblings, a practice referred to as "resurrecting" the name.

In sum, ritual provides a context for us to begin a consideration of the way food and memory are tied up together, particularly if we keep our attention on the ways that "loud" rituals are reinforced by everyday practices. Food is a particularly good medium to lead us to such considerations, as attention to it demands that we look at its ever-present everyday uses as much as its highly-marked symbolism in intensified ritual/religious ceremonies. As I have raised the issue of the cultural value placed on food generosity in creating a memorable reputation or "good name," both during one's life and after death, I will return to a consideration of the role of memory in food exchanges more explicitly in the next chapter, as I look into questions of food's

19. The cultural significance of "generosity" will be discussed in the following chapter in the context of "exchange." In the current context, it is worth noting that Seremetakis describes a *reciprocal* food generosity as integral to Maniat mourning ceremonies, in which the family of the deceased act as hosts to the wider kin group, whose own dead will be there to greet the deceased in the other world. Dead family members will care for the recently deceased and offer him or her a feast of welcome (Seremetakis 1991:109).

20. This is also indicated by the fact that unlike what happens among the Gawa (Munn 1986:106–7), for example, the person for whom a child is named in Greece need not be already dead. Similarly Taylor (1993:659) stresses the importance of forgetting in Jivaro mortuary ceremonies in a universe in which humanity is imagined as "a restricted set of potential human singularities," and names are freed up to be given to newborns after a person is dead and "forgotten."

power to symbolize general social transitions between "modernity" and the good old days, gifts and commodities, community and atomism, holism and fragmentation.

Remembered Gifts, Forgotten Commodities?

In the last chapter I employed some current theories of ritual practice to bring together approaches to food and memory. In this chapter I begin with another classic anthropological topic: exchange. While exchanges of food have been a staple in anthropology, particularly in accounts of feasting (Young 1971; Rosman and Rubel 1971; Kahn 1994), memory has not been considered a relevant category in such analyses except in a few suggestive cases. I begin by reviewing the work of Munn and Battaglia on the relevance of memory to understanding personal exchange relations, particularly involving food, and apply their approach to my Greek materials, suggesting concordances and discordances. I then discuss a different type of food-exchange memory that is not covered in their schema – what I refer to as "memories of *gemeinschaft*." Here the work of those theorists looking at globalization and its incumbent processes sets the terms for the debate over issues of social change and identity, and its implications for the social embedding of memory.

The Circulation of Memorable Reputations

I begin with a quotation from Leach's *Political Systems of Highland Burma* (1965), which provides a classic statement of the relation of exchange and debt:

> Wealth objects other than ordinary perishable foodstuff have value primarily as items of display. The best way to acquire notoriety as the owner (ruler) of an object is publicly to give possession of it to someone else. The recipient, it is true, then has the object, but you retain sovereignty over it since you make yourself the owner (madu) of a debt.

Yiannis Roditis, The Gift of Bread

In sum, the possessor of wealth objects gains merit and prestige mainly through the publicity he achieves in getting rid of them (Leach cited in Gregory 1982:43).

Note that, as we saw with Weiner in the previous chapter, Leach excludes food from his consideration here because it is perishable, while other objects are presumed to be durable. Otherwise the statement encapsulates the anthropological truism that gifts create long-term bonds of reciprocity. But the last sentence contains an important idea for our purposes: "the publicity he achieves in getting rid of them . . ." The giving of gifts must be publicly witnessed and validated in order to be effective, a point brought out by Beidelman in his analysis of Homeric Greek agonistic exchange: "Need for others as witnesses characterizes all social phenomena, yet for Homeric Greeks this extends even to the grave . . ." (1989:249). This points to the fact that one's "name" as a generous person can be manipulated even after death, as we saw in the previous chapter. But it also brings out the distinction between "exchange" and "circulation" made by Turner in his discussion of Beidelman: "The ability of one's name and reputation to circulate separately from oneself and independently of one's physical existence [once again brought out in post-death generosity] is established in large part through successful exchanges" (T. Turner 1989:263). In other words, objects may be exchanged, but what circulates is reputation, one's good name, hence the need for witnesses. But we should not imagine this witnessing as simply a public event occurring in the present. Rather, what is at stake is the circulation of one's future reputation. It is for this reason that I think the distinction made by Weiner and Foster between perishable foodstuffs and durable items is overdrawn. Both work to create an impression, and it is the impression that must be remembered.

Once again we must turn to Melanesian ethnography for a specific consideration of the connection between exchange and memory. In discussing feasting among the Lelet, Eves points to the importance of witnessing, or the talk of others, in creating fame for the feast-giver. "Through successful feasts the renown of the feast host is produced or enhanced, and then circulated to other hamlets and villages" (1998: 264). Eves calls such feasts "tournaments of memory," in which taro and pork act as embodiments of the feast-giver's person that travel, along with his name, accruing renown to him and his kin, a theme we will see clearly when we turn to the Greek ethnography. A feast-giver will sometimes use magic to cause diarrhoea in the feast attenders as a way of marking out his feast as memorable: "If people experience diarrhoea this too will be something for talk and this talk is part of the process by which this feast and feast host is known and remembered" (1998:267).

A second approach, provided by Munn, focuses on the reciprocality of exchange, which, of course, can never be taken for granted, but must rely on processes of memory evocation. She notes a certain type of food exchange among Gawan trading partners called *skwayobwa*. The purpose of *skwayobwa* is to "act upon the mind of the other" and make the partner remember the giver's generosity at a future date when, it is hoped, he will return a Kula shell (Munn 1986:56). Munn argues that exchange and remembering are seen by the Gawans to be inter-linked, and connect the present moment both to the past (fulfilling a past debt) and to the future (creating future potentialities). Of course the notion of debt has been part of exchange theory since Mauss. Gregory, in his classic recapitulation of Mauss (1982), tends to focus in functionalist fashion on gifts as binding society together in webs of gift-debt. But he also speaks of "roads of gift debt", always in danger of deteriorating. In this context he sees food as particularly useful as a gift item because, unlike people exchanged in inter-group marriages, food takes relatively little time to produce, and thus can "keep the roads open" (Gregory 1982:90). But it is Munn who makes the con-nection of seeing this gift-debt explicitly as a process of memory:

> The memory to be induced by the donor in the recipient . . . projects the recipient's mind toward the future . . . in this way extending the trans-action (the past) and the particular media involved beyond themselves and holding them, as it were, in the form of an ongoing potentiality that is not finished. . . . By remembering, one keeps the objective medium or act from disappearing (1986:62–3).

It is this sense that the gift binds time by projecting forward a potential future remembrance of the giver that Munn captures here. Even the ephemeral and perishable medium of food, then, can be extended into the future through memory of the act of giving. Indeed, food may be a particularly powerful medium exactly because it *internalizes* the debt to the other (Battaglia 1999, personal communication). Battaglia confirms and extends Munn's insights in arguing that the preparation of food is a crucial site for the creation of memorable gifts among Sabarl islanders. When feeding visitors it is important that the food be prepared according to "custom" in order to represent the island and make the occasion memorable. Furthermore, in carefully preparing food one is once again projecting the self, in this case the caring, nurturant self, into the external object – the food – which is meant to inscribe a memorable impression on the receiver. The donor becomes, in Battaglia's word's an "absent presence" through the act of giving (1991:76). As Battaglia (1991:47) describes the process:

> Cooking food properly is said to 'show respect for the food' . . . for traditional nurture relations, for the social relationships constructed and honored at present in the giving and accepting of it, for the future that the memory of the food *as an impression* can promote . . . The food . . . is "strengthened" by this attention to tradition by being made 'more like people' – that is, more the model of the memorably nurturant self one projects through giving (emphasis in original).

I will have more to say about the memory of food "as an impression" in a later chapter. For the moment we can turn to the Greek materials to develop these points in examining the dual attention to the preparation and giving of food, specifically because they are seen as potential sites for the promotion of memory.

On a day-to-day level on Kalymnos, when you go to someone's house you must eat or drink something before leaving. Many people actually showed signs of distress at the prospect of my leaving their house without having eaten or taken with me some piece of food, even if it only be an apple to take home for my young child. Cowan (1991:183; see also Kenna 1995) similarly comments on the obligatory nature of the coffee and sweets offered to her by women when she would come by for an afternoon visit. When a man from Athens passed through an elderly Kalymnian man's yard and noticed the fresh red mullet (μπαρμπούνι) being grilled, he commented on how expensive such fish was in Athens. The elderly Kalymnian on hearing the comment actually chased after the man holding the grilled fish by its tail, insisting that he take it.

Proper hospitality requires the proper preparation or provisioning discussed in the previous chapter. It is interesting that du Boulay and Williams, in discussing views of "the good life" in a rural Greek village, quote their informants discussing not simply abundance, but readiness to offer hospitality from one's own resources: "'A person comes to visit, and you have everything ready – your own bread, your own cheese, your eggs, your beans. . . .'" (1987:17).

Such hospitality is indeed very much a part of everyday life on Kalymnos. It is part of the creation of a memorable impression, as Munn puts it. But direct return on such memorable impression is often not expected on Kalymnos, unlike Munn's *skwayobwa*, which hopes for a specific future return. Rather, it is narrative that provides a return on the debt. Hospitality must be continually "witnessed" through narration to be thought of as socially effective, much like Eves's concept of the circulation of names through feast hosting. That is why the prototypical outsider/guest plays a crucial role. Unlike the local community, which has already formed opinions about one's character, the guest "is an unprejudiced outside witness – the only witness from the world outside family or kin before whom the family can afford to play out what its members conceive as its proper nature" (du Boulay and Williams 1987:20). The witness, however, is not only the recipient of hospitality, but the recipient of the ongoing narration of past events of hospitality. In the context of feeding me, people would tell me about past acts of generosity in great detail: whether it involved a brother visiting from America, or a tourist passing through someone's yard who was asked to sit down and take a meal. The actual items served are enumerated in detail as an essential part of the veracity of such stories. These stories also include accounts of whether reciprocal generosity was promised or fulfilled. Men told me about the different foods they offered strangers and how some of these strangers later reciprocated their hospitality with packages from abroad or gifts on return trips. Even a postcard from abroad was seen as a valid return on one's gift, as it could be taken as an affirmation of the value of one's hospitality.

Women recounted such tales as well, but also stressed their ability quickly to prepare an impressive meal even when ten relatives dropped by unexpectedly. My presence was the occasion for some to prove their hospitality in the present, by lavishing it on me, as well as to insist that their present hospitality was not unusual, but was a basic part of their character as illustrated by enumerations of similar past acts. Thus a number of Kalymnians who had offered hospitality (and had recited hospitality narratives to me) would ask me what I thought of them, or ask me to comment on their character to other outsiders who might be present. When other Kalymnians would visit with those who had offered me food hospitality, I would often be called upon to testify to their generosity: "David can tell you how many meals we have fed him." This testimony was itself framed in reciprocal terms, since they would at the same time be testifying to my good character, in other words that I had shown myself to be worthy of their generosity. This was not because I had offered material gifts in return (though I had), but because I had offered friendship through my returns over the years, rather than the exploitative relationship that they associate with some outsiders.[1]

While the outsider, in this case the ethnographer, provides the prototypical recipient of hospitality, it is important to recognize that outsiderhood is always situationally defined (cf. Herzfeld 1987a). A neighbor or an affine can be the recipient of hospitality and can be expected to provide stories about one's own generosity. Thus a woman who had heard that her sister-in-law was claiming that she had not been invited to the woman's house for a long time immediately baked a noodle casserole (παστίτσιο) and sent it to her sister-in-law as a way of blocking the generation of negative stories. The point being that "witnessing" and the generation of hospitality narratives is something done by people on their own behalf, by kinsmen (a wife telling me about her husband's generosity in the context of telling me this was his only good trait), by the local community, and by interaction with non-Kalymnians. In a sense the repetition of performances and of stories of hospitality could be seen as an attempt to bring about an isomorphism between an individual's image of their own generosity and that of the community at large. This distinguishes them from prototypical memories in the United States, where memories tend to be represented as individual "snapshots" or "home movies" that "freeze words and images . . . put frames around them . . . [and] resituate memory ostensibly outside engaged experience and the give and take of social relations" (Lambek 1998:238). Witnessing hospitality is a different type of memory storage and retrieval method, inherently more dialogical and social.[2]

Outsiderhood is situational in another respect, since reputation for hospitality has a segmentary character. That is, not all such hospitality narratives are concerned with creating an image of "a memorably nurturant" *individual* self, as Battaglia describes. Rather, through such memorable acts, collective generosity is being established as well as individual reputation. In the segmentary fashion described by Herzfeld (1987a), people would claim that hospitality is characteristic of Greeks,

1. Outsiders would potentially exploit one's home and family either for economic or for sexual gain.

2. Obviously this is a general trend, and social witnessing is important in some US contexts (e.g., the courtroom), just as memory may at some times be totally individualized on Kalymnos. Thus the view found in earlier Mediterranean ethnography (e.g. J. Campbell 1964; du Boulay 1974) that an individual's reputation is *completely* dependent on community assessment must be seen as an ethnographic exaggeration.

Kalymnians, or themselves according to context. Thus they see Greeks as more hospitable than northern Europeans, Kalymnians more hospitable than Greeks and themselves more hospitable than other Kalymnians. As Herzfeld notes, it is narratives that are at stake here, as the importance of hospitality to the outsider is that it creates goodwill and assimilates the stranger "who might otherwise tell disreputable stories about the village, or who might take home a negative image of the entire country" (1987a:78). Thus Munn's description is apt again here: "by remembering one keeps the objective medium or act from disappearing."

It is important to recognize the "humanistic" element of exchange on Kalymnos, that is, that exchange should be seen at least in part in terms of what might be called "true gifts" that do not expect direct returns (Derrida 1992). Exchange should not simply be exoticized as an attempt to increase one's "capital," – material, symbolic, or other – as anthropologists of Mediterranean patronage and honor often seem to do. Exchange is about social relations, yes, but social relations are about identity construction as much as they are about some calculus of future gain/material obligation. In other words, it can be seen as a human attempt to create social relations for their own sake, not just as a pay-out in the present in order to claim benefit in the future (as Bourdieu (1977) often seems to be arguing). This is what I meant in contrasting these gifts to Munn's *skwayobwa*: the return expected is neither specific, material, nor calculable. As Goddard notes for poor families in Naples, women who kept account of every expense would lavish boundless hospitality on a complete stranger, with the expected "exchange" being praise and recognition: "Everything that was done and offered was worthy of praise and the achievement of praise was a constant element in the exchanges of hospitality with non-kin" (1996:211). The value of hospitality and generosity, then, seems to be embedded in the total system of values, and cannot be abstracted out in terms of some calculation of specific reward. Or as Gilmore puts it, "Exchange [is] less a linear sequencing than an expression of core values, less reciprocity than a reflection of the working or flow of the social mechanism" (1991:28).[3]

The fact that hospitality, to strangers or to kin, has to be narrated and re-narrated, then, reflects the reality that it is an important part of

---

3. For a more humanistic approach to gifts and exchange in terms of the possibility of "true gifts," see Bernasconi's (1997) discussion of Derrida, Levinas and Aristotle on the ethics of exchange.

MEMORY <-> IMMORTALITY

the construction of an honorable personal, local or national identity. Thus it is not simply the impression made on the other, as Eves, Munn and Battaglia discuss, that is crucial here. It is a matter of how that impression feeds back into one's construction of a personal narrative. As Hart, writing on rural Greece, describes it: "It was . . . as if the most important part of the giving were the validation, to the giver, of her own character" (1992:187). Or, as one Kalymnian woman described her husband's generosity, it was "so that his name would be spoken in the community" (γιά να λέει το όνομά του στην κοινωνία). "Name" here has the larger meaning of reputation, or "fame" in Eves's and Munn's discussion. Thus such narratives, predicated on the remembrance of specific acts of generosity relating to food, become key elements in the construction of a personal history – extending to the grave and beyond – that makes claims to being hospitable rather than "hungry" (πεινασμένος). Narratives of past hospitality can draw on a context, as the researchers on memory and cognition Hirst *et al.* (1997:164) argue:

INTERPRETATION

> If someone remembers that she treated four people to dinner, this recollection . . . must be placed in a larger context: that her behavior is a life-long pattern, or that her dinner companions were influential and could be professionally helpful, or that her friends had recently complained about her stinginess. The narrative one would tell about the dinners would differ, depending on what background details one incorporated. What makes the autobiographical recollection important to the self is not the memories *per se*, but the interpretation of the memories, or more specifically, the narrative told around the memories.

In the Kalymnian context, hospitality narratives sometimes contained implicit or explicit contrasts with the ungenerous, inhospitable behavior of neighbors. Thus the narrative frames the hospitality event, and provides a proper interpretation of it, since the possibility for other interpretations, or for reinterpretation *by others*, is great. The discussion of a neighborhood woman and her daughters, all considered "hungry," releases a flood of recent and not-so-recent occasions to substantiate this judgement. Times were recalled when they offered hospitality considered too small – "tiny pastries for a wedding feast, when we Kalymnians are accustomed to large portions." Or when they brought okra to their neighbors, expecting return hospitality when the okra "was not fit for pigs." Or when they didn't want more people to come to their pre-wedding meals whom they would have to feed, even when these people had brought gifts with them. Or when the woman's husband had come to them begging for food because it was during Lent, and the woman had refused to cook. As with the positive stories of one's own generosity, these negative stories are remembered and renarrated as part of one's ongoing judgement of the character of one's neighbors, with whom one is often in competition for neighborhood reputation.

Another factor to be considered is the problematic nature of obligation in Greek society (see Hirschon 1992 for a detailed discussion). Hospitality can be aggressive because debt can be thought of as a threat to one's own, highly valued, personal autonomy. As a result, many stories revolve around the refusal of the hospitality of others, which, as is illustrated in the following case, may be false hospitality in any case. One man in his 70s recounts receiving a meal forty or so years earlier, at the house of someone he was working for. It was a bowl of spaghetti covered with wonderful-smelling cheese, but underneath were fish heads, bones and other rotting things "not fit for dogs." The woman who served him told him not to worry, "they're just a little sour." But he refused the meal, and from then on, even when presented with wonderful meals, such as luxurious tomatoes out of season, he would always make an excuse and refuse the meal. I asked him why he refused a luxurious meal, since it was part of a workman's wage back then, and you didn't make more if you refused it, and he insisted it was "out of pride" (από εγωισμό). While this story illustrated the man's self-sufficiency and his preparedness for the potentially "false-hospitality" of others, his admission to "pride" in a sense recognizes his failure to uphold the social contract: he was willing to offer hospitality to increase his reputation, but unwilling to allow others to do the same.

As with all such narratives, these stories were directed both at constructing a past and at a specific context in the present. As we saw above, oftentimes one act of hospitality provides the context for the recollection of previous acts of hospitality, as part of the process of building and reaffirming one's reputation. Other narratives can have more specific targets. One man was having a two-day-long shouting match with his wife over claims that she was stealing money from his bank account. He had been hurling a string of abuse at her, claiming that she and her daughter were scheming behind his back to take away the money he had worked to provide the family with.[4] During a break

---

4. This in part reflects the realities of matrilineal inheritance on Kalymnos, where men's control over property is always tenuous at best (see Sutton 1998:105ff.).

in the argument, he turned to me, unprompted, and told me the following story:

> I was working on Rhodes with a number of other Kalymnians as part of a work crew during the Italian Occupation. We came upon a field overflowing with peaches, figs, watermelons, bananas . . . "paradise!" The field belonged to an old Turk, 80 at least, and his wife, a "good quiet woman." I asked the Turk the price to buy some fruit, and instead the Turk invited us to keep him company and to eat all the fruit that we wanted during the few days we would be working nearby. Despite the hospitality of this man, the other Kalymnians were secretly stealing fruit from him in the middle of the night, cutting a piece out of each watermelon to see if it was sweet, and if it were not, putting the piece back and turning it over so it would be undetectable, but would rot soon afterwards. I stayed awake one night and caught my fellow Kalymnians at it, telling them that they should be ashamed of stealing from an old married man who had offered them hospitality.

This story has a number of interesting elements, including the positive intercommunity relations established through food, the vividness of the description of events from forty years earlier (discussed in Chapter 3), and the affirmation in this case that he was honorable in accepting hospitality. But its immediate point was to show that other Kalymnians, like his wife, were scoundrels who did not know how to maintain proper exchange relations.

Remembrance of Things Past: The *Gemeinschaft* of Community Exchange

Munn thus provides a useful framework for conceiving of individual exchange in terms of processes of memory, impression-creation, and the binding of past, present and future in the work of everyday social relations. But Munn's schema does not capture a different type of memory of exchange common on Kalymnos. These are the narratives of the past, the "old years" (τα παλιά τα χρόνια) as they are called on Kalymnos, where food exchange provides a metonym for the community values that many people feel are under threat from the forces of modernization. Thus perhaps relevant here is Battaglia's notion of preparation according to custom, which respects the sanctity of "true foods." But on Kalymnos, such customary practice is most definitely situated as part of the past, something to be remembered and mourned, but only occasionally impinging on the present landscape. Debates over modernization and globalization thus become germane to our making sense of what is going on in what I am calling narratives of *gemeinschaft*.

The past is imagined on Kalymnos as a time when food was exchanged freely, and when communal rituals had a greater role to play in people's lives. Thus these narratives are highly nostalgic, and tend to be told in the imperfect tense, "we used to . . ."[5] This includes nostalgia for simpler times on Kalymnos when foods were seen both as more natural, i.e., less processed, and more commonly shared.[6] Such narratives are often told among families. Though they might be stimulated by a question from me about changes in a particular food or agricultural practice, these narratives seemed to take on a life of their own, with one person building on the memories of another and suggesting other examples of the shift from earlier times to the present. This modernization is seen ambivalently by most, as many laugh at the "backward" hygiene practices of the past, while lamenting the lost social world that went with them. In reminiscing about the past, for example, one woman noted that tomato paste used to be sold from a large container at the market, scooped out on to a piece of paper from a common spoon. Now it is sold in cans, which, she noted, is much more hygienic. And yet, she insists, the tomato paste, like most things in the past prior to chemical processing, "tasted better." We can see in this contrast – on the one hand tomato paste the substance of which is shared through the community, and in the other case paste that is locked away in separate cans – a metaphor for social relations more generally. Such reminiscences are not always elaborated as narratives, but may take the form of offhand comments, where narrative context is felt to be unnecessary. A woman cuts a slice of watermelon off the rind and hands it dripping to her grown-up son, saying to him, "here, like the old years." When I questioned her about this, she noted that that's the way they used to eat it, not in a plate with a fork, but with their hands. Here the "old years" intrude on the present through the gesture of the

5. See Sutton 1998:35ff. for a full discussion.

6. This is in contrast to the period of the war itself, which was remembered as the great hunger, when social rules were in fact inverted. Since Kalymnos produced little food in contrast to other islands, many Kalymnians were forced to flee the island during this period, or exchange their treasured possessions with other islanders for food. The sense of social inversion is captured by the Kalymnian writer Niki Billiri. She recalls the horror of this period in her story "Grandmother's Bread" (1982), in which children celebrate the death of their grandmother because they will get her portion of bread.

old woman. Mostly, however, such narratives indicate the separation of past from present, the fact that the past is indeed past. The off-handedness of this particular comment suggests how common these associations are, while once again bringing home the point that in the past there was less separation between people, in this case represented by the handling of a sticky food substance with one's hands rather than with a plate and fork, as Kalymnians commonly consume water-melon today. For another woman in her sixties it was eating out of a common salad bowl, rather than on separate plates, that represented "the old years."

Such narratives of food and community thus dovetail with other stories about the pre-Second World War past and the legacies of modernity. One major theme of such stories is that in the past it is claimed that people were more neighborly, i.e., they didn't treat each other as strangers.[7] A number of people remembered how when you used to go to the bakery to get your bread every Saturday, you would give some of it away to neighbors you met on the street.[8] More generally, foods have an almost pre-capitalist aura, as things of nature that could not be bought and sold, but could only be given as gifts. One particularly expressive example is provided by the folklorist Themelina Kapella. As she puts it:

> You couldn't buy fresh figs. Whoever had leftovers didn't sell them, it was thought to be shameful. Everyone had the right to enjoy figs, along with fresh air, the sun and the sea. You were free to cut as many figs as you wanted when you passed a fig tree, and the owner would urge you to cut some more (1987:103).

Kapella compares this to her disappointment in tasting dried Vassilika figs bought in Athens, which had none of the flavor of those free figs available on Kalymnos.[9]

7. While there is no doubt some truth to this, it should also be seen in terms of Herzfeld's (1990) notion of "structural nostalgia", in which people talk about the past in terms of its ideals rather than in terms of the regular transgressions of these ideals.

8. This suggests a religious significance, given the importance of "blessed bread" discussed above, though this religious dimension was not made explicit by my informants.

9. Indeed such attitudes still linger, as is reflected in the pleasure one woman expressed in eating fish that her son-in-law caught in his spare time, or that she received from neighbors in exchange for letting them graze their animals in her fields or providing them help with weaving. As she noted, "we can eat fish all summer without money!"

Another fig narrative from the folklorist Niki Billiri recounts a specific memory, though with similar intent. She tells of a fall evening when the women of the neighborhood of Farangos were in the habit of gathering to chat and to eat together their gathered fruits: figs, grapes and prickly pears. While she doesn't date the story, the first names of the women are those most associated with the "old years" – Limnaina, Atoumissa, Foukaïna,[10] Kastrovakina, Ksarsena – placing the story back in pre-war times. One woman, Kastrovakina, has been eating the others' figs while not offering any of her own. When her neighbors discover that her fig trees are heavy with beautiful, firm, sweet figs (ρακχουνιστά άβόσυκα), they gather several baskets and bring them to their evening meeting-place. They offer them to Kastrovakina, who eats several and then asks curiously where they are from. They refuse to tell her, and after she has eaten several more she figures out that they are her own figs. At this point the neighbors burst out laughing, telling her that she has been eating without sharing her abundant figs, and she demurs, saying "you're welcome to them as my gift, the fig tree has plenty, especially when I can sit here and enjoy them already cut and rest my body in your company" (Billiri 1993:113). The easy sociability and easily rectified transgression against sharing proprieties once again suggests nostalgia for the pleasures of *gemeinschaft*, which are represented here by those products of nature that "cannot be bought and sold," precisely because they are already seen as gifts of nature or of God: "we sit once again around the brazier (μαγκάλι) with our neighbors to have our portion of fish that God has saved for us" (Billiri 1993:89). Here we see the view presented by Sahlins (1972:167ff.) that the *Hau* of the gift is the idea that one cannot profit from something that has been received as a gift. This idea has been traced by Lewis Hyde (1979:Chapter 1) across Western and non-Western folklore, where those who pass on the gift are eventually rewarded, while those who attempt to benefit directly from the gift are punished. This is reflected in Kalymnos in the common wisdom that one's generosity will be repaid tenfold: as one woman told me, "I can't not offer a plate of food to someone in need, and I find that God watches and I receive many times what I have given." Hyde contrasts this with the market mentality in the following indicative passage:

10. The name Foukaïna has itself come to mean "old" or "old-fashioned, illiterate neighborhood woman."

Yirogos Mixas, Fishing for snacks in front of his grandmother's house, 1992

Where, on the other hand, the market alone rules, and particularly where its benefits derive from the conversion of gift property to commodities, the fruits of gift exchange are lost. At that point commerce becomes correctly associated with the fragmentation of community and the suppression of liveliness, fertility, and social feeling (1979:38).

Note in this passage the metaphor of "fruits," suggesting once again the Kalymnian view that these are the ideal objects of free exchange, gifts by nature. Fruits are ideal gifts in another way, because fruit trees, like houses, are inalienable property, which ideally cannot be sold but must be transferred to future generations. Thus in giving the fruit of one's tree one is giving part of oneself and of one's line of eponymous descendants.[11]

This view of the past as made up of pre-capitalist relations to food is further substantiated, then, by Kalymnian attitudes toward "negative

11. Ideally houses and agricultural fields are passed matrilineally from the grandmother to the granddaughter or another descendant who shares the same baptismal name (see Sutton 1998:181ff.).

reciprocity" or stealing. As indicated in the story above, stealing fruit has the aura of semi-legitimacy, as long as it is done on a relatively small scale (though this is a matter for debate and negotiation).[12] First, it should be noted that negative and positive reciprocity are intertwined. A woman who caught her neighbor stealing figs from her trees queried her as to why she needed to steal when she had her own fig trees. The woman responded by saying that her own figs trees were not enough, because she had many people to whom she needed to give gifts!

Memories of past episodes of stealing were usually situated within a particular neighborhood: one would recall one's own raids against a neighbor's fruit trees, as well as the particularly well-known or humorous deeds of a neighbor. A woman and her parents recounted to me, and to each other, childhood fruit-stealing raids against neighbors which, the woman noted, were not undertaken out of any economic necessity, but were a way to pass an evening before people had things like TVs and VCRs available. Much like sheep-stealing on Crete (Herzfeld 1985), what was important here was both the challenge and display of cunning, and the humorous stories that would result from such excursions. Through these stories, a semi-regular activity could become marked out and remembered as part of a past when people were more sociable.

This led the woman's parents to recount an ambiguous story about olive harvesting in "the old years." Up until just after the war people would gather together at the beginning of every October to collect their olives. Back then you were not allowed to go and pick olives whenever you wanted, even off your own trees, because many people who did not have land had made agreements to plant trees on other people's properties, in exchange for some share of the harvest. So in order for no one to be accused of stealing from anyone else, everyone gathered together on a certain day to go together to the olive fields; they would gather together at around six a.m., waiting for the person in charge to give a rifle shot, and then everyone would run off into the fields to collect their olives, while keeping an eye out that no one took anything from their own trees, this whole activity being encapsulated in the Kalymnian word *tzioma* (τζιώμα). As Maria recalled, people would gather

---

12. In his ethnography of grocery shopping in North London, Miller (1998:42) notes, but does not comment, on the fact that many shoppers almost ritually steal and consume a few grapes when passing through the produce aisle. Aside from the convenience of consuming grapes as opposed to other supermarket goods, it is interesting to speculate that a similar attitude toward fruit might be expressing itself here.

around at lunch and gossip about who they saw stealing a handful of olives and such things, and it all had the feeling of a big celebration.[13] Yiannis added his memories of boys, usually starved for the sight of girls, getting a chance to look at their legs as they climbed up on ladders to knock down the olives. When the olives were collected they would be taken to the olive presses, which were owned by the church, and you would give the church one-tenth of your olive oil in exchange for the use of the press. Maria and Yiannis commented that the priests would often turn around and sell this to some family who did not have olives, making the whole thing into a business. When the olives were pressed you always tried to remember to bring along some dried figs, Maria told me, to dip them in the thick oil as it's coming out of the press: "I still remember the taste of that."

Why was this custom abandoned? People didn't trust each other any more, Maria noted. If you had trees in other people's fields then there would be disputes if they wanted to sell the field. People were much more tied together back then and loved one another, she concluded. This statement seems contradictory, given that the whole point of the *tzioma* was to keep people from stealing from one another. At first sight such a view suggests that the discourse of nostalgia can assimilate even contradictory facts into its schema. But given that people are recalling feelings of community connection and contrasting these to the feelings of atomization in the present, this statement by Maria makes sense. Negative reciprocity – stealing – is still reciprocity, in that it creates lines of community, social relations good and bad, in a time "before TVs and VCRs were available." Thus just as the individual stories of food exchange address both positive and negative aspects of *gemeinschaft*, so with these collective remembrances there is a recognition of both the joys and the burdens of a thick network of social connections.

Global Food: Memory Destroyer?

The ancient, gnarled, familiar, idiosyncratic, almost human olive tree survived in the place where the family had its roots. It gathered to itself all the connotations of peaceful constancy, historic continuity, and unshakable dependability which were accepted as human ideals. Nowadays, we cannot wait (Visser 1986:231).

---

13. Cf. Theodossopoulos's subtle description of the olive harvest on Zakynthos as "a jolly, gregarious project in which gossip thrives" (1999:618).

Are these sorts of food-based memories indeed under threat by TVs, VCRs and the forces of modernity? This question, that is the changing shape of food memory, will return to us in different forms in the following chapters. But some preliminary remarks on the subject seem appropriate here. Two anthropologists whose work is directly relevant to this question are Counihan, who has done research on Southern Italy, and Seremetakis on Greece. Both of their works accord with the Kalymnian perception that the food-based reciprocity that made for thick social relations and social memory is indeed being eroded. As Counihan notes for rural Italy, there has been a considerable decline in the social activities of women organized around food. While bread-baking used to be an opportunity for women to "act out standards for 'good bread,' 'good work' and a 'good woman,'" today:

> with the decline in local primary production and the increasing reliance on the market, the incessant mutual giving and receiving of foods slows and becomes less crucial to survival. Thus one of the most important forces in linking people together – reciprocal prestations – is fading away, and with it goes people's interdependence (Counihan 1984:53).

Counihan further argues for a decline in the significance of seasonal food patterns such as frugal daily consumption within the family context and prodigious feasting on religious holidays to reconnect family and community. "Opulent" consumption has increasingly moved out of the public sphere and into the private sphere, where it "becomes a private, stratifying and individualizing act rather than a public, altruistic and communalizing one" (1984:54).

Seremetakis makes a similar argument for the loss of reciprocity, identity and memory as a result of the standardizing regulations on food on the part of the European Union. She begins with the idea that peaches and other fruits have now become "insipid," (άνοστα), a word that she interprets to mean unable to produce memories and identities. Standardization, producing food and fruits out of season, placing health regulations on certain processes of production and fermentation (one could think of the Kalymnian woman's tomato paste here), strips food of its regional diversity, and strips people of their sensory experience.[14] One recent example of this was the EU response to "mad cow" disease, which placed a ban on the internal organs of farm animals more than

14. For recent approaches to the question of EU health regulations and regional diversity, see Leitch 2000; Leynse 2000; Sartori 2000.

two years of age. This was perceived as a threat to the Greek dish "kokoretsi," made from the stuffed entrails of lambs, and led to a variety of protests, including the establishment of a "Free Kokoretsi" website for people to register their dissent. In such processes of regulation Seremetakis sees "a reorganization of public memory":

> Sensory premises, memories and histories are being pulled out from under entire regional cultures, and the capacity to reproduce social identities may be altered as a result. Such economic processes reveal the extent to which the ability to replicate cultural identity is a material practice embedded in the reciprocities, aesthetics, and sensory strata of material objects (1994:3).

Here Seremetakis nicely ties together the issue of identity, which has been prominent in the literature on food, specifically with questions of memory, suggesting that the ability of foods to produce memories is intimately tied to the possibility of reproducing social identities. The memories that she is discussing here are the type of integrated memories that place an individual in a collective life, where any individual memory is in fact a memory of the whole society. This is the view

Demetra and Konstantinos Panourgias, preparing kokoretsi and lamb for Easter

These pictures come from an EU-sponsored seminar on the use of Greek saffron in cooking, held in the village of Krokos in Northern Greece, in 1999. The first picture shows bread rusks with saffron (tied with pink ribbon), as well as two soups prepared with saffron. The second shows a saffron chicken dish, and the third shows women cutting a cheese pie made with saffron. This area produces high-quality saffron, but people in the area had never incorporated it into their cooking (saffron was part of ancient Greek cooking, and is part of the cooking of a few Greek islands today). The seminars were part of the EU "Structural Adjustment" policy, funded by the "Business Programs in the Periphery" section (partly funded by the Greek government). Their purpose was to teach people a

craft or art related to a strictly local product or resource in order for them to be able to find employment, and in order for the region to develop based on its own resources, "sustainably." The students (mostly women) are local producers of saffron. Does this suggest that local products are being preserved (through supporting the economic viability of villages), or does it suggest the loss of memory of local taste histories as argued by Seremetakis, as cultural "diversity" is literally created from above? These issues are explored in a forthcoming dissertation by Vassiliki Yiakoumaki looking at food and national identity in Greece, at the Department of Anthropology, New School. See also Yiakoumaki 2000. (Photo credit Vassiliki Yiakoumaki) argued by Halbwachs in *The Collective Memory* (1980), that all memories are inherently social. Seremetakis suggests that such memories that are under threat may go underground, become hidden or fragmentary, as the dominant culture is replaced by the modernizing and standardizing protocols of consumer culture. Counihan suggests something similar in the replacement of traditional Easter bread baked by Sardinian women with the standardized loaves produced by bakery machines. The traditional bread symbolizes, through the form it is shaped into, a loose "V" form "recall[ing] birds in flight", while still carrying the baker's personal touch. The machine-made bread symbolizes, by contrast, through words: conveying the message "Happy Easter" through the letters "B.P." (Buona Pasqua). The traditional bread carries specific community meanings and can be read by community members sharing the baker's restricted code, while the machine-baked bread communicates through a generalized code shared by any literate Italian.

Another way to frame what Counihan and Seremetakis are describing is in terms of Marx's notion of commodity fetishism. Commodity fetishism is the process by which objects are compared based on a price derived from their market value rather than on the history of labor relations that went into producing them. The relevance of this to our discussion of memory is that commodity fetishism can be seen as a "memory disorder" (Terdiman 1993:12), that is, a purposeful forgetting of the pasts that went into the making of the present.

Are such meanings and memories disappearing on Kalymnos? Do the memories of *gemeinschaft* recorded above reflect a general pattern discussed by Mintz (1985:201), that is, the "elimination of the social significance of eating together"? One could find parallel examples on Kalymnos of the processes discussed by Counihan and Seremetakis. At Easter 1993, a number of women commented on the fact that it is rare for women to bake Easter cookies any more, that they are now available ready-made at the store. As one woman in her 30s commented, because of this, Easter will pass by this year and we won't realize it (δε θα το καταλαβαίνουμε: lit. "we won't understand it").[15] "Understand" here

---

15. These sensory-rich descriptions resonate with Bahloul's account of reminiscences of the anticipation of the Shabbath on the part of Jewish Algerian migrants to France: "'We'd feel and smell Friday nights back there. It wasn't like here in France: here you don't really *see* the *shabbath*. But in Algeria, you'd *feel* it. . . . In households, one could smell the odour of food cooking, that good food which we wouldn't cook during the week; those dishes simmered slowly, while during the week, well, we'd eat anything'" (Bahloul 1996:105).

is used to mean "feel" in a visceral sense. Lacking understanding is felt to be an incompleteness, while having it suggests wholeness, as in the phrase used by numerous Kalymnians to explain dynamite throwing at Easter: "When you hear the dynamite then you know it's Easter" (see Sutton 1998:71–4). I believe it can be compared to Seremetakis' discussion of "tasteless" fruits as unable to generate meaning or memory. When I asked the woman why she did not bake the cookies she insisted that the store-bought cookies were of good quality and she simply didn't have time to spend fussing over baking. Here, as elsewhere, what is being lamented is not a changing food practice, but a changing lifestyle that people feel that they have little control over.

Another obvious way in which Kalymnos fits with the above material would be in terms of the erosion of the place-identifications of food so central to the generation of social and sensual memories. The figs in people's stories were not simply any figs: they could be traced to a field owned by a person whose history, as well as the history of the previous ownership of the fig tree and field, would be known. Thus a stolen fig could be placed in a long-term cycle of family histories, as well as in seasonal cycles, i.e., the time and method of harvesting and the feel and taste of freshly picked figs; the way, for example, that a bead of white liquid forms on the stem after picking, and methods of home preservation. As Berry (1998:63 [1990]) polemically puts the connection between knowledge of production and memory:

> People who know the garden in which their vegetables have grown and know that the garden is healthy will remember the beauty of the growing plants, perhaps in the dewy first light of morning when gardens are at their best. Such a memory involves itself with the food and is one of the pleasures of eating.

Such food/memory pleasures have been eroded or destroyed, according to Berry (and Seremetakis), by the commercialization of agriculture.

At the same time the picture has been made more complex by studies of the way transnational capitalism has in fact co-opted difference and diversity as part of its marketing strategies. While radical authors and activists such as Berry have focused on de-fetishizing the commodity by revealing the labor processes and histories involved in the production of products from clothing to food to beer, to "ethnic restaurants" (see also Heldke 1992; Narayan 1995; and Mintz 1985, who provides the prototype for such an approach), many marketers have gotten the message, and "package" information about the production process as part of their advertising strategy. Playing on a generalized nostalgia for *gemeinschaft*, all sorts of products claim to be small-scale, traditional, and "authentic," even if produced by huge multinationals: "The objective [of the multinational food industry] is far from that of producing the homogenized 'world steer' . . . Rather, it is necessary to provide a whole range of differentiated food commodities as if instantly harvested from the local field for the suburban and urban platter" (Arce and Marsden, cited in Cook and Crang 1996:134). Such knowledge of production has been used in the past and continues to be used in the present in the construction of class-based differences in consumption taste. At the same time false, fetishized and romanticized images abound of "a paradisiacal Golden Age [of] tropical produce . . . with images of fruit falling off trees for relaxed collection and consumption" (Cook and Crang 1996:146). Such images of romanticized or in some case "savage" others who produce the products consumed in the West have been debunked by numerous authors (for example Enloe 1991 on bananas; Terrio 1996 on *Grand Cru* chocolate).

While these types of memories may seem inauthentic and lend support to Seremetakis's argument, a more complex picture is provided when one looks at how people actually *use* the images and products produced by these multinationals. One woman, a grocery store owner, told me that the prepared food available in her store was "five pieces of bullshit in a can" (πέντε μαλακίες μέσα σ' ένα κουτί), and that, in buying them, Kalymnians were acting as stooges for multinational food companies, instead of retaining their independence by relying on locally grown food. But not all Kalymnians had such positive associations with local food, and they sometimes found creative uses for global products. For example, an older man had the following comment about local products: shepherds make cheese using the pus from their lambs' teats. They "fool everyone," parading this cheese through town, calling it "authentic" (γνήσιο πράμα) local cheese. He showed me his own localizing strategy for cheese: he bought a piece of Roquefort and a piece of Feta made by Dodoni, known to be high-quality Feta. He would pound the two together in a bowl, resulting in a cheese spread called "pounded" (κοπανιστή) a "traditional recipe" that he associated with the old years on Kalymnos. In this case, as in other examples of rejected hospitality, we see how local food can be caught up in both the negative and positive dimensions of Kalymnian social life, and foreign food can be adapted, through local *processing*, to memories of things past and the negotiations of dependence and independence on local and transnational scales.

In examining the implications of changing consumption on Kalymnos, then, we must be careful to understand these different dimensions of "local knowledge" and their implications for the construction of situated or nostalgic memories. The knowledge that certain peaches grow in Manolis's field at a certain time of the year, and that they have a different flavor from the peaches in Irini's field, is of a different order than the knowledge of how different grades of single malt Scotch are produced (a knowledge not absent from Kalymnos, given that Scotch has replaced ouzo as the best-selling alcoholic beverage in Greece (see Stewart 1989:87)). More ambiguous is the knowledge of some older Kalymnians, who could tell me what Greek islands produce the best watermelon or grapes because they have worked at planting and harvesting such fruits, but were also interested in comparing the gustatory values of British vs. Spanish potatoes. Or those who knew that good kiwis were grown in Vathi, the agricultural center of the island, but not that kiwis came from New Zealand. Availability of foreign products has certainly grown dramatically since I first observed Kalymnos in 1981, when only Amstel Beer competed with the Greek brand Fix. By 1997, Kalymnos had several coffee shops purveying Cappucino and Espresso (and competing for a different clientele than the traditional Greek coffee shop – see Cowan 1991), as well as a shop selling "Dunkin Donuts," opened by Kalymnian return-migrants who had learned the techniques of making these donuts during their time in Boston.

But while the pace of such influxes has certainly increased, the question of foreign products has been a long-standing one, a fact that can be missed if one takes the dichotomizations of Kalymnians between "Now" and "The Old Years" too literally (not to mention the anthropological dichotomizations implicit in "Salvage Ethnography" (Clifford 1986). One Kalymnian man reminisced fondly concerning the wonderful meats and cheeses – mortadella, prosciutto, provolone – available on Kalymnos during the time of the Italian occupation of the Dodecanese (1912–1942), as well as the intoxicating smell of all the various canned preserved meats, fish and vegetables brought from Italy. He recounted specific memories of the food-related generosity of certain Italians to him when he was a boy, recollections that might take on the status of "counter-memories" to the Greek nationalist vision of the unmitigated evil of the Italian occupation of the Dodecanese (see Doumanis 1997). He also noted that Kalymnian priests told people not to eat any of these Italian foods or they would become "Franks" (φραγκολίβανοι), and threatened that those who did eat Italian foods would not be allowed to take communion.[16] The man scoffed at the priests' ideas, and at the narrow-mindedness of those who went along with them, as did several others who remembered the time. As one woman put it: there used to exist such racism back then, the idea of the separation of different peoples. She provided her own debunking of tradition, noting that the "famous Greek *pastitsio*" is in fact something learned from the Italians, though another woman insisted that it was "aristocratic" (αρχοντικό) Greek food.[17]

Influxes of unusual food also came, in the past, from returning sponge divers, who would bring dates, chickpeas, spices and sweets, among other luxury items, from the Middle East and North Africa. The wealth of the sponge industry also provided luxury goods from Europe.[18] Kalymnians contrasted themselves with the neighboring Koans in this regard, whose complete reliance on locally-grown food was cited as a sign of their "backwardness" (cf. Sutton 1998:40–5 for a discussion of Kalymnian views of other islanders). As one man derisively noted, "the Koans would come to Kalymnos to sell their children for a sack of flour!" Return migrants and Kalymnians in the merchant marines still account for influxes of food and other objects from abroad. As the folklorist Kapella describes it, the arrival of such goods from abroad (ταξιέρικα) was a special event, as family members, friends and neighbors all gathered to see what the returnee had brought, to compare with the returnings of other migrants, and to hear the migrant talk of the magical things in the land where he had been: "refrigerators always full of steaks, and even bird's milk was kept in there" (1981:43). While this event shares aspects with the food exchanges discussed earlier in this chapter, in that it was meant to create a memorable name for the migrant,

16. He also recalled a childhood rhyme that kids used to chant: "English, French, potato-eater, Italian, pasta-eater, Greek, brave bean-eater" ("Αγγλος, Γάλλος, πατατάς, Ιταλός, μακαρονάς, Έλληνας, Φασσουλάς, παλληκαράς). This is indicative that the totemic relation to food is not a recent one, nor one discovered by anthropologists.

17. A recent discussion of *pastitsio* on the Modern Greek Studies Association bulletin board seemed to agree that it was of Italian origin, though some ambiguity remains on the subject. As one contributor to the discussion notes: "*Pastitsio* is from Italian (Pasta, of course) and is a dish particularly associated with Corfu and the Ionian islands, and was presumably introduced by the Venetians. The word is derived from Italian, but the dish seems to be Corfiote in origin."

18. A travel writer at the turn of the last century describes the pressures on sponge divers: "to keep pace with the growing needs of a plentiful age that supplied silks and satins, Italian marble and French furniture, family portraits, and exotic foodstuffs" (Travis, cited in Kalafatas 1998: 25).

Kapella's hyperbole is also meant to convey the sense of amazement for those who remained on Kalymnos at what is available in foreign lands.[19] Combined with the discussion of Italian products, this gives us a sense that the influx of foreign goods could be a site for memory as well. A different kind of memory than that of the situated peaches, but one rooted in the play of the imagination in creating images of foreign lands for those who stay behind. Such memories, as Kapella describes the scene, supplemented, rather than displaced other types of memories, and also were part of Kalymnian identity practices: their claims to be both localists and cosmopolitans. Kapella captures the sense of mystery and imagination evoked by objects from abroad:

> A package of goods (πάκο) that comes from afar, from the outside, brings with it the charm of the unknown, fixes one's interest in what could be inside, what could be brought from so far away, from a world that you imagine (πλάθεις, lit. create) as different from the world you see everyday (1981:44)

This could be seen as commodity fetishism, as described by Cook and Crang (1996): forgetting actual knowledge of production while inventing presumably false knowledge in its place. However, in this instance it seems far from a passive process, as recent studies of consumption have indicated (Lunt and Livingstone 1992; Miller 1995). Hoskins, working in Eastern Indonesia, struggles with similar contrasts between objects in Western and non-Western contexts, and concludes: "Though the way possessions are imagined in modern capitalist societies is colored by the ubiquity of commodities, and on Sumba by ideas of ceremonial exchange, the deployment of the imagination is equally important in each case" (1998:197).[20] The "deployment of the imagination" described

19. The phrase "bird's milk" (του πουλιού το γάλα) is used to refer to something extremely rare and luxurious.

20. See also Helms (1993); Orlove and Bauer (1997) on the power of foreign goods. Orlove & Bauer in particular focus on the power dimensions of exotic goods: "since they indicate specific sorts of connections with distant powers that balance and compete with local bases of power" (1997:17). Also Wilk (1999) addresses the significance of the foreign/local contrast in the context of the development of ideas about a specifically Belizian cuisine. As he argues, "The taste for foreign goods over local equivalents . . . can be seen as a consequence of the desire to know more about the world, to become more sophisticated, to acquire new forms of knowledge and to make that knowledge material" (1999: 248). He looks at the shifting meanings of Belizian and foreign foods over a twenty-year period. An interesting ethnography could be written along similar lines on the

here by Kapella and Hoskins is, I am arguing, a rich source of memories and of what we social scientists have taken to calling "identity."

Of course, with this example of packets of food brought by return migrants, we are a long way from the economic restructuring implicit in Seremetakis's discussion of EU market dominance. The active appropriation of commodities by consumers should not blind us to such larger realities of production.[21] However, the preceding does suggest that questions of change in people's experience and memory of material objects such as food must be approached ethnographically, with attention to localizing strategies as well as to global forces. This is implicit in the fact that the man who remembers the socially situated theft of Manolis's peaches remembers equally vividly the Italian Mortadella (equally socially situated within its implied critique of Kalymnian church leaders or extreme nationalists). That is, if social density is a key factor in generating food memories, such social density can be generated even in the absence of knowledge of production.

In this chapter we have seen some of the ways that the flow of food exchanges and their continued narration provides a key feature in the construction of identity and social relations within the local community

---

way foreign products have been brought into the Kalymnian social system, and how local goods have been revalued. The wife of the leading sponge merchant, Ekaterina Vouvali, who was known for her control over the island for several decades earlier in the century, was also remembered as the person who brought the first automobile to Kalymnos. The greater ability of ordinary Kalymnians to bring back all sorts of foreign products more recently suggests that this might have shifted away from being a domain of class status/control.

21. This is the problem with an otherwise quite interesting collection edited by Watson (1997) on the spread of McDonald's restaurants to East Asia. The overwhelming focus of the ethnographic studies in this collection is the way in which McDonald's occupies a different niche in the meal-system of East Asian countries, and how customers (and to a lesser extent employees) use the spaces of McDonald's for different purposes than are specified in management manuals at Hamburger University (i.e., young women using McDonald's as a legitimate place to linger and meet boyfriends), as well as the rejection of customer discipline represented by the refusal of customers to bus their own tables. Although this approach provides a needed corrective to the "McDonaldization" thesis of global standardization, it is nevertheless curious that there is no mention of issues of the *production* of beef and all the subsidiary products sold by McDonald's. This absence is all the more striking given that such issues have been very much the focus of the organized protest generated against McDonald's in the West, as well as of writers concerned with the deadly effects of monocultures and other industrial agricultural practices (see Shiva 1999).

and between Kalymnians and various outsiders on a transnational level. I have explored how the flux of new foods provide a threat to certain types of memories rooted in local knowledge. But at the same time I have suggested that such foods also provide opportunities for the play of imagination and the creation of different types of memories as well. In some cases, new foods revalorize old foods, and make these old foods epigrammatic of other temporalities, a site for what I have called "memories of *gemeinschaft*," or what are perceived by Kalymnians as compensatory memories for the trade-offs of modernity as they have experienced this process. While I have suggested some of the different sites and everyday uses of food memories in this and the preceding chapter, one question remains unanswered, and will motivate what follows in the rest of the book. That is, what is it specifically about food that makes it such a powerful source of memory? This question will take us into an exploration of two seemingly opposed theoretical currents in anthropology: first, the anthropology of the senses and bodily experience as seen through the synesthetic properties of food, and second, considerations of structure and history, as seen through the structuring of meals.

Sensory Memory and the Construction of "Worlds"

"Every man carries within him a world which is composed of all that he has seen and loved, and to which he constantly returns, even when he is travelling through, and seems to be living in, some different world" (Chateaubriand, cited in Kahn 1994: xvii).

This chapter looks at food memory from the perspective of the senses. That is, it addresses issues of how and why food is memorable as a sensory as well as a social experience. It does this through a consideration of cross-cultural, cognitive aspects of sensory memory, but without neglecting how such cognitive potentials can be culturally elaborated or downplayed in specific ways. I begin with a type of exchange not discussed in the last chapter – transnational food exchange, which has, I argue, interesting aspects as part of a process of revitalization or "returning to the whole," through multisensory or synesthetic food experiences. I then describe certain synesthetic qualities that are elaborated in Kalymnian and Greek experiences of food. Finally I consider more general questions regarding synesthesia, memory, and categorization that lead back to the social quality of food memories.

Travelling Food: Memory and Globalized Identities

A flower-pot of basil can symbolize the soul of a people better than a drama of Aeschylus (Dragoumis 1976 [1914]).

At the end of the last chapter I suggested some possible implications for memory of the inflows of food from the global marketplace to Kalymnos. In this section I turn the telescope the other way to consider outflows of food from Kalymnos (and Greece in general) to other parts of the world. Once again my purpose is not to provide an extensive ethnographic picture, but rather to suggest some useful avenues to explore in the study of food's relation to memory practices.

The reference to basil by the Greek historian Ion Dragoumis provides a point of entry into my subject, the power of tangible everyday experiences to evoke the memories on which identities are formed. Dragoumis's aphorism was given substance by a comment passed on to me by Eleana Yalouri, a Ph.D. student in anthropology living in London, who was visited by a recent migrant from Greece. Smelling a pot of basil on her window sill, he told her with evident longing "It *really*[1] smells like Greece!" Although basil is not used in cooking in Greece to the same extent as in the United States, basil-dipped water is a component of the ubiquitous leavening (προζύμι) used for bread-making, and the smell of basil a part of the general kitchen ambience in Greece.[2] That this basil-inspired memory is not an uncommon experience is further confirmed by Papanikolas, in her account of Greek immigrants in the American West in the early years of the twentieth century (1987: 156): "Basil plants grew in dusty cans on the window ledges of the restaurants and coffeehouses; men broke off sprigs to put in their lapels and from time to time brought them to their noses and breathed in the piquant scent. 'Ach, patridha, patridha,' [homeland, homeland] they said." This association is interesting at a number of levels. First, it suggests the importance of the sensory in reconnecting and remembering experiences and places one has left behind for short- or long-term migration. Secondly, the association with Greece, while particularly appropriate in this case given that basil has been taken as a national symbol in Greece, suggests that objects can shift levels of identity when experienced in new contexts, becoming a symbol not just of home or local place, but of countries or perhaps regions. Closer examination of Greek migrant experiences reveals that basil is merely the tip of the iceberg of a vast array of transnational odorific and gustatory travelling companions.

1. I am translating loosely the phrase "πο ρε γαμώτο" as "really", since it is used as an intensifier and a phrase that frames the accompanying statement as particularly emotionally charged. A more literal translation might be "fuck it all," or "for fuck's sake."

2. Hart (1992:148) notes that basil is blessed in church and brought back to the house to convey the blessing to the bread leavening. Dhosithios (1995:18; my translation) describes the process as follows: "We pass a branch of basil Into the water [being used for starter] we 'baptize' the basil, making a cross in the water three times . . ."

That food frequently accompanies people in their travels across national borders may be obvious to customs officers worldwide, but its significance has only begun to be explored by anthropologists. While there has been some interest in the way migrant food has transformed eating in the US and other migrant destinations (Raspa 1984), less attention is given to the implications for identity of the food that migrants might bring with them, or have sent from home (but see Knight 1998; Narayan 1995),[3] indeed its importance is explicitly dismissed by Hannerz in his theorizing concerning "cosmopolitans" and "locals" (1996:103). Yet Fog Olwig and Hastrup (1997) argue for the importance of "cultural sites," localized cultural wholes that become points of identification for people displaced by migrations caused by larger global processes. Here I suggest that food might be analyzed as just such a cultural site, and is especially useful in understanding Kalymnian and Greek experiences of displacement, fragmentation, and the reconstruction of wholeness.

In using the concept of "wholeness" I am drawing on the ongoing work of Fernandez on the process of "returning to the whole," which he first discusses in the context of religious revitalization movements in West Africa. Bwiti, the revitalization movement among the Fang of Gabon where Fernandez worked, is seen as a response to the alienation and fragmentation brought on by "the agents of the colonial world and simply modern times" (1982: 562). In the face of these radical changes in their society, Fang use Bwiti to reintegrate the past and the present, to "recapture the totality of the old way of life" (1982: 9). Thus, as against the celebration of fragmentation in post-modern analysis, Fernandez provides an analysis of some of the ways that those whose worlds are being rent asunder attempt creatively to reconstruct them. Fernandez's approach is potentially applicable to many sorts of alienation, from that of victims of war, to that of refugees, migrants, downsized workers, those caught in major political shifts such as the fall of Soviet socialism, and all those who in the midst of change "are looking for firm ground under their feet" (Thomassen 1996: 44).

---

3. Knight considers how packages sent from rural villages to urban centers in Japan are imagined and commodified. Narayan focuses on the way that Indian food has been "incorporated" into British society, but also gives brief attention to the gendered meaning of Indian food for women migrants expected to be the upholders of tradition, while men are given more leeway to break the rules, including dietary rules (1995:74–5). See also Petridou's analysis of Greek migrants in London which runs along similar lines to that which follows (Petridou, n.d.).

The originality in Fernandez's work comes in his focus on the symbolic processes by which the "return to the whole" is attempted. Fernandez describes the "whole" as a "state of relatedness – a kind of conviviality in experience" (1986:191). He suggests some of the difficulties of imagining or experiencing the whole given the atomization and fragmentation of present-day Fang society. It is the sense that there is a "lack of fit" or coherence between different domains of experience that leads to attempts to return to the whole. Returning to the whole requires a "mutual tuning-in" based on shared sensory experiences that are explicitly synesthetic (crossing sensory domains). "Hearing, seeing, touching, tasting – in primary groups, families, ethnic groups, fraternal or sororal associations, etc. If we don't have these things to begin with we have to somehow recreate them by an argument of images of some kind in which primary perceptions are evoked" (1986:193). This is where revitalization comes in, the process by which a domain of experience that is experienced as fragmented or deprived is revalued by simply marking it for ritual participation: "The performance of a sequence of images revitalizes, in effect, and by simple iteration, a universe of domains, an acceptable cosmology of participation, a compelling whole" (1986:203). While Fernandez focuses on elaborated ritual revitalizations, he also suggests more mundane venues for such processes, and even that the teaching of introductory anthropology is an attempt at revitalization through "taking the student's too individuated awareness and . . . in some sense returning him or her to the whole" (1986:210). It is revitalization in a more everyday context, the effects of which may certainly be less durable than a full-scale revitalization movement, but nonetheless are a key component for the construction of identity in exile, that I examine here.

Fernandez's final image is of "returning to the depths" (1986:211), an appropriate image for understanding the experience of Kalymnians. Until quite recently, Kalymnos relied on sponge diving for its livelihood. Sponge divers, prone to the crippling effects of the bends, can only temporarily regain use of their limbs and a sense of themselves as whole people by returning to the ocean depths where they contracted the disease. Fernandez's notion that wholeness requires a coherence of domains, a "structural repetition," also resonates with the words of a Kalymnian schoolteacher to whom I described my project of studying food and memory: noting that the study of food evokes a "whole way of life not divided into pieces," he pointed to sea urchins as an example. When a Kalymnian desired them, he had to take the time to go and find them . . . one couldn't buy them at the store. In diving for sea urchins "you became a sponge diver in miniature," and in the process, you were enculturated into Kalymnian life. Here "wholes" already exist; but for migrants, I suggest, food is essential to counter tendencies toward fragmentation of experience. And we can use Fernandez's terms to analyze this process of "conviviality" evoked through food in a way that brings out the aspect of memory that I believe is a key part of the experience of the return to the whole left implicit by Fernandez in his use of the term "iteration," i.e., repetition.

The experience of absence from one's home is culturally elaborated in Greece under the concept *xenitia* (ξενητειά). *Xenitia* has a long history of commentary in Greek oral tradition, as examined by Sultan (1999). Sultan examines *xenitia* in the context of heroic poetry, and notes that for men *xenitia* means absence from the physical comforts of home: "The woman will not be with her man in *xenitia* to cook his meals or serve his needs . . . [thus] he will experience hardship and isolation with his horse as his only companion. The analogy is to misery and death" (Sultan 1999: 48). More generally in the modern Greek context, *xenitia* is described as a condition of estrangement, absence, death, or of loss of social relatedness, loss of the ethic of care seen to characterize relations at home (Danforth 1982:93ff.; Seremetakis 1991:85, 175–6). It provokes a longing for home that is seen as a physical and spiritual pain, as Frantzis describes for the Dodecanese migrants to Tarpon Springs, Florida: "The sun-drenched shores of Florida [are] verdant with pine-trees, orange trees, palms, beautiful tropical trees, and multi-colored fragrant flowers. All of them resemble and remind them of their islands. Nevertheless, and in spite of it all, their heart withers, and the longing for the wild beauty of these chunks of rocks where they were born is alive in them" (Frantzis 1962: 105). Here the sensual landscape of Florida serves as a painful reminder of the home they have left.[4] More usually, however, migrants are moving to an urban environment where there is a more striking sense of disjunction. Hence the need to have some physical object carried along

---

4. And indeed, Tarpon Springs was chosen as a migration spot for Dodecanese islanders because of its similarities, because it allowed them to extend their sea-going profession to a new locale (see Buxbaum 1967; Frantzis 1962). As Georges (1980 [1964]:33) notes, "Unlike their countrymen in other parts of the United States, the Greeks of Tarpon Springs had to make few *immediate* concessions to their new environment. The Florida climate was comparable to that in the Dodecanese islands. Households were re-established to emulate those in the mother country . . . Dietary habits and modes of dress were retained . . . Theirs was a life transplanted in the fullest sense of the word."

or sent as a tangible site for memory, as expressed by poet Y. Drosinis (cited in Sederocanellis 1995:230) in the idea of carrying Greek earth with him in his travels:

> Now that I leave for foreign lands,
> and we will be parted for months, for years,
> let me take something also from you,
>
> . . .
>
> Earth scented by the summer seasons,
> blessed earth, earth bearing fruit –
> the muscat vine, the yellow grain,
> the tender laurel, bitter olive . . .

Here it is agricultural soil (though elsewhere in the poem he speaks of "blood-imbued" national soil) that can be seen as a link to home. But food itself is more commonly sent to migrants, whether they have left a home village for Athens, for a sponge-diving expedition, or for Europe, the US or Australia.[5] Such packages of food sent abroad are given the local word *pestellomata* (πεστελλώματα)[6] and described by Kapella as a part that recalls the whole: "*pestellomata* are a piece of homeland, carrying inside them its sun, its sea, its wonderful smells" (Kapella 1981: 35). Kapella stresses the symbolic nature of this transfer in recounting the bitterness of a Kalymnian mother whose son had married an Athenian and moved to Athens. She is told by her daughter-in-law not to send anything because "the refrigerator is full."[7] As Kapella notes, "in order to appreciate a *pestelloma* you need to have lived in a place, and to love it" (1981:39).

Such packages sent within Greece often include fish pickled in rosemary and vinegar (often red mullet, available in Athens but at much inflated prices), locally produced cheese (μυζήθρα), locally-grown

---

5. Gavrielides (1974:68) indeed notes the function of ceremonial feasting associated with name-day celebrations in providing a mechanism for maintaining ties between villages and their migrant populations.

6. From the standard Greek ἀποστέλλωμα, a dispatch.

7. Buxbaum notes similar concern expressed among Dodecanese islanders in Tarpon Springs, Florida in cases of mixed marriages between Greek men and non-Greek women: "Greek-American mothers of sons who have married American girls frequently prepare Greek foods and bring them into the house of the married son as a means of making contact often against the wishes of the wife" (Buxbaum 1967: 232).

tangerines and a variety of homemade sweets.[8] Those sent further abroad can include Kalymnian oregano, thyme, mountain tea, locally produced honey, figs, almonds, hard cheese and dried dark bread rings,[9] all items that are particularly fragrant markers. The desire for such food is referred to by Kapella as a "burning of the lips" that comes from missing something deeply (1981:36). Similarly a Kalymnian woman describes her brother's longing for a Kalymnian bivalve prepared in brine (σπινιάλο) as his *kaïmo* – the noun form of the Greek "to burn," which translates as both "psychic pain" and "uncontrollable desire" – which led him on his return to consume an entire bottle and become sick. Another story that a man told me concerned his son's time spent in the merchant marine, when during a long and unhappy stint in England in the late 1970s he bought a small vial of olive oil from a chemist's shop (at the time olive oil was not generally available for cooking in England), to soothe his desire for the taste and smell of it. That this tiny vial would be satisfying seems surprising, but it relates to a local practice that if you smell a food cooking at someone's house and strongly desire it, you must at least taste a small piece or lick the remains (for example, of lobster shells). Otherwise the desire might cause men's testicles to swell (να μπουζευθούν) or pregnant women to lose their babies (perhaps a transfer of desire from one domain to another).

In some cases it is not specifically Kalymnian food that is sent abroad. A man in his thirties who had migrated back and forth to Italy for schooling mentioned that his mother sent him all kinds of things, feta cheese, grape leaves, even flour, "as if they wouldn't have flour in Italy!" Another woman speaks of sending her daughter a special sweet

---

8. Kremezi (1999:14) describes the food packages received by Athenians from "home" villages: "My brother-in-law still gets parcels from his mother, who lives in Volos, Thessaly, containing not only fantastic baklava and squash pie made with hand-rolled phyllo pastry, but also *katsamaki*, a kind of cornmeal porridge. *Katsamaki* is something that most of us would not like to eat unless we had been starved for a couple of days. But what for most of us is tasteless mush is, for him, a reminder of happy, although difficult, childhood years."

9. Arnott notes that in Mani festive Easter *kouloures* have a mnemonic function for those abroad: "a *kouloura* is made for each member of the family who is away from home, and it is either sent to him or, if the distance is too great, it is hung on the wall and eaten 'for his health' by other members of the family while they are gathered together. Then the family speaks of his absence, of the work he is doing, and of his childhood activities" (1975:302).

(Φοινίκι);[10] when I asked if it was Kalymnian she replied: "no, it's Greek, but there are variations, whether you use oil or butter, almonds – and in any case it reminds her of Kalymnos." In speaking with Greek students studying in Oxford, I found that the food they received from home (either through the mail or brought by friends or family members on visits) fell into three categories: (1) olives, olive oil, meat (in one case, two whole goats for Easter), eggs and other products produced by family members on family land; (2) baked goods associated with Easter and other festive times (τσουρέκι and Φτάζυμο), either prepared by family members or store-bought; (3) mass-produced Greek products such as Feta cheese. The first type of item produced immediate local knowledge: one woman, who had lived in London for ten years working in various jobs while taking courses in art and design (with hopes to become an icon painter), told me about the olive oil that her father makes from family trees in Crete, and that the olives were especially good for oil because they weren't watered, but raised only on rainwater. She said it had zero per cent acidity; that it sometimes becomes more acidic if you let the olives fall off the tree, but her father used a stick to knock them off the tree, and you must knock in a certain direction, otherwise the olives won't grow again.

Aside from such local knowledge, sensory aspects of food sent from Greece are also stressed. Another woman, studying environmental planning, who had been in England for five years, spoke of the eggs sent from her father's farm, which she contrasted with "plastic" eggs in England, which had a particularly unpleasant smell (μυρίζουν αβγουλίλα), while eggs from Greece had a deep orange color to the yolks and an "intense" (έντονη) flavor.[11] The second category had an obvious connection to "Greek traditions" as well as to the family, usually mothers, who had baked some of these items. But it is certainly not only mothers who put together such packages. Fathers, grandmothers and grandfathers may send separate packages of foodstuffs, items that they have actually produced or that they have shared in the past with the receiving child.

10. An Athenian friend tells me that the equivalents of *foinikia* are made in Athens. Called μελομακάρονα, they are typically available only at Christmas time.

11. This tendency toward hyperbole in describing Greek products is captured by Papanikolas (1987:10) in her account of her mother and other Greek women drinking coffee and eating Greek "honey and nut" sweets and pining "for 'sweet *patridha*' (homeland) where grapes were sweeter, lemons larger, water colder." On the "plastic flavor" of foreign products as experienced by Greek migrants, see also Petridou n.d..

This direct connection with the family through food takes place in less tangible ways as well. Currently, with the availability of Greek products in the United Kingdom and the United States (even on the internet) one has the possibility of shopping for and cooking many Greek dishes.[12] If this makes packages of food from home somewhat less special, the contact through food remains. Elisabeth Kirtsoglou, a doctoral student in anthropology in Wales, notes that her mother invariably asks her what she is making for Sunday dinner: "She is satisfied when I tell her roast lamb, or other Sunday food. It symbolizes for her that I am doing OK."

The third category of mass-produced Greek products was less common in the late 1990s. One man noted that now (in 1998) it was possible to get these same products at British supermarkets, so that the only connection they had to Greece for him was the thought of his mother sending them. But others spoke of the importance of Feta at earlier periods of migration, when Greek Feta was not widely available. Dimitris Theodossopoulos, an anthropologist at the University of Lampeter in Wales, notes that new students who come from Greece wouldn't realize how much they were going to miss Feta. "When they would return to Greece for Christmas, they would really stock up, fill their suitcases and bags with Feta in all different kinds of containers. One trip I came back from Greece with a 10-kilo tin of Feta cheese, which I preserved in brine. . . . I would cut a little piece with my meal every night. It was like 'white gold' to me (laughing)."

What is the actual experience of such food events? As was seen above, they are often experienced in terms of a "burning desire" that is satiated through a sensory experience evoking local knowledge, at the same time that a domain of experience that has fallen into disuse, in Fernandez's terms, is revalued. They often explicitly evoke a wholeness, or fullness in experience, as in the following report by Kapella of a letter from a woman living in Germany, written in local Kalymnian dialect, on receiving a *pestelloma* from Kalymnos at the post office: "My joy was indescribable, I laughed and cried at the same time. I took the package, left the post office, and in the street I felt like I was holding

---

12. There is an economic component involved in these transfers as well. Up until the early 1980s the Bank of Greece strictly limited the amount of money that could be transferred to relatives abroad, which posed a particular problem for parents of students studying abroad. Packages of food were one way of making up for the 'poverty' that children of middle-class parents were undergoing while studying abroad. Indeed, it was not unknown to smuggle cash inside various types of food packages.

the whole world [in my arms]" (Kapella 1981:36). The woman notes that she used the honey to make doughnuts (ψευτοϋριστές, a Kalymnian word) and she "soothed her insides" (ηβαρσαμώθηκα τα μέσα). She contrasts this feeling to her experience of the sensory deprivation of work in Germany in a few descriptive images: "we've made money, but we've moldered (ηραχλιάσαμε) in the factories. We don't see outside and we're dying of cold . . . Thank you for the *pestelloma*" (1981:36).

This gives a clear sense of one strategy for returning to the whole: through what Fernandez calls the shock of "recognition of a wider integrity of things" captured in the metaphor of the "whole world," but specifically triggered by *memory* of taste and smell. It is this memory that leads to the emotional affect described in the passage: simultaneous laughing and crying, and then a sense of soothing fullness, suggesting the evocation of other memories. The expression "laughing and crying" implies that such moments of wholeness are bittersweet and temporary, a reminder of a homeland the return to which is deferred. Yet the soothing fullness also suggests that such moments give the migrants the strength to carry on with their *xenitia*. This sense of emotional/ embodied plenitude evoked above is echoed in the following passage from Papanikolas (1987:217), describing several Greek immigrant men, cousins who were working in Idaho in an endless task of clearing sagebrush to homestead:

> One night, working nervously, swearing obscenely, Louis made a *pita*. He could have waited for Sunday, gone the six miles to Pocatello . . . and had one of the Greek women who ran boarding houses make it for him, but he wanted it right then. Louis rolled out the pastry leaves, layered each sheet with butter and eggs mixed with crumbled feta. The helper gazed with tearful eyes, Yoryis avidly. That night they fell on their cots, satisfied.

Once again, the terrible emotional overload of *xenitia* – living in a foreign land – is temporarily relieved in the experience, which demands and receives immediate satisfaction.

And once again it is the iteration of a neglected domain, metonymically described ("Louis rolled out the pastry leaves . . .") that revitalizes it for the participants. Implicitly, the revitalization of one domain brings others with it, a point made by recent theorists of refugee displacement. For example, Nordstrom (1995) describes the everyday and ritual practices of resistance to the destruction wrought on people's lives by war in Mozambique. She concludes: "Worlds are destroyed in a war;

they must be re-created. Not just worlds of home, family, community, and economy but worlds of definition, both personal and cultural" (1995:147). Bahloul's (1996:28) description of Jewish Algerian refugee memories also resonates in this context with Fernandez's concept of the return to the whole: "The remembered house is a small scale *cosmology* symbolically restoring the integrity of a shattered geography" (emphasis mine).[13] As Fernandez describes, integrity is restored through a remembered coherence, or structural repetition between domains. This occurs because the food event evokes a whole world of family, agricultural associations, place names and other "local knowledge." Even memories of water have this characteristic, partly owing to the fact that different qualities of water are said to produce different qualities of food (for example, water used for olive trees or water used to soak beans before cooking them). Papanikolas recounts migrants' memories of water sources from home (1987:167), illustrating the almost sacred power of invocation:

> The men talked constantly of the water in their part of Greece, which often had to be carried a long distance over rocky trails, how cold it was, a special taste, its curative qualities, how its fame was known throughout the province and people came from afar to drink it. They spoke the names of waters with reverence: Kefalovrissi – Head Springs, Palaios Platanos – Old Plane Tree, Mahi Topos – Slaughtering Place, Nifi Peplos – Bride's Veil, Nerolithi – Water Rock.

It is this same sense of the part that holds the key to re-vivifying a whole structure of associations that I found when I followed the advice of my colleague cited in the introduction to "try Proust." Here is Proust describing the memory of the senses evoked by food, in his famous *madeleine* description:

13. See also Bardenstein (1999) on Palestinian memory in exile, and the metonymical association of trees and landscape (especially fig trees) with homeland and wholeness. Bardenstein cites a poem that describes the joy of a Palestinian man who grows a fig tree in his backyard:

> There, in the middle of Dallas, Texas,
> a tree with the largest, fattest, sweetest figs in the world.
> "It's a fig tree song!" he said,
> plucking his fruits like ripe tokens,
> emblems, assurance
> of a world that was always his own. (Nye, cited in Bardenstein 1999:152.)

But when from a long-distant past nothing subsists, after the people are dead, after the things are broken and scattered, taste and smell alone, more fragile but more enduring, more unsubstantial, more persistent, more faithful, remain poised a long time, like souls, remembering, waiting, hoping, amid the ruins of all the rest; and bear unflinchingly, in the tiny and almost impalpable drop of their essence, *the vast structure of recollection* (Proust 1982:50–1; italics mine).

Of course Proust was not speaking of migration, as I have been. But if the past "is a foreign country," then similar processes can be at work in temporal as in spatial or spatio-temporal displacement. And indeed Proust directs us once again to the power of sensory parts to return us to the whole, of the unsubstantial fragment to reveal the vast structure. Like the memories discussed above, Proust also points us to the emotional charge of the moment of consumption for keying, involuntarily, these associative memories. But why taste and smell? The question still looms before us.

I would also suggest another reason for the sense of "fullness" stressed in these descriptions: that there is an imagined community implied in the act of eating food "from home" while in exile, in the embodied knowledge that others are eating the same food. This is not to deny that real communities are created as well: Dimitris Theodossopoulos notes how he would bring pieces of his 10-kilo Feta cheese to friends with whom he was sharing dinner, and the joy evoked in the shared consumption of this "most valuable object." But even in this case of shared consumption, a wider community of homeland is being referenced in the act of eating "food from home."

Here I am drawing on Anderson's notion of imagined communities, made famous in his primal scene of the "secular ritual" of the newspaper reader who, in the everyday act of reading "is well aware that the ceremony he performs is being replicated simultaneously by thousands (or millions) of others of whose existence he is confident, yet of whose identity he has not the slightest notion . . . What more vivid figure of the secular, historically clocked, imagined community can be envisioned?" (1991:35). What indeed? Anderson's image, despite its appeal, is perhaps far too literary as a conceptualization of processes of identity formation and reproduction (see Wogan n.d., for a critique of Anderson's literacy-oriented biases). It lacks Fernandez's sense of the importance of immediate, synesthetic experience as a primary strategy of dealing with the inchoate. As Palmer, drawing on Billig's concept of 'banal nationalism,' argues: food is one of the mundane reminders that keep national identity "near the surface of daily life" so that people do not forget their nationality (Palmer 1998: 192).

Here things become interesting, because the processes I have been describing work at multiple, sometimes contradictory levels of identity – the family, personal or village history that needs only to be remembered, or reimagined, as well as at higher levels of imagining such as the nation. Just as people's identities shift levels in changing contexts such as migration, local products can take on shifting identifications as well. I have suggested that Feta cheese evokes a national "Greek" identity in migrant contexts. Within Greece Feta can shift between representing a "national" cheese (part of the diet of most Greeks and the single most-consumed cheese within Greece) and also having strong local associations (i.e., strong differentiating between Feta produced in different parts of Greece). The same man who shared Feta with other "Greeks" also had very localized memories of buying Feta as a child from the small shop in his neighborhood: how it was kept in large cans of brine, and the shop-owner had a "magical way of dipping his knife in the brine and simultaneously spearing and cutting the Feta." In the mid-1990s, In the wake of challenges by Denmark to the EU to have the right to produce a cheese called "Feta," Feta gained new "national" significance. The "purity" of Greek Feta, represented by the "whiteness" of ewes' milk (as opposed to the "yellowish" cows' milk that predominates in Danish Feta) became a rallying point in Greece, thus associating Feta with the whiteness of ancient Greek statues.[14] What was a taken-for-granted national product with local associations became a national symbol in which to debate issues of Greece's relation to the European Union.[15] Like Feta experienced abroad, the basil sniffed in a pot in London reminds the new migrant of "Greece" in this instance, rather than any more localized association. Though it is interesting to note that the phrase cited by Papanikolas "Ach, patridha, patridha" (homeland, homeland), is inherently ambiguous in Greek, and can be used to refer to both local and national "homes."

14. See Petridou (2001) for a full discussion. For a review of the issue of food and place names, or *appellations d'origine*, see Moran 1993.

15. See Petridou (2001) for a full discussion. An interesting discussion was provoked in March 1999 on the Modern Greek Studies Association Electronic Bulletin Board by an article in a college newspaper by an American student complaining about the anti-American politics of her Greek roommate, whom she refers to by the pseudonym "Feta." Here a "smelly" cheese comes, through synecdoche, to stand for an entire national identity as well, but in the negative context of ethnic slurs, rather than the positive one of ethnic identifications.

The power of smell and taste is not fixed to specific references then, but can take on many levels of identity, which normally don't contradict one another. However, local and national experience are not always congruent. A Greek couple living in England recount, half-jokingly, their fights over bean soup (Φασολάδα), which the woman believes is "properly" made with tomatoes, and the man equally vociferously insists cannot be made with them. As the woman put it, "call it something else: call it some French recipe for making beans, and I'll eat it. Just don't call it authentic bean soup, and don't call it Greek!" The man noted that they no longer made *fassoladha*; it was only when his partner was away, and perhaps his sister (also living in England) was over for dinner, that he enjoyed this dish. Here it is the fact that he comes from the Peloponnese region and she from Thessaloniki that makes for the clash in attempting to make their local experience a metonym for national identity. And although local divergences in cooking, dress and custom are part of discourse within Greece as well,[16] I would suggest that they become more intensified in the migrant context, where cooking is not simply an everyday practice, but an attempt to reconstruct and remember synesthetically, to return to that whole world of home, which is subjectively experienced both locally and nationally, if not at other levels as well.

This brings us to a deeper consideration of the sensory aspects, or the synesthesia that forms a key component of these memories. Or, as I asked a moment ago, why taste and smell? I address this question from two directions, first: a general consideration of the socio-cognitive aspects of the senses and synesthesia in cuing, storing or creating memory, and, second: an examination of the specifics of Kalymnian sense worlds that argue for the particular potency of food memories in this cultural context.

Taste, Smell and Evocation

Although I focused in the preceding section on the power of migratory food among Kalymnians and Greeks abroad, the themes of fragmentation and the search for the whole permeate US migrant experience.[17]

---

16. See, for example, my discussion of perceived endo-Greek differences in Sutton 1998:40–5.

17. See, for example, Pettis (1995) for a rich discussion of fragmentation and the search for wholeness in the novels of Paule Marshall describing the experience of West Indian immigrants.

I could just have easily found similar materials in the experiences of other diasporic groups and individuals, as shown in the beginning of the film *Il Postino*, in which an old woman tells the postmaster that she is sending her own pickled capers to her son in the United States, to which the postmaster replies: "He will be pleased." Sarah Franklin, an American-born Anthropologist living and working in Britain, provided me with the following list of items brought back from a recent trip to the States:

- Maple syrup produced by Aunt and Uncle in New Hampshire
- Velveeta processed "cheesefood" (a vastly underrated food, she says)
- Karo Syrup (a sweetener)
- Bisquick pancake mix (Here she talks about how she shows her English friends how to cook with Bisquick: "mix it in a bowl with water, 'watch carefully,' and it's done!").
- Indian Corn and corn flour for tortillas (made from the inside of the kernel that has been soaked in wood ash, lye or lime. She never cooked much corn in the US, but has a corn fetish now out of "pure chauvinism." British call corn "maize," and use it as animal feed. She has even planted corn in her backyard, from seeds brought back from Guatemala).
- Reese's Peanut Butter Cups (Despised by the British because of the mix of chocolate and peanut butter; but in fact she has got her whole office on to these).
- Arm and Hammer Baking soda (she buys this for the packaging, a distinct orange, old-fashioned color, because she likes the way they look in her kitchen).
- Limes from California and other fresh fruit from Latin America (brought in illegally).

This list shares many aspects with those of Greek migrants in its mix of items involving personal connection or local knowledge of place with those associated with a particular home activity (Bisquick and breakfast), and items of significance in maintaining a broader national identity experienced as different from "the British."[18] Along similar lines many friends, knowing of my interest, have shared "Proustian memories" focused more on temporal than spatial displacement. If this is clearly a general, if not universal phenomenon (remember our Oxford

18. See also Goddard (1996:207) on the nostalgic longings for food from home on the part of Neapolitan migrants in northern Italy.

don), some wider consideration of the issues involved in sense memory seems in order.

Evocative Senses

Note that in his *madeleine* description, Proust does not single out taste, but rather taste and smell, as the senses that hold the promise of the return of the memorable whole. Taste and smell, it is generally noted, are interrelated senses. The chewing of food forces air up through the mouth to the nose, and a blocked nose can cause considerable reduction in the ability to taste (Vroon 1997:24). In his 1975 work *Rethinking Symbolism*, Dan Sperber directly addresses the Proustian phenomenon in a consideration of the evocative power of smells. I believe his discussion could equally well be applied to taste, as will become clear from what follows. Sperber begins by contrasting smells with colors. While colors have a fairly elaborate classificatory terminology, hierarchically arranged so that we recognize shades of the same color, smells are organized much more simply along an axis of good–bad, and in terms of their causes and sometimes their effects: "the smell of coffee brewing," "a nauseating smell" (see also Engen 1991: 86). Attempts at scientific classification of smells in something equivalent to classes have led to little consensus concerning what might constitute clusters of smells and "primary smells," and attempted taxonomies seem forced and vague, such as Linnaeus' division of smells (on a gradient of best to worst) into (1) Aromatic, (2) Scented or perfumed, (3) Ambrosia or musk-like, (4) Sharp or garlic-like, (5) Stinking or goat-like, sweaty, (6) Repulsive and (7) Disgusting.[19] Sperber continues his contrast by noting that it is fairly easy to recall colors to mind, even when not in the presence of the actual stimulus. In other words, if asked to imagine the color of a Granny Smith apple, most people experience little difficulty seeing the color in their mind, or the apple itself. The same is not true for smells, or, I might add, for tastes.[20] As Sperber notes, if one does want to recall a scent, one often employs an image: the church where one smelled a certain type of incense: "and I will almost have the impression that I sense that scent – a misleading impression,

19. Vroon 1997:47–51; see also Lawless 1997 for a recent attempt at different classification schemes.
20. Though some people claim to have this ability to recall smells or tastes, experimental evidence seems to indicate that it is a relatively rare phenomenon (Vroon 1997:101; Lawless 1997:155).

however, which will fade as soon as, relinquishing the recollection of the object it emanated from, I try mentally to reconstitute the scent itself" (1975:117).

The failure to recall scents is related for Sperber to the way they are categorized, or rather, not categorized; in other words, there is no "semantic field of smells." By contrast, in the presence of a stimulus, smells can be recognized over a distance of many years.[21] Recognized, but not analyzed and described in the fashion one might do for a color. Or for the face of someone one has seen before whom one runs into at the supermarket: once recognized, one can access or invoke prior information one has about the person to whom the face belongs, and add the fact that you shop at the same supermarket. With smells, however, because of the difficulty of analysis and invocation, one attempts evocation: "in the case of smells, the evocational field comprises all recollections likely to corroborate the feeling of recognition, and it is these recollections that evocation passes in review" (1975:121). In other words, smells evoke what surrounds them in memory, what has been metonymically associated with the smell in question. Smells are prototypical symbols, in Sperber's terms: "by virtue of the accepted definitions according to which the symbol is the part for the whole, or the object that gives rise to something other than itself, or the motivated sign, etc." (1975:118).

Recent research has borne out Sperber's view of the relation between smell and memory. First, the idea that memory often works by synchronous convergence, i.e., the association of diverse things occurring at the same time, is "well documented" (Fuster 1997:451). "If, for example, you are reading Dante's *Divine Comedy* about Beatrice while watching scenes on the television of refugees, then images of Beatrice and the suffering of refugees are likely to be associated in your memory" (Reyna, n.d.:284; see also Engen 1991: 3ff.). But this property is more true of smells, as Vroon notes, because smells more easily connect with "episodic" than "semantic" memories (i.e., life-history memories as opposed to "recognition of a phenomenon" memories), and also because of the tendency for smell memories to be emotionally charged (Vroon 1997:95, 104). This emotional charge is touched on by Sperber in noting that in trying to place a smell that one is re-experiencing

21. As Vroon (1997:102) notes, smells are not recognized under experimental conditions in short-term situations as well as visual stimuli, but those that do manage to be stored are recognized quite well over long periods.

"one may revive memories that are more captivating than the smell itself, more insistent than the original desire one had to identify it" (1975:122). Or to quote a food author discussing the phenomenon of taste memory: "the hunger is in the memory, not in the biscuit, berries and cream [your mother's strawberry shortcake]" (Lust 1998:175).

Once again, if we extend this view to taste, which shares limbic system location, and low semantic/high episodic recall, then we have a confirmation that, on both counts, Proust was right! And this gives us a context to understand the bag of apricots with which Yiannis began his story of forty years ago that so puzzled me, since it was not at all about apricots. The apricots provided the taste and smell that could continually cue for him all the local knowledge of time of year, of places on Kalymnos where apricots could be found, and that unlocked a vaster structure of recollection of different times on Kalymnos.

Sperber speculates on the absence of other analyses of smell in anthropological discussions of symbolism, given that they are for him "*symbols par excellence,*" and places the blame on their seemingly individual and idiosyncratic nature which "bypass[es] all forms of coded communication" (1975:118). In other words, apricots evoke the Second World War for Yiannis, but they just give me hives. But say the words "Chinese Pressed Duck" and I am sent into reveries of early college years and love in bloom. However, Sperber goes on to argue that culture does in fact play a role in these types of phenomena. Through repetition in ritual and other forms, cultural symbolism "focuses the attention of the members of a single society in the same directions, determines parallel evocational fields that are structured in the same way, but leaves the individual free to effect an evocation in them as he likes" (1975: 137).[22]

These ideas form a bridge to our consideration of the sensory worlds within which Kalymnian evocative fields are shaped, if not determined. And it is a bridge that, while hopefully leading us forward, also returns us to Fernandez's conception of the whole, since, as I will argue, it is the notion of synesthesia that best sums up the sensory experiences with which I will be concerned.

---

22. Stewart (1997:879) makes similar points in discussing the cultural aspects of seemingly individual phenomena such as dreams in Greece. When five different informants from the same village told him that they had had dreams about going to dig up treasures only to find coal instead of gold, his first reaction was to be sure that they were pulling his leg.

"Listen to That Smell!": The Cultivation of Synesthesia

In studying phenomena in comparative, cross-cultural perspective – from concepts of personhood, gifts and commodities, to embodiment – recent anthropological work has stressed that we are dealing not, for the most part, with radical cultural difference, but with shifting emphases, with cultural elaborations on a continuum of experience. Thus ideas of the "individual" vs. the socially embedded "dividual" do not characterize entire cultures, but rather may represent dominant understandings without precluding the co-existence of subordinate understandings opposed to these within the same culture. Such a view is applicable to the attempt to describe different, "non-Western" sensory worlds: we are not dealing with phenomena of radically different perceptions, but rather with the cultural elaboration of certain sensory registers and the relative dormancy of others.[23] The study of smell and taste in one society might lead one to look at the realm of myth and the afterlife (Bubant 1998), in another to issues of healing (Rasmussen 1999), and to the domain of advertising in a third (Classen, Howes and Synnott 1994: Ch. 6). In trying to give a sense of Kalymnian smell- and taste-scapes, I will focus on the domains of religious experience and cooking, stressing the cultural elaboration of the synesthetic nature of these domains that leads to their prominence in memory processes. Cultural elaboration is reflected, but not completely comprised, in linguistic elaboration. Thus, while I will focus on Kalymnian discussions of taste and smell, which of course provide the easiest access for the ethnographer, I will also describe ways in which these senses may be elaborated non-linguistically.

"Orthodox ritual stimulates the senses – sight, sound, touch, taste and smell" (Hirschon 1998: 21). Indeed, it is difficult to enter a church on Kalymnos and not feel overpowered by sensory stimulation, from the smells of myrrh and frankincense that are spread by the priests swinging censers rhythmically back and forth, to the flicker of the candles that each person lights and places in front of the icon when

---

23. Bubant is particularly critical of the "radical alterity" approach to non-Western sensory experience, as well as the view that certain senses are more power-laden, while others move us into the realm of freedom from social constraints. This view is explicit or implicit in post-modern critiques of the hegemony of vision or ocularcentricity (Bubant 1998:48–9). That smell and taste are both capable of hegemonic uses is clear from recent studies (Corbin 1986; Classen, Howes and Synnott 1994: Ch. 5; Howes and Lalonde 1991).

entering the church. One experiences the kinesthetics of making the cross and kissing the icon, the press of bodies in the often confined space of many of the small chapels on Kalymnos, and the reverberating nasal pitch of the liturgy being sung by the cantors. And, of course there is the multicolored sight of the icons, illustrating key stories from the Bible, and the taste of the communion bread and wine mixed to the consistency of gruel and presented by the priest on a spoon. Kenna (n.d.: 5) sees this in terms of reinforcement of the message of sacredness: "An Orthodox Church service is a synesthetic experience: every sense is conveying the same message."[24] The sensory experiences are not confined to the church, but extend outward into the community. The liturgy itself, projected by loudspeaker, is heard throughout each neighborhood every Sunday morning and on other special days. At other times it is the bells of the church being rung that peal through the streets of each neighborhood usually to announce a funeral. Incense, basil, icons and blessed bread are a few of the many items that either pass between church and home, usually through the mediation of women, or are reduplicated in each setting (Hart 1992:148; Hirschon 1998:139–140; Kenna n.d.).[25] When liturgies are held at the many local chapels that dot the island, usually on the name day of the saint of the chapel, these sensory aspects are extended through the serving of a variety of sweets and Greek coffee at the end of the liturgy. And on Kalymnos in particular sensory aspects of the church are heightened by the throwing of dynamite from church courtyards on Saturday at midnight when Christ is officially risen.[26] People expressed the importance of dynamite by using a language of feeling: "If I didn't

24. Forrest (1988:225ff.) provides a useful contrast, in his ethnographic description of a Baptist church in North Carolina, where he argues that other senses are shut out of the church experience in order to provide a sensory focusing on the experience of sound. It is only in religious activities that take place outside the church (church suppers), that multisensory experience is encouraged.

25. Kenna distinguishes between incense use at home, which marks a transition from profane to sacred activities, and in the church, where all is sacred, but incense is used to "'sharpen our attention' and indicate that we are going to get in touch now, this particular moment, with something which is always there" (n.d.: 19).

26. As I have argued elsewhere (Sutton 1998: 73ff.), the practice of Kalymnian dynamite-throwing is one of heightened sensual experience: "the sight of the explosion itself, the smell of dynamite going off around you, the thickness of the air created by the pressure of numerous explosions, and finally the sense of relief after you throw and are still in one piece. I have been told that it is something so basic and primal that you can only experience it by throwing yourself."

hear the dynamite I wouldn't feel it was truly Easter," was a common sentiment. And many migrants are known to phone home on Easter specifically to hear the sounds of the exploding dynamite.

The stress on the material and sensory aspects of religious experience is a part of the official doctrine of Orthodoxy, as seen in the notion of the deification of matter, or the idea that "it is the human vocation to manifest the spiritual *in and through the material*" (Ware 1979: 64; emphasis in original). Panourgia, for example, stresses the corporeality of Greek religion, crystallized in ritual and epitomized in the *epitaphios*, the funeral procession of Christ on Good Friday (1995:151ff.). And these sensory aspects of religious experience were often remarked upon by Kalymnians as well, and seen as what distinguished their religion from the perceived "coldness" of Western Christianity. Two men in a coffee shop discussed with me and each other at length the power of different cantors on the island to evoke religious sensibility through the sound impressions they created on the tympanum of the ear. This is a common topic of discussion, as frequent church attenders compare the services at different churches in terms of the beauty of their cantors' singing voices.

Another key sensory aspect associated with Orthodoxy is the question of the smell of decay associated with sin and death. Although the body and other matter is not inherently sinful, matter is corruptible as well as redeemable, a distinction made by Ware between "body" and "flesh" (1979: 79; see discussion 59ff.). On Kalymnos this distinction tends to play out in the realm of smell, with sinful flesh smelling putrid, while redeemed flesh smells "wonderful," perhaps an association with the incense that envelops priests and the church (cf. Classen, Howes and Synnott 1994:52). The corpse of a bad person is said to putrefy quickly, and to stink very soon after death. One man told me a story about someone on his deathbed who feared he might have such a fate. He instructed his wife to place a small vial of perfume in his funeral jacket when he was buried, so that later people would smell it and say "mmm (making a gesture of smelling) this must be a saint, he smells of frankincense"; and thus gravediggers checked the pockets of the people they were burying against such frauds.[27] Similarly, the proof adduced by many people that a Kalymnian man who had died in the 1960s

---

27. Similar associations can be found in Medieval Western Christianity. Classen, Howes and Synnott (1994:53) for example, note that "the body of St. Isidore . . . showed no signs of decay and emitted a ravishing odour when it was disinterred forty years after the saint's death in the twelfth century, and then again four hundred and fifty years

was indeed a saint was the fact that his remains, on display at one of the island monasteries, had not putrefied after all these years.[28] A considerable part of this was seen as related to a rejection of food and animal flesh in particular, the food most directly associated with religiously required abstinence from certain foods (see Sutton 1997 for a full discussion). One man told me of the decayed smell of meat that remains overnight caught between his teeth, as compared to vegetables, which he claimed did not have such a smell.

Good and bad smells also make claims for social distinction, as a number of writers have noted (Classen, Howes and Synnott 1994: 165–9; Corbin 1986). Thus a man in the heat of an argument with his wife about family financial dealings shouts "I'm a sweet-smelling flower, and you are stinking meat!" (είμαι μυρισμένο λουλούδι και 'συ βρωμοκρέας). This indicates his claim to have had "clean" financial dealings with the world, in contrast to his perceptions of his wife's corrupt schemings.[29] On Kalymnos smell can be used as a put-down for poorer families, such as a neighborhood grocer who was nicknamed "dirty," and whose store was reputed to smell. But smell can also act as a leveling mechanism "from below" on Kalymnos. Thus a man, describing to me a neighbor who was planning to open a hotel, mocked him, saying "he puts on a tie every morning [here the man acts out

---

after his death when it was exhumed once again . . ." They also note the practice of using herbs and spices on the bodies of the well-to-do at their funerals in the Middle Ages. Gonzalez-Crussi (1991: 74 ff.) also discusses the "odour of sanctity" and notes that smell was in some cases tied to taste as well. On describing the smell of St Lydwine, a contemporary notes: "'It was as if one had eaten ginger, clove, or cinnamon: the strong and spicy flavor softly bit the tongue and the palate'" (1991: 75).

28. I refer to St Savvas, recently canonized by the Church. See Papanikolaos 1989 for an account of his life and works.

29. Corbin (1986) stresses the use of smell by higher classes to distinguish themselves from the lower class, and one finds similar ideas concerning rural/urban contrasts in Greece. For example, a woman from Athens expressed to me her surprise at the bad smell of Kalymnians, indicating to her that they did not bathe. However, such odoriferous characterization can apply to Greece as a whole, as is shown by Zinoviev in her discussion of Greek men (kamakia) who look for tourist women for sex because they are seen as superior to, often expressed as "cleaner than," local women: "When a kamaki approaches a woman who turns out to be Greek, he may return to his friends, and say disparagingly 'She smells of sheep' (mirizei provatila), an insulting reference to Greece as an agricultural society, and to its backward womenfolk" (Zinoviev 1991: 216). It should be noted that Zinoviev interviewed women who claim that one of the benefits of having local men interested in tourist women is that at least these men now show concern for bathing and keeping clean (1991: 206).

tying a tie], he acts like he's important, but his house still stinks." In making the argument that this man could not claim to be of higher class than other people we see how vision is associated with surface acting, while smell reveals inner essence, a common theme noted by Classen, Howes and Synnott (1994:4).

A more positive discourse on smell, as well as a synesthetic orientation, can be found not only in ritual contexts such as the church, but in everyday discourse and practices related to food. As was noted in Chapter 1, basic recipes and ingredients seem, from an outsider's perspective, to be somewhat limited on Kalymnos. But this did not preclude a lively discourse on the quality and preparation methods of different ingredients. When I asked a woman about why locally produced honey was so expensive on Kalymnos (at $8/lb), she noted that it was produced from many different flowers, which gave it its extraordinary taste and medicinal properties. Her husband then went and got his "special stash" of honey, which had been given to him by a beekeeper friend, and we all shared a spoonful, while they asked me to identify all the different flavors it contained. On another occasion I inquired about different prices for store-bought olive oil which was of similar quality (i.e., "extra virgin"). She suggested we "do an experiment" and brought out some store-bought oil along with locally fresh-pressed oil. She noted that the oil must "sit for three or four months in order to take its scent" (να πάρει μυρωδιά). She poured each into small glasses and advised me to note the differences in color and viscosity, noting the thickness and deep-green color of her local oil, before giving me each to taste on a piece of bread. Such attention to quality does not only focus on local products, and I noted that Kalymnians debated the differences between different brands of rice and pasta with equal interest. Even salt was carefully distinguished, with iodized salt being acceptable for some cooking uses, but coarse sea salt (rock salt) being insisted upon for use on homemade french fries and in salads, especially when it is collected fresh from small sea caves around Kalymnos.[30] Similarly, special preparation methods were said to make a great difference, and I was lectured upon the importance of soaking beans in rainwater rather than spring water to make them puff up better. This

30. At the time of this writing exotic salt had recently become a new "hot" ingredient in some US culinary circles (following on the heels of the rise of "exotic" pepper). I am tempted to see this as another example of the post-modern commodification through diversification that has been so successful in remarketing coffee in recent years, given that a variety of salt produced in Brittany called *artisan paludier* was selling in New York in late 1999 for twenty dollars a pound (Acocella 1999).

entailed a visit by one woman to her mother-in-law's house and an opportunity to socialize, since her mother-in-law was the nearest person she knew who had a cistern. She also used the opportunity to ask her mother-in-law for fresh parsley (μαϊντανός), a much coveted seasoning for preparing bean soups, particularly during the deprivations of Lent.

Discourse surrounding food focusses on sensory qualities as well, smell in particular. A woman in her twenties living at home with her family describes her culinary preferences as follows: "I prefer salty foods, cheese, cheese pies, to sweets. When I eat something I wanted it to have a smell and a flavor (να μυρίζει και νά'χει γέυση)." But she also told me that she did not eat meat, because she couldn't stand the smell of it. One way to refer to a tasteless food is "water-boiled" (νερόβραστο), in one case used by a woman to describe the noodle casserole (παστίτσιο) made by her cousin on the neighboring island of Kos without nutmeg to give it its proper aroma. Metaphor is also prominent in Kalymnian discourse on food. A particularly delicious batch of bean stew is called "Turkish Delight!" (λουκούμι, a word that doesn't have the modifier 'Turkish' in Greek. It also directs attention to the tender texture, as well as the sweet flavor, of the beans). A man tells his friend that he ate prickly pears the other day and they were tasteless, but today "they were honey!" A woman refers to fresh-caught tuna as "souvlaki!" and a man describes a batch of oranges he bought as "banana!" In these cases it seems that a superordinate category of "sweet foods" is used to relate prickly pears and honey or oranges and bananas, as in an "attributive categorization" view of metaphor (see McGlone 1996). What is interesting is the vividness of the metaphors, so that in the latter two examples, any conjugation of the verb "to be" is dropped entirely: "I ate one of those oranges . . . banana!" The Kalymnian practice of using multisensory terms and metaphor is not in itself unusual. In his study of restaurant workers, Fine (1996: 207ff.) discusses the imprecision of discourse surrounding food taste, even among chefs. The tendency is either to use superlatives ("it tastes wonderful;" "it tastes like shit") or to rely on similes and metaphors, although interestingly all the examples he provides are of similes rather than metaphors, while in my Kalymnian examples the seemingly more direct and vivid metaphor is employed: "the prickly pear today, it was honey" (ήτανε μέλι).[31]

---

31. Tilley discusses the greater immediacy of metaphor when compared to simile as follows: "The power of many metaphors may be held to reside in the fact that they are not similes. A statement such as 'the interviewer hammered the prime minister' is not particularly well expressed by stating that 'what the interviewer did to the prime minister

These materials have a number of suggestive implications. First, memory theorists note the importance of "encoding specificity" for later recall: "'What is stored is determined by what is perceived and how it is encoded, and what is stored determines what retrieval cues are effective in providing access to what is stored'" (Tulving and Thompson, cited in McGlone 1996: 557). Second, as Tilley notes: "A vivid metaphorical image, such as saying 'they cooked the land', is likely to be remembered far longer than a statement such as 'they burnt down the forest'. In so far as metaphors can evoke vivid mental images, they facilitate memory" (Tilley 1999: 8). This suggests some basis for the Proustian phenomenon of remembering through evocation of a powerful sensory image: the sweetness of a banana hardly seems similar to that of an orange, and yet, as an image of a food with a strikingly sweet flavor, "banana" does have a certain evocative power. It should be pointed out here that, as noted in my discussion of Sperber, the significant quality of smell and taste is that *it is possible to recognize them, but much more difficult to recall them.* As Engen (1991: 80) notes, in cases in which people do claim to be able to recall odors, as with perfumers working on creating a new scent, it is more likely that a visual image is what is evoked. Through metaphor, Kalymnians seem to be providing the powerful images that might facilitate recall.

One other aspect of odor memory stressed by Engen (1991: 81 ff.) is that time seems to have no effect on dissipating recognition ability. Indeed, a powerful (positive or negative) first experience of the smell of a certain food may color all subsequent sensory experiences of that food (or other odor). In the cases discussed above, the food referred to had been consumed recently. However, in one case I recorded a man discussed the meats and cheeses that the Italians brought to Kalymnos during the Occupation (sixty or more years previously) first by a metonymical listing: "mortadella, prosciutto, provolone," and ending with the declaration: "Aroma!", here citing the sensory experience directly through invocation rather than metaphor. He did follow this, however, with a striking metaphor, phrased in the infinitive: "to eat and to have your insides open up from joy" (να τρώως και ν'ανοίγουν τα σπλάχνα σου!). Through use of metaphor, as well as through invocation, the sensory intensity of the experience is either stressed for the interlocutor or recalled to mind by the person him- or herself.

---

was like someone hammering a nail into a piece of wood' . . . A statement . . . is produced in the metaphor in a particularly vivid manner impossible by the conversion of the statement into a simile or literal statement of comparison" (Tilley 1999: 12).

Several other distant memories of food similarly rely on striking images, for example the plump purple figs a woman served to her fiancé who had returned from years working in the US. As she notes, she knew that he would be longing for Kalymnian figs, having been away so long. This memory combines a visual image with the memory of migrant longing discussed above, as well as, in the context of a marriage negotiation, the noted sexual suggestiveness of figs. Another memory focuses on the sensory qualities of the first loaf of bread consumed after the Second World War by a woman who was a child at the time:

> I remember when the Red Cross finally came at the end of the war, with flour that was from America, or Australia, it wasn't Greek flour, and when my mother shaped it into a bread ring (κουλούρα) and it was baking in the oven, my sisters and I kept opening the oven 'look how big it's getting!' 'shut the door, you'll ruin it!' 'But look, it's getting all red on top like a rose!'

Once again a striking, synesthetic visual image captures the food memory and preserves it as narrative that the woman can return to.

In his discussion of chefs, Fine draws out another aspect of discussions of taste: the tendency of chefs to see themselves as artists, and to use a synesthetic vocabulary in describing their activities, focusing sometimes on visual imagery of brightness and hues, and in other cases on musical analogies: taste seen in terms of musical octaves (Fine 1996: 212). The synesthesia evidenced in Kalymnian/Greek church experience is also strongly present in food experience and food discourse, as I have been suggesting throughout. Seremetakis has written an extended essay discussing the evocation of such synesthetic qualities in Greece. She notes the bringing of children into this synesthetic world through cooking and through verbal play (often by grandmothers) in the following passages (1994: 27):

> The cook 'has to be fully alert', because cooking is a sudden awakening of substance and the senses . . . most of the time she does not eat the food she prepares for others, for she is 'filled with the smells' . . . The entire act of feeding the child and naming the points of the body [e.g. 'my eyes'] is an awakening of the senses. The act of talking to the child engages hearing. Naming the eyes awakens vision, the transference of substance from mouth to mouth [referring to the softening of bread with saliva to feed to infants] animates taste and tactility.

Seremetakis significantly locates synesthesia at the very heart of the enculturation process in rural Greece through the feeding and the teaching of language to children. She also describes the journey from urban to rural spaces (to visit the grandmother who remains in the largely abandoned village) as a journey from the implicitly anesthetized city to a world of sensations, "tactile and auditory smells": a bunch of oregano hanging over a sheep skin of homemade cheese, the smell of bread baking mixed with the ashen smell of the outdoor oven. As she notes, nothing that gives off smells is sealed, "to do so would mean to silence the smells preventing them from being heard" (1994:29–30).

This last comment brings us to the discursive elaboration of synesthesia in Greece. While it is fairly easy to find synesthetic discussions in the cookbooks that line the walls of Barnes and Noble and on the pages of the food sections of major newspapers, there are a few distinctive aspects of Kalymnian/Greek synesthesia, and in particular the focus on the auditory qualities of food. This is reflected in the expression found on Kalymnos, and in other regions of Greece (but not, apparently, in Athens), "listen to that smell" (άκου μυρωδιά) which is used, usually in an approving context, to refer to the odor of food cooking, and often accompanied by a noisy intake of breath through the nose. The opposite, to indicate the failure to taste an element of a dish, is "it is not hearable" (δεν ακούγεται).[32] Seremetakis sees this as directly tied to the encoding of memory discussed above: "The memory of one sense is stored in another: that of tactility in sound, of hearing in taste, of sight in sound" (1994:28). Seremetakis sees this as a violation of the Cartesian segmentation of the senses characteristic of modernity, and the point of her many examples is to show that the lack of such segmentation is what gives ordinary experience its depth and historical connectivity: the cup of coffee with the rich foam on the top – "the top implies sedimentation, texture in taste" – supplies a pause in the day, a chance to reflect on the past, and provide meta-narratives on the felt losses of "modernity," or of the exile of migration (1994:17; 26).

The ways that such experiences of synesthesia do or do not pervade life in the United States and Western Europe must be left somewhat of an open question at present. Intuitively, one could contrast the swirl of sights, smells and sounds at open market-places in many parts of the world to the packaged, deodorized, muzak experience of the modern

---

32. Also notable is the phrase common throughout Greece to emphasize what you are saying: "listen to see!" (άκου να δεις).

supermarket. Writers who do discuss the senses in the modern West stick to analyses of the commodification of taste and odors. For example, Classen, Howes and Synnott (1994) describe the marketing of scents and flavors in a chapter entitled *the aroma of the commodity*, arguing that "marketers have discovered what academics and other arbiters of culture have ignored: smell matters to people" (1994:197). Indeed advertisers, with their concern for consumer memory, have focused on the transmission of mood and image rather than information to sell their products (1994: 187–9). They seem at least intuitively aware of the importance of synesthesia: one need only think of the well-remembered jingle for Rice Krispies: "snap, crackle, pop!"[33] But surely the sensory experiences of those living in the United States or Western Europe aren't limited to the experience of commodity transactions. We certainly don't need to fall into global dualisms of a rational "West" and a sensory "Rest," even if we revalidate the sensory side of the equation.[34] Rather in the study of "experience" or "the everyday" we need to recognize that all experience is synesthetic to some degree, and cultural differences, to the extent that they exist, will fall along a continuum of the elaboration or validation of different senses. Forrest's (1988) ethnography of "everyday aesthetics" in a small, relatively isolated fishing village in North Carolina is suggestive in this regard. It provides an analysis of how the aesthetic realm is unequally gendered, with men by-and-large suspicious of appeals to the aesthetic,[35] as well as being divided between inside and outside (of the home, of church). Forrest also suggests the importance of Baptist doctrine in dividing the "spiritual" and the "material" senses in ways that could be both compared with and contrasted to Kalymnos: "Food, being material, feeds the material body, but sounds, being nonmaterial, feed the nonmaterial

33. See Heller's (1999) discussion of "appetite appeal," advertisers' attempts to engage "the eye and all the senses." He discusses such ploys as billboards in Times Square, New York City, that could project coffee aroma into the air at regular intervals (1999:218). Nelson and Hitchon (1995) discuss the ubiquity of synesthetic appeals in advertising, but argue that the effectiveness of such appeals has been under-researched.

34. See also Herzfeld's (1995a) concise critique of Classen's tendency to promote "occidentalism," a simplification of Western modernity's sensory apparatus that ignores alternate traditions within the West, and suggests an evolutionary progression from greater to lesser olfactory sensibility.

35. Forrest argues that men publicly scorn the aesthetic, but have a complex aesthetic appreciation in certain private realms, such as the making of duck-decoys for hunting (1988:160ff.). This contrasts strikingly with Kalymnos, where it is not uncommon to see a man on a bus holding a flower and savoring its scent.

spirit. Sounds can feed the soul because they can be used to express spiritual concepts through a variety of linguistic modes" (Forrest 1988:230–1). Unfortunately, apart from literature and film, we have almost no other descriptions of everyday sensory experience in the West on which to ground our comparisons and contrasts.

While the relationship of synesthesia and memory seems to be an open question from the point of view of experimental psychologists (see for example Jones 1976; but cf. Cytowic 1993: 129 fn.2), intuitively it seems to be the case that synesthesia is an aid to memory. This relationship has been particularly described by Luria, in his classic study *The Mind of a Mnemonist*. According to Luria, S. used synesthetic associations to code words and other objects for future remembrance. This additional information acted both as a prompt to recollection, and as a screen for false memories, i.e., if a word was altered by the experimenters, it would not produce the same taste, sense of weight, or emotions (Luria 1968: 28). S. was, of course, synesthetic in a clinical sense, rather than having been culturally encouraged toward synesthesia, so his case must be used with caution. But his subjective perception that synesthesia aided his memory is what is of interest to me here. For my purposes it is these subjective associations that are crucial, rather than experimental assessments of synesthesia and memory, since I am looking at *claims* to remember food, the accuracy of which I have little way of testing.[36]

Conclusion

> Perfume is symbolic, not linguistic, because it does what language could not do – express an ideal, an archetypal wholeness, which surpasses language (Gell 1977:30).

The experience of synesthetic memory brings us back to where we began this chapter: the return to the whole. In this chapter I have argued that we can understand the evocative power of food by examining some of the properties of taste and smell, which are universal but which can be culturally elaborated to different degrees and in different ways. The fact that taste and smell have a much greater association with episodic than semantic memory, with the symbolic rather than the linguistic,

36. My only assessments of accuracy are based on the few instances in which Kalymnians did remember my own food preferences over a period of years, as noted in the Introduction.

and with recognition rather than recall, helps to explain why taste and smell are so useful for encoding the random, yet no less powerful, memories of contexts past than, say, vision or words. But at another level there is no need to counterpoise the senses in this way, since I have argued that the experience of food in Greece is cultivated synesthetically and emotionally, so that eating food from home becomes a particularly marked cultural site for the re-imagining of "worlds" displaced in space and/or time. The union of the senses in synesthesia has a powerful effect, much like Turner's descriptions of the power of ritual (e.g., V. Turner 1969). The Desana of the Amazon, for example, place the synesthetic experience of Ayahuasca-induced hallucinations "at the core of their culture, saying that it reveals ultimate truths about cosmic reality" (Classen, Howes and Synnott 1994: 156). But the union of the senses is not only a metaphor for social wholeness, as this last quotation suggests (cf. Fernandez 1988); it is an embodied aspect of creating the experience of the whole. Food is not a random part that recalls the whole to memory. Its synesthetic qualities, when culturally elaborated as they are in Greece, are an essential ingredient in ritual and everyday experiences of totality.[37] Food does not simply symbolize social bonds and divisions; it participates in their creation and re-creation.

37. Much the same has been argued of music, and for similar reasons I believe (music fits Gell's and Sperber's description of the symbolic rather than the linguistic). Once again, Melanesianists seem to be in the forefront of connecting music and memory (e.g. E. Schiefflin 1976; Feld 1982).

Memorable Meals

"It is the play between fixity and novelty that makes possible the creation of meaning" (Deborah Tannen 1989:37).

From the Union of the Senses to the Structure of Meals

In the preceding chapter I made an argument for an ethnography of the sensory experiences of food as a way of interpreting its evocative power. In the spirit of theoretical ecumenicalism, I will argue in this chapter that food memories can equally be illuminated through structural analysis (ideally the two approaches would be combined; here I separate them for theoretical clarity). Though it is structural analysis of a particular kind, it is not a re-excursus of Lévi-Strauss's division of the world into the Raw and the Cooked. Rather, I will begin with Mary Douglas's insights into the structural interrelationship of meals, and use them to ask, and answer, the question: how do people use one meal to recall another. I will argue that repetition works both at the level of the meal, and at the discursive level (linguistic repetition) to make certain types of meals memorable in certain cultural contexts. I began to consider the issue of fixity/repetition vs. novelty in my discussion of the influx of "new" foods to Kalymnos in Chapter 2. Here I extend this discussion, and broaden it, to suggest parallels between how food is remembered and how the past is remembered more generally. Thus I look at the workings of historical consciousness, the play of repetition and change in structuring the memorable and the forgettable.

From One Meal to Another

As was noted in the Introduction, Mary Douglas provides a starting-point for my discussion, in so far as her work looks not only at the structure within a meal, but at the structural relationship between meals. I quote her in detail below (and from diverse sources), because I believe that her contribution to the study of meals is sometimes overlooked in focusing only on her work on "Deciphering a meal" and on the Hebrew pork taboo. Douglas notes the problem of distinguishing the significance of the meal-as-event. How do we determine the significance of any particular meal? How does a migrant, returning to his village after a long absence and coming upon a large meal in progress, recognize and categorize the type of feast being enacted? "As we trace the problems of identifying the event, we realize that though the possibility of very detailed discrimination of one event from another is a potential in any system of celebrations, it cannot be recognized in any one event seen by itself. It is a potential that lies in the system as a whole" (Douglas and Gross 1981: 5). As she argues, these meal systems, or patterns, have different rhythms: daily, weekly, yearly and, at the furthest extreme, over a whole life cycle "when we have moved from the christening cake, to the wedding cake, to the funeral baked meats" (Douglas 1982:109). In this structural view, meals fit together because "the smallest meanest meal . . . figures the structure of the grandest meal, and each unit of the grand meal figures again the whole meal, or the meanest meal" (Douglas 1971:67). In other words, the "part," to be recognized as part, must recall the whole, and the whole, in turn, reveals the structure of the parts. This interrelation between part and whole, "a well-known technique in music and poetry for arousing attention and sustaining interest," can reveal to us the musical and poetic characteristics of food events. She waxes poetic herself in summarizing this point:

> Food, as the music of love, structures the days and the years with its rhythms. Leading up to great moments and down through diminishing cadences, its temporal framework plays the accompaniment to gifts and countergifts in other media. It can surely not be understood by being considered item by item ('piece-meal' is always a term of reproach). Its regular structure can stabilize shifting emotions and make promises of fidelity to be kept. Looking back on a marriage through a pergola of meals, small deviations from the main structure can be seen for what they were, nothing that disturbed the grand pattern" (1982: 116).

Now Douglas recognizes that not all meal systems are equally structured, that the intricacy of structuring of meals itself bears some relationship to the degree of social structuredness (Douglas and Gross

1981:22ff.). Leaving aside the issue of correlations with social structure, the key point for our purposes is that a more highly structured meal system will tend toward conservatism. Of course, she does not claim that there will be no variation in ingredients and their combination in such a system. Indeed, Goode, Theophano and Curtis apply Douglas's approach to an Italian American neighborhood to argue that continuity and consistency exists not mainly at the level of ingredients and their combinations (recipes), but rather in the predictable alternation of "meal types" over weekly and yearly cycles.[1] Douglas's point, then, is not that meals are reproduced without change, but rather that change tends to be more in the realm of "variations on a theme" (a musical metaphor, this time implicit), rather than radical breaks with the past and daring leaps of experimentation (1982: 89).

Kalymnian meal patterns can be fitted rather well into Douglas's frame. Certain meals are associated fairly generally on Kalymnos with particular days of the week, with Lent's restrictions tending to make for even more structuring, because choices are further limited. The weekly meal system builds to a small climax every Sunday, when many families serve stuffed grape leaves (Φύλλα), described to me as the "national dish of Kalymnos" (το εθνικό πιάτο της Καλύμνου). Below I present two meal diaries kept over a two-week period. The first was kept by Nina, a Kalymnian woman who grew up in the United States and moved to Kalymnos in her early twenties. Married to a fisherman, Manolis, she shares her meals with her husband and her mother. The second week is somewhat sparser than the first, using leftovers, because Manolis has left for seasonal migration to the US. Most dishes were prepared with their own stock of olive oil produced from their trees, and garnished with their own olives.

Day	Main Meal	Comments
Sunday	Dolmadhes (filla), lettuce, fruit	lettuce from garden
Monday	White bean soup, olives, fruit	
Tuesday	Pork chops, lettuce, fruit	
Wednesday	Smelt, greens, fruit	Greens from garden, fish from husband's friend
Thursday	Pasta with tomato/meat, lettuce	
Friday	Octopus stew, fruit, cake	Octopus from husband's friend

1. Goode, Theophano and Curtis 1984. The two main meal-types they distinguish are "platter" or American-style dishes, and "one-pot" or Italian-style dishes.

Day	Main Meal	Comments
Saturday	Chicken soup	Husband leaving, wanted "light dinner" for boat trip
Sunday	White bean soup, olives, fruit	
Monday	Leftover chicken soup, fruit	
Tuesday	Leftover Bean Soup,[2] fruit	
Wednesday	Lentil soup, fruit	
Thursday	Sausages, macaroni and egg salad, fruit	
Friday	Lentil soup, olives, fruit	
Saturday	Grilled mackerel, fruit	
Sunday	Meat stew with potatoes	

Aggeliki is married to the retired secretary to the mayor, Yiannis. Their meals are taken regularly with their 13-year-old goddaughter who lives next door, and irregularly with their unmarried son in his late thirties. Her diary as follows:

Day	Main Meal
Sunday	Dolmadhes, tzatziki (yogurt/cucumber sauce), fruit
Monday	Fish soup, fried fish, tomato salad, fruit
Tuesday	Pasta with tomato/meat sauce, fruit
Wednesday	White bean soup, fried potatoes, lettuce, fruit
Thursday	Baked chicken, fried potatoes, lettuce, fruit
Friday	Lentil soup, lettuce, tomato salad, fruit
Saturday	Meatballs, mashed potatoes, tzatziki, fruit
Sunday	Meat stew with potatoes, fruit
Monday	Fish with tomato, salad made from cooked, chilled greens (χόρτα), fruit
Tuesday	Pastitsio (pasta with meat and bechamel sauce), fruit
Wednesday	Chick peas cooked with tomato and rice, fruit
Thursday	Chicken with peas, zucchini and mushrooms
Friday	Squid with rice, cauliflower salad, fruit
Saturday	Steak, mashed potatoes, salad made from greens, fruit.

2. Women tend to see leftovers as more acceptable than do men, and in some cases may finish a leftover bean soup, while cooking a small piece of meat for their husbands. One woman would complain bitterly to me over the fact that her husband insisted on newly-cooked food each day, so that the previous day's food would go to waste if they could not find someone to give it to (I often became the recipient of this benevolence, particularly when I was staying on Kalymnos without my family).

All meals, it goes without saying, are accompanied by fresh bread from local bakeries. All the fruit consumed in both families is seasonal: figs and prickly pears (for those who have trees), oranges and tangerines all produced on the island, watermelon, grapes and strawberries imported to it. Despite the differences in life histories and socio-economic trajectories of these two families, meal patterns are remarkably similar and recognizable. Sunday meals rotate between *dolmadhes* and meat and potatoes (occasionally chicken). Wednesday and Friday, as light fasting days, are days for fish, seafood or legumes. White beans and lentils are the most common, with chickpeas and occasionally fava beans (κουκιά) making an appearance. In the case of Nina's meals, fish or seafood is obtained through a fishing friend; for other families with less reliable connections, a good purchase at the market may determine what fish or seafood is chosen. Other days allow for more flexibility, with a rotation of meat and chicken dishes, which would include pork chops, steak, sausage and meatballs. But note that both families have spaghetti with meat sauce as part of the cycle, which tends to be almost as common as beans and lentils. Self-provisioning in lettuce, fruit and olives is common. It is part of the diet of Nina, who has a garden near her house, as well as land on the west side of the island with fruit-bearing trees. It is not a part of Aggeliki's diet, who does not have land for growing vegetables or fruits. Most of all, Nina's list would be completely recognizable to Aggeliki, and vice versa. Thus we can speak of a "common cuisine," defined by Mintz as a shared community of people that eats similar foods "with sufficient frequency to consider themselves experts on it. They all believe, and care that they believe, that they know what it consists of, how it is made, and how it should taste" (1996:96; emphasis in original).

Given this common cuisine, what might Douglas's notion of meals as variations on a theme mean for food memories? Clearly, no one remembers every meal they have eaten, nor anything close to that. That is why many of our food memories are in the past habitual tense: "I used to eat." Ordinary meals on Kalymnos are prototypical non-events. When this is commented on, people will use the expressions "it passes the day," meaning that it leaves no reason for further discussion, nothing memorable except re-establishing the structure that can later be referred to in the past habitual. Linguistically speaking, these meals are "unmarked categories," i.e., default values (Battistella 1990:41ff). Kalymnians, however, often alter their standard meal patterns in purposeful ways. For example, a man may spend free time fishing or hunting; the return with his catch will be the occasion for a special meal. A woman may take advantage of living near the water to bring up a bagful of sea urchins, which are eaten live on the spot, or snails may be brought home by children and become dinner fare. A return from a neighboring island to visit relatives may bring with it special greens that are not available on Kalymnos. Or more generally, the normally available fare may be prepared with extra trouble on a grill or on a wooden stove. Cooking greens on a wooden stove, I was told, imparts a desired, smoky flavor to them. In all these ways, Kalymnians break up the normal routine in patterned ways, and create the variations on a theme that are marked out as in some way special or memorable. The basic similarity of meal structure means that one meal *calls others to mind*, other meals that share many similarities, but are worth narrating for their differences, their divergences from the recognizable pattern. This point was implicit in my discussion in Chapter 2, that each act of food generosity calls others to mind, which form a narrative attesting to the person's good (or bad) character. Here, I am extending this idea to the structure of meals more generally. In other words, meals by their very structure provide for the similarity and difference that can become the stuff of narrative. The discovery of a fish available in the market-place brings to mind the last time that fish was served, who was present, the changing prices and availability, the relative freshness, bargaining involved in acquiring it, the differences in serving it fried or on the grill, who forgot to buy the lemon this time, how some men are not very good at cleaning a fish from the bones, while others are considered experts.[3] The meal may end with some watermelon, leading to a discussion of the different countries that produce watermelon, and the differences between light- and dark-skinned watermelon. A linguistic analogy to what I am describing is provided Jakobson's comment that "by focusing on parallelisms and similarities in pairs of lines, one is led to pay more attention to every similarity and every difference" (Jakobson and Pomorska 1983:103). Tannen (1989:50–1) gives the example of the repetition of a phrase, "and he knows Spanish/and he knows French/and he knows English/and he is a GENtleman," which both foregrounds and intensifies what

---

3. At one meal I attended two wives jokingly complained about one of their husbands' inability to clean fish, and thus his general unwillingness to eat it. The woman who was not the man's wife held up a piece of grilled fish and insisted to the man "isn't this better than meat?" To which he replied, "we all have our preferences." Then the woman's father-in-law, who claimed to love fish, joked that "fish, like women, requires good hands."

is similar *and* what is different in the phrase. Indeed, what I am suggesting is that "table talk" on Kalymnos works largely by analogy, and that the process of analogy structures memory.[4]

Here Douglas's work on part–whole relations in meal structures dovetails with cognitive anthropology's approach to schemata as a sort of collective memory. Shore, for example, begins his discussion of schemata with an analysis of Meno's Paradox, i.e., that any understanding of a piece of something points to a prior knowledge of the whole. This led to the Platonic doctrine of "recollections," by which all learning is a form of memory, a "calling up to mind of that which has been buried" (Shore 1996: 327). Forrest makes a similar argument for fried chicken dinners made as part of church festivities in a fishing village in the United States: each time a dinner is made, critical commentary is elicited comparing this meal to previous chicken dinners. He contrasts these meals to another festive meal, "Brunswick Stew," which is uncommon because it takes considerable time to prepare, but does not leave much room for variation in preparation, and thus leads to a simple state of unreflexive communion and nostalgia:

> Each mouthful a person eats is the same as the next mouthful, the same as each mouthful for other people at the table, the same as mouthfuls eaten in previous years, and so on. A sensual, subjective link is created between all those present at the meal and between all those who took part in similar meals in earlier years (Forrest 1988:228).[5]

These two meals both involve memory. The first fits well with the notion of repetition with difference that I have been developing. In the second case it is repetition that is savored. But this is the case, as we have noted, because the meal is uncommon. Thus it might be compared to an unvarying Thanksgiving meal, which might potentially

4. See Shore (1996: 326–72) for a discussion – from the point of view of cognitive anthropology – of meaning construction as analogy-formation, as memory. West (M.L. West 1999:27–8) provides a more poetic example of such food talk and the workings of memory spurred by analogy: "From the pond a bullfrog croaked. Then Aunt Tempe would sigh and say she'd been meaning to catch that frog all summer. He'd sure fry up good. Then the talk veered back to food – the last time they'd eaten fried frog legs, the best recipes for frog legs, and every meal that had ever involved amphibians" (1999: 27–8).

5. Forrest contrasts Brunswick Stew to other meals which leave more room for individual variation and commentary.

provoke such silent memories of similar meals under different circumstances, rather than a full-blown discourse. In each case, however, repetition forms the baseline for the construction of memory.

If these analogies form the basis of discourse, let us look at Kalymnian food discourse in greater detail. Mintz has argued for the importance of food talk in creating a shared food community. As Mintz argues, the fact that people in France and Italy (and Greece) eat bread every day does not make it mundane or trivial. "How bread tastes, how the dough is prepared and baked, are subjects of sufficient familiarity and importance to be the basis of discourse" (1996:97). While I have indicated above that mealtime is a time to talk about likes and dislikes, different preparation methods, the sources and qualities of different foods, in the next section I turn to what I consider an interesting particularity of Kalymnian food discourse, which, for lack of a better term, I will call "retrospective listing of the everyday."

Talking Food: Everyday Metonymies

Kalymnian stress on similarities that set off differences has, I will argue, its parallels at the discursive level. But here what is striking is less the "variations on a theme" than the repetition of the known, particularly the drawing out of descriptions through a detailing of the parts of any whole: meal, recipe, etc. Here are some samples:

1. Mihalis, a man in his late 30s, describing to his neighbor Maria a recent nice evening with his family at their summer house: "We had the meat in the freezer. We got pita bread from downtown, we cut some tomatoes, onion, a little parsley. It was nice."
2. Froso, a woman in her mid-twenties, describing to me some of the things she likes to eat: "I can't stand cheese unless its cooked in something. Sometimes I make cheese pies (τυρόπιτες). I put in feta, a few eggs, a little salt . . . and I make cheese pies!"
3. Overheard conversation of a young woman on a boat talking with two friends about the different prices and qualities of restaurants on Kalymnos and Kos: "It's important not to pay too much, but more important to get a proper meal (να Φάς σωστά). Not tiny portions. At one restaurant, we had taramasalata, tzatziki, tomato salad, calamari, octopus meatballs, spanakopita, fish, then for dessert they brought out grapes, cantaloupe, watermelon . . . in a few words, we ate well!" (με λίγα λόγια καλά Φάγαμε).
4. A mother writing a letter on the airplane back to Greece to her daughter whom she has just left in the US to start graduate studies

(Tannen 1989:157–8): "It's 10:30. I have just eaten rice, beef, a beer, salad with small shrimps, sweet coffee. . . . But it's 4 o'clock in the morning . . . We have just eaten breakfast, coffee, milk, marmalade, butter, cheese, bread, orange juice and croissant."

These different conversational fragments describe different temporalities: No. 1 is a vignette from a few weeks before; No. 2 is a repeated action; No. 3 is unclear, but possibly several months old or more; and No. 4 is written down almost simultaneously with its occurrence. They all, however, share an attention to detail that goes beyond any informational function. While Nos. 3 and 4 provide information to some degree – the daughter would not know what the mother had eaten on the plane, nor would the friends know what had been served at the restaurant, though in the latter case it is notable that the dishes mentioned are so standard that they are what the vast majority of people do order, and thus could have been collapsed by a phrase such as "we ate the normal restaurant fare" – Nos. 1 and 2, on the other hand, list the obvious and the familiar, as the recipes they describe are completely standardized: indeed to make *souvlaki* or cheese pies without any of those ingredients might seem more worthy of comment.

How to interpret the inclusion of such details, then, beyond noting that if they are not "informational" then they are, by default "phatic," i.e., they use language to maintain and to build social relations rather than to communicate new information. Certainly food detail has the potential to be highly symbolic: Caroline Babayan (1997:113) describes her grandmother's glass of tea: "It was big as a drinking glass, through which I could see the spoonfuls of sugar accumulating in the amber liquid until it became half white." With this brief reference we see the author watching the glass, which seems overlarge from her small-child's perspective, the white sugar falling through the glass an arresting image, the white sugar perhaps also symbolizing the age and perceived purity of her grandmother. But certain details seem to resist this type of interpretation, the bag of apricots in Yiannis's story that I discussed in the previous chapter having no clear narrative or symbolic function. The listing of foods above, similarly, seems to resist any symbolic interpretation, except, perhaps, in No. 3, in which the list might be interpreted as forcing the conclusion "we ate well" (though not, of course, "in a few words"). Literary approaches to the question of details provide some suggestive materials. Friedrich notes the popularity of listing in modern American poetry, such as Gary Snyder's "Hunting 13", which begins "'Now I'll tell you what food we lived on: mescal, yucca fruit . . .' and so on through 47 other nature foods of sorts" (Friedrich 1991:36). He notes that listing is also popular among American ethnographers, but sees it as a "clear, obvious" trope, which does not lend itself to further analysis (1991:37). Roland Barthes (1986) sets a similar problem for himself in trying to interpret realist prose, such as that of Gustave Flaubert, in which many details included seem to have neither a symbolic function (to set the mood in some way) nor a narrative function (to move the story forward). He concludes that such details constitute "the reality effect," that is, they signify that "we are the real," and lend verisimilitude to the rest of the text.[6] Hollander, looking specifically at literary lists of food, draws a similar conclusion: "The sheer joy of naming. . . . As a way of authenticating the veracity, as well as the very powers of representation of the speaker or narrator" (1999: 201).

Could these meticulous food details be seen as a Kalymnian version of the "reality effect"? Such a notion seems to fit well with Yiannis's bag of apricots, the detail that attests to nothing more than the fact that Yiannis does remember the events he is describing from forty years earlier. It fits less well, however, with the mother describing the meal to her daughter as she consumes it. Perhaps it is more in line with Hollander's "sheer joy of naming," as well as Friedrich's description of Whitman's tropes, in which lists of things "are reeled off in rich profusion" (1991:36). Note that this is rather different from an "image trope," in which a detailed picture is presented to the readers' eyes to be savored. Once again, here is Babayan describing one of her grand-mother's Persian specialities: "Cubes of fried lamb or beef, cooked slowly together with black-eyed peas, chopped onions, and a huge amount of five sorts of herbs, finely chopped. Again served with steamed rice which had formed a thick bread crust underneath" (1997:113). Here the author asks us to savor this "exotic" dish, lamb, five sorts of herbs, cooking slowly, along with her. The closest any of my examples comes to such an image trope is in the description of "chopping the tomatoes" for *souvlaki* or "putting in the feta" for cheese pies, though, once again, these are mundane descriptions of common ingredients (using common verbs: βάζω κόβω), and the focus, unlike that in Babayan's description, is not on the food, but on the person cooking it.

6. Kelly (2001:256) sees the inclusion of recipes in recent culinary memoirs as serving a similar function: the reader is not supposed to stop reading and actually make the recipe that has been provided, but rather to experience the verisimilitude of the text through reading the recipe.

How else, then, might we usefully interpret Kalymnian listing? Let us return to the notion of the phatic uses of language. In her book *Talking Voices* (1989), Deborah Tannen discusses the use of repetition and detail (among other devices) in creating conversational intimacy. I find this useful in discussing the examples above, which clearly employ detail, but also repetition, in the sense that the detail given in examples Nos. 1–3 does not involve "new" knowledge, but a replication of the familiar. Tannen discusses the use of repetition as an "involvement strategy" that draws the listener into the conversation.[7] While her overall argument is to show that repetition and detail are strategies prevalent in all languages (and most of her examples are taken from American English), she also notes some differences between languages in users' attitudes toward repetition. For example, while "set phrases," or proverbs, are fairly common in everyday speech in modern Greek and Yoruba, they tend to be viewed with suspicion in American English, since Americans tend to "assum[e] that sincerity is associated with novelty of expression and fixity with insincerity" (1989:40). Or as Urban, discussing the discourse patterns of the Shokleng of South America puts it (1991:102): "In 'hot' models, the present is unique, distinct, just as the discourse instances are; each is ideally different from those that have come before it. In the Shokleng model, emphasis is not on uniqueness or distinctiveness but on similarity." As noted, American English is, in fact, shot through with repetition, just like any other language. But from the point of view of speakers and listeners there is a cultivation of the "new" at the expense of explicit connection with the linguistic past (see Urban 1991:81). Tannen continues her contrast of modern Greek and American English in ways that elaborate this contrast: for languages such as Greek, which "value verbosity," repetition "is a resource for producing ample talk, both by providing material for talk and by enabling talk through automaticity" (1989:48). I would hypothesize, though I cannot confirm, that examples Nos. 1–3 are "set pieces" in the speakers' repertoire, texts that are evoked at certain moments of interaction, that may be reshaped over time (Becker 1994:165). That's from the speaker's point of view. From the point of view of the listener, repetition also serves the function of creating familiarity, the linguistic equivalent of "the pleasure associated with

---

7. Repetition can, of course, be rhetorically used to express tedium, as in the following excerpt from a Javanese servant's memories of the Dutch Colonial diet: "'The only food [the Dutch] ate was potatoes, potatoes, always potatoes, potatoes with this, potatoes with that . . . potatoes, potatoes, potatoes non-stop'" (Stoler and Strassler 2000:34).

familiar physical surroundings: the comfort of home, of a favorite chair" (Tannen 1989:52). This seems to be what is going on in a number of our examples, less a "reality effect" than a "comfort effect," creating a sense of the known, the habitable, through a laboring over the familiar, the recipe for *souvlaki* or *tiropita* recognizable to anyone in the community. Detail serves many of the same functions as repetition according to Tannen, and shows much the same metalinguistic contrast: i.e., detail may be believed to be more appropriate in many Greek conversational exchanges than in similar American ones (there is no Greek equivalent for the American imperative "cut to the chase"). Once again, Tannen uses examples concerning food to illustrate her point:

> a list that is too detailed for its context can be comic, as in a cartoon showing a priest delivering a eulogy: "He was a man of simple tastes – baked macaroni, steamed cabbage, wax beans, boiled onions, and corn fritters." The cartoon is funny because the level of detail is inappropriate to the occasion, and also because of the banality of the items in the list (1989:161–2).

Contrast the "inappropriate" and "banal" detail above with the seemingly banal detail of the mother's letter to her daughter: "coffee, milk, marmalade . . ." etc. Of course, the different contexts of these two examples make the contrast a bit unfair. Neni Panourgia provided an interesting anecdotal and somewhat more appropriate example in discussing the use of food detail in her book *Fragments of Death, Fables of Identity* (1995). In one section she provides a description of the activities of several women in preparing a meal directly after the death of the grandfather of the family. In her initial text she included a description of the meal: fish and potatoes in a lemon and olive oil sauce. To a US colleague of Panourgia's these details sounded "funny," and out-of-place, and he suggested that she delete them if they could not be given a specific symbolic meaning. Once again I take this to be suggestive of cultural variability in attitudes toward the relevance of the "mundane" when it comes to food.

If we can agree with the sociolinguists that the kind of detail and repetition of recognizable quotidian knowledge represented by descriptions of meals and cooking that I have described are strategies of involvement, it is also important to note their mnemonic function. Linguistic repetition has long been noted for such properties in the context of oral storytelling (Ong 1977). It is also discussed in ritual contexts, such as the Maniat funeral laments described by Seremetakis, where choral repetition is not only a mnemonic technique but has "jural" and "historical" functions to produce truth in the community, or collective memory. The memory function of repetition is somewhat less remarked in everyday conversational contexts. But we have seen in Chapter 1 that we need to be wary of too strong a distinction between the ritual and the everyday, given the abundant evidence that they are mutually reinforcing. Thus I do not think it is too great a stretch to apply Urban's conclusions concerning Shokleng mythic discourses to Kalymnian repetition of mundane food discourses: "Cultural sharing consists in the replication of discourse instances over time and their dissemination throughout the community. When someone tells the origin myth, he is not only telling about culture; he is actually replicating it" (1991:96). Talk of meals past not only tells of food; it is part of remembering and replicating the culture of food on Kalymnos.

Historical Meals

Now if Kalymnian meals and Kalymnian food discourse structure the memory of food in particular ways, I want to make the following leap: I will argue that this same relationship of structure and event, schema and particular case, the familiar and the new, can be seen as an aspect of Kalymnian views of the past more generally. Thus I want to argue that certain attitudes toward the familiar and the new influence multiple domains of life, linguistic, alimentary and historical. To make this point I will contrast Kalymnian attitudes toward meals/history to an ideal-typification of attitudes prevalent in US mainstream middle-class culture as depicted by a variety of writers. I refer to these latter attitudes as ideal-types because they are not based on ethnographic fieldwork in the United States, and because I do not want to deny the diversity that exists within US culture based on class, ethnicity, region, rural–urban contrasts or other social markers. Having grown up in New York and Chicago, and living now in a town of 400 people next to a city of 25,000, in which a recent survey noted that 3/4 of the region's restaurants serve fast food, I can hardly deny that attitudes toward food cannot be easily broken down into Kalymnian/US contrasts. However, I do believe that what I am calling US mainstream cultural attitudes (which some describe as "post-modern") have some descriptive validity, and at the very least are good heuristically, to help us think, by contrast, about Kalymnian attitudes.

In my earlier ethnography of Kalymnian historical consciousness (Sutton 1998) I argue that Kalymnians see a particular relationship between historical structures and individual events. For Kalymnians, "history," like the meal, is constituted by events organized around certain accepted themes (structures) that break up the flow of everyday life in which "nothing happens" (1998:121–2). Debt and betrayal are two interwoven themes that one can find at the national level in discussing Greece's relationship to the West as well as at the local level in relations between family members and neighbors. If "History" on the national level is contrasted to periods of time when nothing happens,[8] local level "histories" are explicitly contrasted to actions that simply "pass the day" uneventfully. Making history, in a Greek context, then, implies doing something out of the ordinary, but that at the same time is something that fits an accepted pattern and can be narrativized as such. This does not mean that history is a simple repetition of a pattern. Appeals to the past are not necessarily appeals for stasis. As Valeri (V. Valeri 1990:161) argues for Hawaiian histories, "Since the relationship between past and present is analogical and not merely replicative, the past need not exactly replicate the present to function as its precedent . . . the perception of difference plays in fact a great role in th[e] comparison." Similarly, for Kalymnians events are chosen to construct historical narratives both for their similarities to accepted structures and for their differences – once again the notion of variations on a theme.[9]

By contrast, in US mainstream popular culture as depicted in the mass media, "making history" is not explicitly imagined as the repetition of structures or themes (however much such repetition still objectively occurs). It has the explicit sense of doing something that has never been done before, for example, the first manned space flight. When it does involve repetition, "history" still has the connotation of the never-before-done: setting a record for the most home runs, the hottest day, etc. (while at the same time consigning the previous record to "history," i.e., to oblivion and forgetfulness, rather than to narrative).[10] The popular expression "it's ancient history" then implies that the past

8. One such period is the Ottoman occupation of Greece, considered to be 400 years when Greece left the stage of history. The Greek revolution is widely referred to as the "awakening" (αφύπνιση) from the historical slumber of the previous period. For another example, see Sutton 1998:175. For a discussion of "History" vs. "histories" see Herzfeld 1987b:41–6; Sutton 1998:135–8.

9. See also Herzfeld's (1992) discussion of the repetition of themes in Greek historical narratives. For a fuller explication of these ideas, see Sutton 1998:163–5.

10. I believe that Seremetakis (1994:33) is making a similar distinction between the narrative gluing together of events and sensory memory that she sees as exemplified by

should have no hold over the present consciousness. As the critic Greil Marcus (1995: 22) explains the phrase: "It means there is no such thing as history, a past of burden and legacy. Once something (a love affair broken off, a fired baseball manager, a war, Jimmy Carter) is 'history,' it's *over* and it is understood that it never existed at all." Thus Americans are enjoined to look to the future and not get stuck in the past, to think in terms of personal destiny rather than collective history, and to act in a continuous present that the oral historian Studs Terkel diagnoses as "a collective Alzheimer's disease."[11] If Kalymnian meals parallel Kalymnian historical consciousness as described above, can the same argument be made about US mainstream (or post-modern) attitudes toward memorable meals? I will not be suggesting that meals are not remembered in the United States; analogies are not a Greek invention but part of our shared cognitive inheritance. Rather I will suggested that *what is remembered* and how it is remembered can be usefully contrasted, based on divergent attitudes toward the familiar and the new.

In the US there is very little ethnographic work on food and memory to draw on, apart from the odd suggestive paragraph in larger works such as that of Forrest (1988). However, the observations of several anthropologists of food on what they see as dominant trends are suggestive, as is work on the post-modern "consuming body." As was noted in Chapter 2, marketing of diversity is a key aspect of late capitalism (see Harvey 1988). What this implies for subjective experience is analyzed by Baumann in what he describes as the postmodern "consuming body," the receiver of sensations. Because sensations cannot be objectively measured, the occupant of such a post-modern body lives in a state of restless uncertainty as to whether any experience is indeed "optimal." Thus, one must always be as open as possible to "new," "improved," products and experiences that might lead to heightened sensory delights (1996:116–17).[12] At the same time the consuming body must

---

the figure of the Greek grandmother as contrasted to the repression of memory and erasing of the past that she identifies, not with the United States in particular, but as a general condition of "modernity."

11. Such a view of the relationship of past, present and future might be seen as a more general characteristic of the project of Western "modernity." As Osborne (1995:xii) notes: "Modernity is a form of historical time which valorizes the new as the product of a constantly self-negating temporal dynamic."

12. Campbell's hallmark article, "Romanticism and the Consumer Ethic" (C. Campbell 1983) makes a historical argument for the development of the spirit of modern

be kept in a constant state of "fitness" to receive these sensations and not become compromised by the lassitude induced by previous sensation-experiences. This leads to what Baumann describes as a schizophrenic situation, which finds expression, interestingly enough for our purposes, in the endless popularity of cookbooks and diet books:

> Not just ordinary cookbooks, but collections of ever more refined, exotic, out-of-this world, . . . recipes; promises of taste-bud delights never experienced before. . . . Side by side with the cookbooks, as their undetachable shadow, the dieting/slimming books, the no-nonsense recipes for self-drill and self-immolation, instructions how to heal what the other books might have damaged: . . . the capacity to live through wondrous sensations (Baumann 1996:121).

I will have more to say about cookbooks in the next chapter. For the moment, Baumann's image of the sensation-seeker seems very much in line with anthropological descriptions of mainstream American and Western European urban middle-class eating habits. Discussing the ethos of American eating, Abrahams notes that there is hardly a dearth of interest in food. On the contrary, "one is overwhelmed by the sheer amount of discussion in middle American culture of different diets, of the new restaurants and speciality food stores that have opened, and of the great meals one has eaten" (1984:23). Abrahams also notes that "we are equal opportunity eaters. . . . We seem to want to be able to say of ourselves as eaters that we will try anything once." MacClancy writes in a similar vein:

> Psychobabble about your sexuality has become *démodé*; instead foodies score conversational points by name-dropping the best restaurants or by describing their latest visit to one of the culinary paradises (France/ Japan/ China). Novel or strange edibles are no longer scorned but prized, dinner-party fare is judged according to its surprise value, and new types of ethnic restaurants are opening in even the dullest suburb (1992:209).

---

consumerism as part of the Romantic movement in the early nineteenth century. This "spirit" is defined by the search for novelty: "not merely the treatment of the consumptive experience as an end-in-itself but the search for ever more novel and varied consumptive experiences as an end-in-itself. It is the desire to desire, the wanting to want which is its hallmark . . . Above all, this continuous sequence of dissatisfaction and desire is propelled by an underlying sense of obligation and duty" (1983:282).

→ *status → diet*

MacClancy links these changes in part to affluence, status-seeking and individualism, rather than to a renewed interest in taste itself: "[people] do not go to an expensive foodie restaurant because of the chef, but because the place is in vogue" (1992:210). Visser similarly concludes that the post-modern taste for novelty is "a wonderful marketing milieu" (1999:124). All this suggests that continuity, or reproduction, is being recuperated at the level of attitude or of class structure rather than of ingredient or recipe. Mintz is more charitable in his assessment of "eating American," noting that "we tend to try new foods, seeking novelty in eating, as we do in so many aspects of life. We are inclined to identify that novelty with knowingness, with sophistication; and certainly being open to new experience is a good value, most of the time" (1996:16).[13] Whatever one's assessment of the goals, in terms of memory such an eating pattern has certain implications. As Mintz notes, the "taste" for novelty characterizes many aspects of life in the US. I thus do not think it's stretching the analysis too far to see similarities in attitudes toward food and toward history itself. Here again what is memorable, what is "history," is the new, the different, the in vogue, the never before tried. In the world of new taste treats, restaurants and "exotic" fruits, durian is hot, kiwis are yesterday's news – which, from the perspective of mainstream attitudes toward the past, is the same as saying that they are "ancient history." People may still eat kiwis, especially now that they are reported to have much greater quantities of vitamin C than oranges. But without the cachet of novelty, they, like the banana before them, seem to provide no longer a source of distinction, discourse, and hence memory. At least not in a society that bases memory on such principles.

On Kalymnos there is a paucity of non-Greek restaurants. A few restaurants serve a combination of Greek and Italian food (pastas), and tend to cater to younger Kalymnians and tourists. And there are a growing number of fast food places serving pizza, hamburgers and *souvlaki*. Many older Kalymnians, particularly those of a more working-class background, never go to restaurants, and would often point out to me that you could cook seven meals for the price of one restaurant meal. Indeed, before the tourist influx of the 1970s, restaurants were specifically for those who did not have a family on the island, or who

13. Note that Baumann also concludes with some hope that the openness to experience of the post-modern body may imply a more positive stance toward "the Other," whose otherness must be preserved, rather than annihilated, in order to continue to provide a source of the "new" (1996:124–5).

worked too far away to return home for the main meal. Thus eating at a restaurant was a solution to a particular problem, not a leisure activity. Today younger working-class couples are more likely to rely on *souvlaki* or pizza for an outing with their children, rather than an elaborate sit-down meal. Others with middle-class aspirations might go out to a restaurant with friends or relatives on holidays, such as Greek Independence Day (25 March), or on namedays and for other personal celebrations. Such restaurants would in general serve typical Greek restaurant food (a variety of salads and dips to be shared, perhaps fish or steak as a main course), and are typically chosen for their seaside location or because the owner is a friend or relative. In other words, variety and novelty are not at a premium. I was struck that even at one of the trendier restaurants (serving Greek and Italian dishes), the menu had not changed in a four-year interval between my visits. An Asian-American woman who had married a Kalymnian was living on the island and working in a restaurant and as a caterer. She complained about the difficulty of introducing any new foods to Kalymnians, or even serving familiar foods in new contexts. She recounted the shocked reactions of several customers to okra because it had been cut into little slices and served with rice instead of being left whole and cooked with olive oil and tomatoes. Dimitris Roditis, a Kalymnian computer programmer who has traveled and tasted widely in Athens and other parts of Europe, and with whom I often discussed different, "exotic" cuisines in post-modern fashion during the long months of fieldwork when I sought in vain for local sources of tamari sauce, added the following nuancing/update after reading the above:

> Kalymnians ARE food lovers, but still they will not change their eating preferences easily! There used to be a restaurant in Melitsaha [a seaside area], run by two people from Athens, that made fresh pasta! The quality was absolutely marvelous, and we enjoyed many excellent dinners there. But you just wouldn't believe the fact that the locals who happen to come in and sit to eat, did not like the freshly made pasta at all! Actually there were complaints directed at a completely shocked cook! The guy couldn't believe his ears when he heard that these "were experiments, and the only 'makaronia' that's edible is the one in the packages" !!!!! And of course Kalymnians couldn't understand why the price was three times an average "makaronada" (pasta dish) of another restaurant! However, I've heard a lot the complaints about the non-existence of restaurants with other kind of food. There are five Chinese restaurants on Kos, and many Kalymnians who have worked or work there now, bring those influences here too. One of the restauranteurs of Kos is

considering starting a Chinese restaurant here, which is absolutely fine by me!!!!

If restaurants do not provide the novel fodder for memory on Kalymnos they seem to in the US, what of ordinary, home-cooked meals? For the US and Britain information is ambiguous, partly because, as noted, studies are not directed to the subject of memory. Mintz has suggested that in modern society the tendency is toward fewer and fewer "meals" as set events displaying a particular structure. Instead, meals are replaced by individualized consumption and snacking at all hours of the day. Mintz also points to studies that suggest that such eating patterns lead to a 50 per cent disappearance in memory of what one has ingested by the following day (1985:205). Falk (1994:29ff.) similarly sees the collapse of the notion of an "eating community" as a structuring principle of social life in modern society, manifested in "a tendency toward a marginalization of the meal" and the rise of non-ritual eating (snacking), which is not categorized as "eating" and thus, as Mintz argues, is less likely to leave memory traces (Falk 1994:43 n.21; see also Fischler 1988). Murcott, however, disputes the idea of the decline of the meal (1997). She suggests that the meal has always been a middle-class ideal, while much more ambiguous attitudes are found among upper and lower classes. She further proposes that the "decline of the meal" has been a standing issue on the agenda of twentieth-century social commentary, which should, until proved otherwise be viewed with as much suspicion as laments over the decline of the "traditional family" and other golden-age nostalgias.[14]

Whether the meal as "structured event" is being replaced by snacking, and what this might imply for memory, is indeed an empirical question.[15]

14. Recent work by Grignon and Grignon (1999) on French eating habits over the last several decades seems to support Murcott's position that changes in meal habits have been negligible. However, their data are quantitative, and based on a distinction between meals eaten outside the home and in the home. They do not provide information on whether the structure of the meal inside the home has changed or stayed the same.

15. That snacking can be a rich vein for certain types of memories – of growing up, youthful rebellion, sensual pleasure (when contrasted to "health food") – is beautifully illustrated by Jill McCorkle, in her playful story *Her Chee-to Heart*, as in the following: "I bite into my Hostess snowball and retreat to a world where the only worry is what to ask your mother to put in your lunch box the next day or which pieces of candy you will select at the Kwik-Pik on your way home from school. Ahead of you are the wasteland of years: a pack of cigarettes, some Clearasil pads, a tube of Blistex, and breath spray. But for now, reach back to those purer, those sugar-filled, melt-in-your-mouth, forever-a-kid years" (1998: 154–5).

But as we discussed at the beginning of this chapter, meals can change in many different ways. Even if we accept Murcott's points that meals are likely not to disappear as social events, they may be changing in other ways. To judge by anecdotal evidence from students in my classes on food and culture, most still claim childhood experiences of meals as social events in the sense of eating with other people (even if many reported that this eating might occur in front of the television rather than around a dinner table).[16] However, students report increasing individualization of fare, so that a family of four may be eating four different meals at the same table to accommodate special diets, vegetarianism and different taste preferences. This once again suggests an image quite different from Mary Douglas's structured meals. It also militates against food's providing a common ground for discourse, or for a sense of a "common cuisine," as discussed for Kalymnos. In attacking the notion of "American cuisine" Mintz notes: "I find it difficult to understand how a people can have a cuisine without ongoing, active producing of food and producing of opinions about food, around which and through which people communicate daily to each other who they are" (1996:198). If the family more and more does not even form a micro-community of shared food, what chance is there for larger discursive communities that might form the basis of a collective memory? Or perhaps food communities are fragmenting along the lines of other communities in US society – you might not be sharing the same food with the person sitting next to you at the dinner table, but you can find a virtual community of other vegans, Atkins' diet enthusiasts, or Kosher seekers of the thrill of imitation seafood. What might such disembodied, virtual food communities mean in terms of memory? For the moment we must scratch our heads and crunch on another Thai basil-flavored "Kettle-style" potato chip.[17]

16. Mintz sees this as part of a trend toward saving time, by maximizing one's simultaneously stimulating activities (1985: 202–3).

17. One might speculate that fast food restaurants constitute one of the remaining common meals that could form the basis for discourse and community. This might be true particularly for children, who seem, again anecdotally, to discuss the comparative virtues of different pizzas and burgers in ways similar to what I am describing for Kalymnian meals.

Conclusion

"What is for some people a radical event may appear to others as a date for lunch" (Marshall Sahlins 1985:154, discussing the events of Captain Cook's crew eating with Hawaiian women).

While Sahlins meant his *bon mot* to be a comment on the fact that "events" do not exist outside the cultural categories that give them interpretability (and cultural categories do not exist outside their instantiation in events), I take this to return us to Douglas, and the point that history and meals need to be read (or eaten) together. I have argued in this chapter, in my rhetorically overdrawn contrasts between different attitudes toward the familiar and the new, that it is crucial that we pay attention to the implicit assumptions behind meal structures and table talk. If we are indebted to Mary Douglas for the profound insight that meals, like historical events, have structures implicit in them, the type of structuring has profound implications for the type of memories and histories created through food. Equally, it is important that we examine different styles of telling when it comes to food for what they can reveal about styles and mechanisms of discursive memory.

As we engage in anthropological histories that attempt to transcend the dualism of structure and event, to see continuity and change in the instantiation of schemata (Shore 1996) or the "putting at risk" of cultural categories (Sahlins 1985), we must pay attention to the particular ways actors perpetuate the familiar or inaugurate the new (or perpetuate the familiar in the guise of the new, or vice versa), lest we are left with "gaping holes" in our theories (Reyna 1997). Urban gives us one possible model in discussing the replication of Shokleng performances, in which "the younger performer is locked to the older, more skilled performer, forced to copy syllable by syllable the discourse produced by his elder" (1991:103). This replication is far from an exclusively cognitive process, since he argues that the formal and "sensuous qualities of the sound" are foregrounded, and the semantic content is only a small part of the ritual (Urban 1991:88; see also 1994). Such a model of verbatim memory, processed both as cognitive schema and as bodily experience, might describe some phenomena. But does it help us to understand the process of cultural transmission of cooking knowledge, where more active appropriations and *bricolages* seem the order of the day? And what of societies where fewer and fewer of us seem to learn to cook from Grandma? These issues lead us into the next chapter and a consideration of recipes, cookbooks, and embodied learning.

Doing/Reading Cooking

There are no index cards or folded, stained papers. The recipes are written into her hands, into the strata of her calluses. Oregano shards, lemon dust, fossilized garlic essence, petrified olive oil (Kapsalis 1997:27).

It is no doubt one of the primal scenes for hyphenated Americans. A family culinary secret from the ancestors is either lost to subsequent generations, or the attempt to preserve it through writing has dire consequences. The long-time observer of ethnic phenomena Stephen Steinberg comments on the passing of his grandmother and her *challah* bread, noting that "not one of her eighteen progeny . . . had acquired her skill." He wonders whether "Bubbie's *Challah*" was by definition unreproducible, her signature gift, "kneaded by *her* hands . . . purveyed by *her* outstretched arms." But this leads him to reflect on how his grandmother had learned to make *challah*, and the process of cultural reproduction itself:

How, after all, did my grandmother acquire her culinary magic? It required an elder not just willing but determined to share her powers with a neophyte. And it required an upstart who craved to follow the path treaded by forbears. Is it possible that as much as my grandmother's eighteen progeny revered her, that none of them wanted to *be* her? (Steinberg 1998:296)

Thus Steinberg suggests that loss of tradition is a necessary part of becoming the modern Americans that his family members aspired to be. That this piece of cultural reproduction was no more part of the future plans for ancestors or progeny, suggested the formation of new identities as much as it did new material relations to the world. But what else is implied as far as the process of cooking is concerned? What kind of relations of cooking and "everyday life" (Giard 1998) accompany traditional transmission of cooking knowledge from mothers and grandmothers to daughters and granddaughters, and what has come to replace this knowledge? And how might these considerations add to our anthropology of memory? In this chapter I sketch some possible approaches to questions of memory and the doing/learning of cooking. I do so by looking first at contexts in which cooking could be spoken of as an "embodied apprenticeship" in contrast to a formal learning mediated through cookbooks and written recipes. I then focus attention on the spate of "nostalgia cookbooks" that in recent years have begun to line the shelves of US bookstores, cookbooks that are not just written stores for memory, but that thematize memory as their central *raison d'être*. I consider what these cookbooks might tell us about how authenticity, loss and nostalgia are conceptualized in present-day US society, and some of the conundrums that processes of commodification through writing and mass-marketing pose for our memories of doing-cooking.

Doing Cooking

Practical Knowledge

Requesting recipes on Kalymnos never elicited a note card, but rather a visit to the person's kitchen to observe and participate. This offer was usually made to my wife, but extended to me as well, and its value was clear when it came to learning such tasks as require a knack, such as rolling grape leaves with just enough filling that they don't burst or turn into a bulging mess. Luce Giard, in association with Michel de Certeau, writes of the transformation of everyday practices, gestures and knowledges in ways useful for an anthropology of cooking. Although their focus is on French society, they provide a model of issues that could be potentially explored, against which I will draw on my knowledge of Kalymnos and other Greek contexts for comparison and contrast. I begin with a review of her work (Giard 1998), which I supplement with recent work in cognitive anthropology on the mental/bodily practices involved in learning tool use in a variety of contexts.

Giard writes of the gestures of cooking as mobilizing the resources of the body as well as of the mind. Cooking requires the knacks both of doing and of planning. It calls on bodily rhythms: "Whether it is done with a tool (chopping an onion with a small knife) or with the bare hand (kneading bread dough), the technical gestures call for an entire mobilization of the body, translated by the moving of the hand, of the arm, sometimes of the entire body swinging in cadence to the rhythm of successive efforts demanded by the task at hand" (1998:202). Before many foods came pre-processed, one had to "actualize a certain competence" in dealing with raw materials, on guard with a "parrying gesture" against fish bones, the worm within the fruit, or the green part of the potato (1998:205). When I asked a woman on Kalymnos why she peeled potatoes, removing what I had been taught to be the source of all the vitamins, the skin, she replied "Potatoes can fool you" (σε ξεγελάσουν), suggesting a judgement and competence in relation to material objects not far removed from the judgement required to not "be fooled" while shopping from a merchant. Here we see the integration of the mental and the manual that goes into each step of the process: "One has to organize, decide, and anticipate. One must memorize, adapt, modify, invent, combine . . ." Note that this is not the strict application of a plan, nor is it "the standardized execution of manual dexterity" (Schlanger 1990:44), given that it calls for constant adjustments not only to the material environment, the ingredients, but shifting social demands, likes and dislikes, rhythms of repetition and accommodation to temporary diets (Giard 1998:200).

In this regard cooking could be seen as the type of "practical knowledge" studied by cognitive anthropologists: "by necessitating an experienced and critical understanding of material realities, by drawing upon repertoires of memories and imaginations – it enables me to design and to create" (Schlanger 1990:44).[1] Lave (1988:155) refers to the interrelated processes of everyday shopping and cooking as a "complex improvisation." Although Lave's study is focused on mathe-matical abilities, she suggests the complex work of memory and foresight involved in shopping and cooking in similar terms to Giard:

> People act inventively in terms of expectations about what has happened, is happening and may happen. And these in turn affect what does happen . . . Thus a cook who uses a whole package of noodles while fixing a goulash dinner generates expectations about grocery shopping – again. In the supermarket, the shopper-actor and setting generate shopping activity partly on the basis of expectations about how the activity unfolds (Lave 1988:185).

---

1. Scott (1998) also discusses "practical knowledge" under the concept of "*metis.*" As he notes, "Any experienced practitioner of a skill or craft will develop a large repertoire of moves, visual judgments, a sense of touch, or a discriminating gestalt for assessing the work as well as a range of accurate intuitions born of experience that defy being communicated apart from practice" (1998:329).

Shoppers "have their heads in the kitchen" (1988:205 n.4), balancing complex possibilities of menus, storage space and durability, personal desires, time and monetary constraints. These portrayals are quite consistent with the shopping practices I describe for Kalymnians in Chapter 1, where ability to face the challenges of getting the best deal while at the same time fulfilling one's social obligations to different storekeepers is taken as a sign of "intelligence."

But aside from such balancing of memories and expectations, how might we usefully describe cooking in terms of a cognitive anthropology of memory? Keller and Dixon Keller provide a clue from their work on blacksmiths and creativity (1996, 1999). In activity blacksmiths draw on a generalized "stock of knowledge" which is made up of "past accomplishments and experience . . . a rich store of recollections of previous productions" (1999:15).[2] Keller and Dixon Keller stress the role of non-verbal reasoning in blacksmith production. The blacksmith must draw on visual and kinesthetic imagery of desired outcomes, which are not templates to be copied but manipulable images of aesthetic qualities and procedures (1996:134). He must monitor and improvise on his work in process. And he draws on retrospective assessments of the work of others to figure out the steps involved (1999:19). Explicit and implicit memory are in dialectical tension as "the unique requirements of situated tasks create an ongoing dynamic between the stock of knowledge and constellations [procedures] applied in practice. An actor has the continuing possibility of expanding his stock of knowledge by reflecting on the results of activity and refining the constellations subsequently employed in goal attainment" (1996: 106).

While it would seem at first glance that smithing is more of a creative process than cooking, perhaps this is simply a gendered assessment born of our Platonic distinctions between things lasting and things ephemeral, things inventive and things repetitive (see Heldke 1992 for a discussion). Both smithing and cooking rely heavily on tradition and

---

2. Ingold (1993) and Pallson (1994) both criticize the idea of a "stock of knowledge" as ethnocentric, and seem to wish to dispense with it altogether. Pallson, drawing on Lave, sees it as "the product of western history and textual discourse, reinforced by the tradition of literacy and the institutions of formal schooling and disembedded training" (Pallson 1994:903). While Lave does criticize the concept when thought of as a "toolbox" of context-free cognitive tools (1988:24), she argues for a dialectic between practices and prior knowledge that seems more in line with the approach of Keller and Dixon Keller.

on constraints of material form, but within those constraints allow room for innovation and personal signatures. As I have noted, Kalymnian cooking seemed at first to be rather restricted from my perspective, and in the light of judgements such as "carrots don't go in lentil soup!" However, as has been noted, a world of fine distinctions lay below the surface of "standard" foods such as bread, olive oil and salt. Despite what I saw as lack of variation, a husband and wife insisted to me that he suffers greatly when he spends summers working on neighboring islands, because other women cannot replicate the way his wife prepares bean stew and other standard fare.

"Tradition," as discussed by Keller and Dixon Keller, refers to a stock of knowledge and procedures, brought together through a combination of planning and improvisation, and often drawn from retrospective assessment of the work of others. No doubt one of the reasons for so much oral discourse about food on Kalymnos is the building of stocks of knowledge, and retrospective assessment of the processes and secret ingredients of neighbors, for example, the effect of substituting flour for cornstarch in the making of the Greek version of a Napoleon (γαλακτομπούρεκο), a subject of discussion at the dinner among friends described in the last chapter. Within the stock of knowledge, there is considerable room for innovation. Few Kalymnian women were interested in adopting our liberal use of cayenne pepper (though one middle-class woman had discovered it on her own). One woman in her sixties, however, came to discuss the flavor of my wife's adaptation of the dish known as "fava," mashed split peas, to which my wife had added bouillon in cooking, so that she could adapt her "traditional" recipe to it.

Dixon Keller first suggested to me the parallels between blacksmithing and cooking:

> Your move to study smells and tastes as cultural mnemonics reminds me of our treatment of visible storage. The latter is simply the observation that artist blacksmiths store their tools in clear sight on the walls surrounding their work space . . . This open storage provides constant visual access to tools, which can then evoke memories of past circumstances in which they were employed. The past memories are useful in constructing present problem resolutions and strategic approaches to current production tasks. While the medium is clearly different, isn't this much like the rich evocations associated for Kalymnos islanders with the smells and tastes of past repasts? (Dixon Keller 1999, personal communication with author).

Indeed, I would suggest that taste- and smell-scapes, what Rozin and Rozin (1981) describe as the different "flavor principles" that go into making up different cuisines, present the mental "images" of desired outcomes with which a cook works in making constant adjustments in the process of cooking. Thus variations on garlic, tomato, olive oil, salt and parsley in different combinations would provide memory markers of acceptable flavors and smells for the cook to work with and adjust "in process" as Keller and Dixon Keller describe. As Fischler (1988:287) points out, within such a system one can introduce some new ingredients and still have the resulting dish be acceptable to the system. It is these "images," I would suggest, that make bouillon in split pea mash an acceptable variation and cayenne pepper, for most, a culinary outrage.

But there are more parallels here. Just as the blacksmith displays his tools in full view as a mnemonic, many kitchens on Kalymnos exhibit this same visibility of tools and materials, rather than having them hidden away in cupboards and under counters. Now, this may in part be due to the fact that kitchens in older Kalymnian homes tend to be quite small. There is a sense in such kitchens that every bit of space is used up, with pots and bags of bread and tomatoes, sage tea, dried beans and other items hanging from pegs in the wall, bowls of home-cured olives and leftover food covered with plates scattered on counters (those that don't need refrigeration), and vats of olive oil and brine-curing cheese placed in corners. The film *Kypseli* (Hoffman, Cowan and Aratow 1974), shot on the island of Santorini, shows a kitchen very similar to the ones I saw on Kalymnos. The camera pans over three walls of the kitchen, which are covered with battered utensils – pots and pans of various sizes, a colander, metal baking dishes and pans for making cheese and spinach pies all clamor for space on the walls of this small kitchen.[3] Just as the landscape provided a wealth of additional sources of food for snacks, main courses and side dishes, from snails and sea urchins to greens and fresh almonds, multifunctionality seems the rule in kitchen tools, spaces and utensils. Most time-consuming tasks such as peeling vegetables or picking through beans, or in older times grinding flour, take place outside, in courtyards or other "public" sociable spaces, where women can share tasks, talk and follow the flow of daily life. Similarly, patterns of outdoor food preparation are noted for other parts of Greece, and other less urbanized areas of Europe more

3. See also the picture provided by Pavlides and Hesser (1986:90) of a kitchen on the island of Lesbos.

generally.[4] One woman would joke to me about the makeshift kitchen at her summer one-room "cottage," on the water. It was a wooden partition on her back porch which her son or son-in-law would construct each year, separating off a small space for a table and a two-burner stove. She referred to it as "Karaghiozis's shack" (η παράγκα του Καραγκιόζη), referring to the Greek shadow-puppet trickster figure. Through this trope she suggested the practical intelligence involved in wresting good food out of such conditions.

Tools and Technology

The issue of cooking utensils points to another aspect of "practical intelligence" – the way that the tool in small-scale societies tends to be "not a mere mechanical adjunct to the body, serving to deliver a set of commands issued to it by the mind, rather it extends the whole person" (Ingold 1993:440). Ingold contrasts the "technique" implicit in such a holistic view of tool use, with "technology," which disembeds the tool from a social context and a context of practical learning and subjective intention, and treats the workman as an "operator." If the tool draws its power from and extends the human body, the logic of technology's operation lies outside human bodies (Ingold 1993:434–5). Giard analyzes this shift in relation to cooking, noting the loss of many "ancient gestures" made obsolete by technology and by the pre-processing of foods before they reach the hands of the consumer.[5] She sees this loss of gesture to be both a bodily and a cognitive de-skilling. In the past, the cook not only furnished the kinetic energy, but supervised the progress of the operations and "could mentally represent the process for herself," much like the artist-blacksmith. Giard sums up:

4. For some good images of women cooking and preparing food in courtyards, see Hoffman, Cowan and Aratow 1974. See James and Kalisperis (1999) on Chios. See Birdwell-Pheasant and Lawrence-Zuñiga (1999) on "pre-modern" house spaces in Europe. See also Booth (1999) on the resistance of women in public housing to the "rationalizing" designs of urban planners in a Sicilian town. When housing was provided after an earthquake in the town, planners attempted to impose functionally-discreet "private" kitchens. Women responded by turning their garages into kitchens, which allowed them to continue food-processing in a public context where they could share information and gossip.
5. Giard does note the creation of some new gestures with new technology, such as the strength and dexterity needed to open jars with airtight lids (1998:210).

In the past, the cook applied her savoir faire each time, she could perfect her dexterity, and display her ingenuity. At present, just about anyone can use an industrial object as well as her, and so she has become the *unskilled spectator* who watches the machine function in her place (Giard 1998:212).[6]

Giard does not wish to wax overly nostalgic for a time when women's work required huge amounts of labor input, but rather to find room amidst "frenetic overmodernization" for the "reasoned differences" that would resist the contagion of conformism implicit in the replacement of all the local variations of gestures and techniques with the hegemonizing force of technological loss of control.[7] Similarly, Kalymnians attempt to navigate between Scylla and Charybdis. In the past, one of the latent purposes of cooking's taking a long time was to prove women's fidelity and faithfulness to their families and their daily chores. As Hirschon (1998:150) notes, "proper food" took hours to prepare; food that could be prepared quickly was referred to as "prostitute food," because it implied that women were saving time in the kitchen to pursue illicit activities. Many Kalymnian women remain suspicious of the time-saving device – the blender, the food processor, the microwave – and see it as a tool of status-seeking, rather than a true kitchen aid, more likely to be used once and to be put away. Disdain for cooking technology can be found in many discussions of "traditional" cooking. For example, a 'culinary memoir' by a Barbadian author begins with the following remarks concerning food preparation:

6. See also Mars and Mars (2000) on the contrast between cooking through "the habit of the hands" and through "assemblage." Kapsalis (1997:32) captures the notion of the "habit of the hands" in a story about a Greek grandmother:

With her sight now gone completely, Yiayia mourns the days when the kitchen was hers. She cries as she recounts a list of the dishes she used to make. Her hands are grasped together, solacing one another as if they are having an agonizing memory of their own. But even with her sight gone completely, occasionally a dish miraculously appears from the kitchen – *pastitsio* or *domates me avga* prepared by hands that remember.

7. Adams (1994:199ff.) takes a parallel balanced approach in discussing the effects of changing technology on farm women's labor in Southern Illinois. She remains critical of the effects these changes have had on women's control over the products of their labor, while at the same time recognizing some of the real benefits that have led women to embrace many "labor-saving devices."

so, we are talking about cooking food with feeling. Feeling is stretched to include 'feeling-up' the food: touching the fish; pulling out the entrails of a chicken with your fingers; peeling potatoes and slicing them with a knife while holding them in your hand – not using a gadget that ensures precision of cut and duplication of each slice (Clarke 1999:3).

Note that the disdain for technology here goes with a disdain for measurement and precision, seen as part of the alienation of modern life. Willingness to get one's hands dirty, to mix one's substance with that of the food one is preparing, is a reflection of dynamic social life. As on Kalymnos, careful measurement of food (or money when shopping for food), as discussed in earlier chapters, is seen as the height of anti-sociality.

Kalymnian memories of past cooking techniques, then, the weekly preparation and baking of bread, are much like their memories of the days before flush toilets. They involve a taken-for-granted materiality and physicality of everyday life that has been eroded by "modernity." Lack of concern with measurement and perfect hygiene in cooking correspond to the sense of less privacy in all bodily functions in the past, as well as to the notion of "pre-capitalist pleasures" discussed in Chapter 3.[8] They are what I have called memories of *gemeinschaft*, of shared substance, but also tinged with a sense that "we were very backward then." This raises issues for feminist analysis of the extent to which cooking represents control, and thus power for women, or is seen as low-status, and thus a source of women's subordination (for opposing viewpoints, see, for example, Williams (1984) and Devault (1997)). In an interesting parallel to Hirschon's "prostitute food," Coontz (1992:165) recounts her mother's awakening feminist consciousness in the US in the 1960s that food manufacturers were putting extra steps in their preparation instructions in order better to occupy the time of homemakers "liberated" by kitchen technology, and keep them from boredom or other activities, an interesting example of the "invention of tradition" applied to cooking techniques.

8. What I am discussing here is nicely captured in the notion of "the joking body" as recently delineated by Graeber, a body "continuous with the world around it." He, too, makes the connection between social and bodily relations of shared substance, between "contact between people (looking, touching, speaking, striking, sexual relations) and eating, excretion, running noses, decomposition, open sores – all of which refer to different sorts of stuffs and substances passing into, and out of, the physical person, with contact between bodies and the world" (Graeber 1997:698). Note that Graeber also makes a connection between such relations between body and world and notions of pre-capitalist, or pre-private-property, social relations.

Learning and Transmission

In terms of our concern in this chapter with cognitive and embodied memory, Giard's discussion of tools and technology leads to another crucial issue, that of changing forms of transmission or enskillment in cooking knowledge and practice. Giard suggests that new technologies, including the "technology of writing" (Goody 2000), have had an influence on the processes by which cooking is learned, since techniques of the past implied *apprenticeship* to a relative, an aunt, mother, grandmother or neighbor (Giard 1998:220–1). Indeed, those looking at practical knowledge have stressed this aspect of its necessary transmission not being through a set of rules that could be abstracted and learned *separate from practice*. Scott discusses bicycle riding as an activity to which we would apply the maxim "practice makes perfect," inasmuch as "the continual, nearly imperceptible adjustments necessary for riding a bicycle are best learned by having to make them. Only through an acquired 'feel' for balanced motion do the required adjustments become automatic" (1998:314). Scott includes cooking under this heading as an activity for which learning the rules cannot be separated from practice: "A complete mastery of the principles may exist alongside a complete inability to pursue the activity to which they refer, for the pursuit of the activity does not consist in the application of these principles; and even if it did, the knowledge of how to apply them (the knowledge of actually pursuing the activity) is not given in a knowledge of them" (1998:316). Learning through practice is being contrasted here to learning through recipes. Schlanger (1990) provides a detailed analysis of all of the knowledge that must be already assumed for one to be able to follow a recipe for making a soufflé. Scott points out that many Chinese recipes call for the cook to add ingredients when the oil is "almost smoking," a direction that assumes the cook has enough experience of failure to identify that turning-point (1998:330). Heldke, discussing the cook Verta Mae Grosvenor, notes that Grosvenor sees written recipes as having a very limited function in relation to cooking. They cannot teach one how to cook, but can serve as memory-jogs for previous learning that has been acquired through experience (1992:219).[9]

9. As Heldke paraphrases Grosvenor: "If you don't know how you like it, what good is it for me to tell you how much rice to put in? And if you don't already know how to cook it, how is my writing it in a book going to help you learn? You need a teacher – a hands-on teacher – for that . . ." (1992:219). See also Tomlinson (1986) on the incompleteness of recipes as instructions.

There may be general agreement that cooking is best learned through an embodied apprenticeship, in which what is remembered is not a set of rules, but images, tastes, smells and experiences, techniques that can only be partially articulated, or memory-jogged, through the medium of written recipes. But there remain substantial questions about *how* cooking is taught and learned in different cultural milieux, by *whom*, and with how much stress on observation, participation, positive or negative reinforcement, etc. All these factors would have implications for memory processes and issues of reproduction/innovation of foods past.

At the end of the last chapter, Urban presented us with a striking image of a teacher attempting to transmit an exact replication (of Shokleng mythic texts) to an apprentice. I would suggest we see this as one end of a continuum, of what is generally a more dynamic process. In his work contrasting oral and written traditions, Goody (2000:40) encourages us to see transmission in oral cultures as much less a process of replication than of flexibility and innovation: "Since there is no fixed text [in oral culture] from which to correct, variation is constantly creeping in, partly due to forgetting, partly due perhaps to unconscious attempts at improvement, adjustment, creation." While Goody argues that written traditions allow for certain other types of self-conscious creativity and innovation based on comparison and critique of traditional texts, there is also a much greater facility for reproduction based upon writing. Approaches to learning have moved away from "blank slate" images to take a dialectic view of learning more generally (see for example, Tonkin 1992:105).[10] Such work goes, perhaps, against the grain of certain recent popular images of learning in the West as simple knowledge transfer from one brain to another through the medium of writing. Perhaps these popular images help to explain the strange enthusiasm (and financial support) in the United States for transferring teaching and learning out of the classroom and on to "the web" and other disembodied media.

In contexts such as Greek villages, the stress remains on informal, socially-embedded learning. Henze begins her study of teaching and learning in a mainland Greek village with the (perhaps stereotyped) image of an American woman requesting a Greek woman to teach her Greek dancing. Rather than starting small with basic steps, the surprised

---

10. Bourdieu (1990) stresses the "practical schemes" learned through bodily imitation of the actions of others, often at an unconscious level. His stress tends to be more on unconscious reproduction rather than innovation. For a discussion see Pallson 1994.

American woman was pulled immediately into the dance circle and whisked along (Henze 1992:xi–xii). Observation is a key value in such learning settings, as Henze notes: "Whenever I asked them directly how they had learned a particular skill, they inevitably replied, 'I watched'" (1992:14). Similarly on Kalymnos learning through observation was a highly valued skill. As one man told me: "I'm very attentive, whenever I see someone doing something I watch and learn it." Herzfeld (1995b:137) stresses the use of multiple senses in apprenticeship on Crete: "a good craftsperson does not speak in order to teach an apprentice; it is the apprentice's eyes and sense of sound and touch that guide the acquisition of technical knowledge."[11] Henze also focuses on direct participation, which may occur in "play" frames, in which the participant (usually a small child) is allowed to pretend to do the action being taught (when it is perceived as dangerous), or in "real" performances. While Henze does not focus on cooking in her study, she does give one example of a grandmother and grandfather teaching their 14-year old granddaughter to make Greek coffee:

> The task was not simplified in any way, and in fact both grandparents insisted on accurate and expert performance of this . . . task . . . Only at one point, when the coffee and sugar were measured into the water, did the grandmother actually take over the task from Kalliope. Once this was done, however, she returned the task to Kalliope to finish. At the end, as Kalliope began to pour the coffee from the *briki* into the four cups, she was reprimanded by her grandfather for not distributing the *korfi* (foam) equally among the four cups. Managing the *korfi* (also called *kaimaki*) is a crucial aspect of expert performance (Henze 1992:98).

Hoffman comes to similar conclusions, based on her work on Santorini, stressing the social nature of cooking, as well as the way that different women have marked out specialities:

> For holiday cooking large groups of women cook together, the leaders being the older, the young as workers, all known for special abilities,

11. Terrio (2000:87) similarly cites an apprentice to a French chocolate maker: "'You see, they could never explain what they were doing. As for my apprenticeship, I was just told to be quiet and watch.'" Terrio goes on to describe the "intimate sensory mastery" that develops through apprenticeship: "by smelling and feeling the heat of the chocolate mass against their skin, by visually measuring the final result for a brilliant gloss, and by tasting the cooled candy for the cleanest bite under the teeth and the smoothest consistency on the tongue" (ibid).

i.e., Maria (an older woman) knows the batter best, Eirini (younger) is known for her delicate fingers for fretting a crust . . . In individual kitchens it seems that girls watch and watch and more or less one day are just told to make the dinner as their mother is busy – and they do! Again it is a sororal setup, so there are plenty of advisors bustling in and out (Susannah Hoffman, personal communication with author; see Hoffman, n.d.).[12]

Like Henze, Hoffman notes the use of play frames, which are set up for the younger girls: for example, making pies that no one expects to eat. Hoffman also suggests that while linguistic elements are not absent in such informal learning episodes, they tend to take a back seat to the combination observation/participation. Language plays a part, however, in another aspect of such collective cooking: the sharing of stories and "gossip" about both the present and the past. In the case of the Kalymnian women who went to Kos to pick grape leaves (described in Chapter 1) the labor-intensive nature of this "traditional" food-processing procedure seemed to evoke memories of *gemeinschaft*, a chance for the older women in the group to reflect on the good and the bad of the past, and to pass on their vision to the younger woman present. Others have also seen the labor-intensive nature of traditional cooking as a space for passing personal and collective histories to the younger generation. Ormondroyd (1997) describes learning to make borscht from her Russian-Jewish grandmother. While part of this process was learning techniques and "tricks" – "'I like to peel mine first,' she told me, 'otherwise they taste like earth'" – the slow chilling process was a chance for her grandmother to pass on stories about life in Russia and migration to the US, as well as poems in Yiddish, all told while her grandfather attempted to interrupt and trivialize her grand-mother's memories. Thus apprenticeship becomes a site of transmission in the broader sense of a woman's culture, history and everyday experience.

12. Hirschon (1998:176) also notes that neighbors may be drawn into such communal cooking: "Time-consuming tasks such as cleaning vegetables or chopping nuts for a sweet pastry were often done in the yard where passing neighbors would call in and offer help. The standard acknowledgment for this help is a small plate of the finished dish, called a 'tidbit' or 'morsel' (μυρωδιά, lit. 'smell'), which is taken to the house of the helper and presented with the words 'Just a morsel/tidbit.'" Hirschon notes that this is also the occasion for the recipient to show off her culinary skill by returning the plate filled with her own speciality dish.

Learning with the hands (1) A presentation on "minority cuisine," Komotini, Thrace (Photo Credit Vassiliki Yikoumaki)

Learning with the hands (2) Komotini, Thrace (Photo Credit Vassiliki Yiakoumaki)

It is also important to recognize the effects of different kinship systems on such recipe/cultural transmission. Ormondroyd describes transmission in the female line, from a maternal grandmother to her granddaughter. Hoffman similarly describes a matrifocal situation common to Greek islands (and also found on Kalymnos), in which the clustering of female kin is common. This is different from mainland Greece, where the rule is patrilocality, and young women are generally separated from natal kin at marriage. Inheritance on Greek islands also tend to be matrilineal, in that there is an explicit ideology of *transmission* of material and intangible goods in a female line (see Sutton 1998:105ff.). In non-matrilineal settings there might be less stress placed on direct transmission from older to younger women. Or contrarily, a matrilineal focus might play against the apprenticeship described by Hoffman. For example, in Forrest's study of a small town in North Carolina (discussed in the last chapter), the fact that an elder matrilineal woman provided all the cooking for the extended family, and desired control over her domain, seemed to work against younger women's being taught to cook, and many women claimed to not have learned cooking until after their mother had died (Forrest 1988:69–70). But this did not mean that women relied on written recipes. Mother's cooking continued to provide an aesthetic standard by which women judged, compared and adjusted their own cooking when they did take on the role.

On Kalymnos, cookbooks and written recipes more generally have yet to make much of an incursion into everyday cooking practices. When I asked one older woman about written recipes, she said experience (η πείρα) was the only source of cooking knowledge for most Kalymnian women. Even if she shared recipes with friends and neighbors, it was always orally. Even a middle-class Athenian woman scoffed at the idea of cookbooks. When asked where she had gained her cooking knowledge, she replied with barely-veiled contempt "from my mother and grandmother, of course!"[13]

---

13. Thanks to Renée Hirschon for sharing this anecdote. The recent development of cookbooks in Greece celebrating regional, minority and peasant cooking, but meant for an urban middle-class audience, is considered in a forthcoming dissertation by Vassiliki Yiakoumaki at the New School for Social Research. While these cookbooks exhibit interesting divergences on questions of the relationship of the local and regional to national Greek identity, Yiakoumaki notes that they share a nostalgic tone, much in line with my analysis of US nostalgia cookbooks below (Yiakoumaki, personal communication). See also Tratsa 1998.

Clearly, then, there is a strong gender component to this type of cooking-doing that I have been discussing. The one man who claimed to me to be a good cook, said that he was self-taught, and had learned by experimenting when as a bachelor during the Second World War he had lived on his own. This image of the chef/experimenter would be more in line with the male "great chefs" in France, who, according to Giard, have the power to impose their family names on their culinary innovations, while women have tended in the past to cook in an oral tradition of kinship transmission in which, even when they publish cookbooks, they remain the semi-anonymous "Aunt Maries" and "Grandma Madeleines."[14]

Cooking by the Book

> Was it true . . . that by writing down her recipes, my mother stole something before her time, took the easy way and tried to pin down what is learned only by being alongside another woman, only by feeling the same weight in your own hand, the same texture against your own skin? (Davidson 1998:259).

What might a shift away from such embodied cooking apprenticeship mean for memory and innovation? To what extent has US society replaced the transmission described above with cookbooks and recipes?[15] Or are cookbooks more commonly used to supplement and expand one's repertoire once "the basics" have already been learned? How much has cooking knowledge come to be replaced by pre-processed foods,

14. In their study of the values articulated by chefs in the United States (who were overwhelmingly male), Peterson and Birg (1988) stress the importance of creativity to self-image. This means that chefs frame their food creations in terms of coming up with new recipes and presentations, rather than working within a tradition. Memory is an important issue, noted by Peterson and Birg, since the ephemeral nature of their creations means that chefs must find other ways to preserve them. They do so both by writing recipes and recipe books, and by keeping a portfolio of pictures of their work, "perserving [sic] the memory of accomplishments in this perishable art form" (1988:69).

15. Pillsbury (1998:118–35) traces the rise of cookbooks in the United States in the nineteenth century to the increased female participation in the labor force during the industrial revolution, but also, interestingly, to the rise in immigration, which tended to separate women from a home community. Both of these factors militated against the type of embodied apprenticeship in cooking that Pillsbury implies was the norm before the nineteenth century.

meals that "taste like homemade,"[16] so that sauerkraut made from scratch, or bread made with homemade starter becomes a nostalgic, "primal" discovery.[17] Processed foods by their very nature would seemingly work to decrease both knowledge and memory. Written recipes could work in different directions: calling as they do for exact reproduction, rather than the variations on a theme that are part of Kalymnian cooking practice, they seem a piece with what Terdiman (1993:37) describes as "extra-individual mnemonic mechanisms," which isolate the "individual *item* of information to the detriment of its relation to any whole . . . such abstraction has been increasingly programmed by the practices of modern socio-economies since the industrial revolution." Warde, examining changes in written recipes over a 25-year period, notes an increasing emphasis on precision, measurement, calculation (Warde 1997:157). Cookery is presented increasingly in recipes "as a matter of technical rationality rather than of practical judgement," the *techne* that makes up "traditional" cooking practices. On the other hand, written recipes are also a key to innovation; Goody (1982) suggests they are one of the factors leading to the development of a "cuisine."

In the absence of studies of everyday cooking practices in the United States, however, we remain in the realm of speculation. In the rest of the chapter I will look at the recent wave of self-reflexive, mass-market "nostalgia cookbooks" in the United States, and how they approach some of the issues of embodied learning I have been discussing above.[18]

16. One study of an English town, cited by Warde (1997:127) claims that 94 per cent of all meals (including breakfast and lunch) involved less than ten minutes' preparation time.

17. On rediscovering sauerkraut, see Lust (1998). On making "primal" bread, see Steingarten (1997).

18. While my claim that "nostalgia cookbooks" are a recent trend is impressionistic, it receives some support from Warde's study of recipes in Britain. Warde notes that between 1968 and 1992 there was no increase in percentage of recipes appealing to "the exotic" or "the new," but there was a marked increase in recipes that claimed to be "traditional." In particular, recipes were touted in terms of their "authenticity," whether they were British or non-British in origin. Some also explicitly stressed the *loss* of cooking knowledge that was being renewed by the recipe: "'How many young housewives know how to make bread pudding?,' to be followed by a reassuring promise 'We have given a really authentic recipe'" (Warde 1997:65). Warde also notes an assumption of "shared and common knowledge regarding appropriate ways to construct a domestic food regime" in recipes from the 1960s. In the 1990s, by contrast, there is much less assumed common ground between readers and recipe writers, reflected in the more detailed instructions contained in these recipes (1997:76).

The quotation with which I began this section suggests the ambiguous and problematic issues being dealt with in books that attempt to capture culinary memories. But what is interesting is how many of the issues of embodied vs. abstract knowledge, tools vs. technology, practical knowledge vs. precise measurement are raised in these cookbooks in different ways. Now this embodied knowledge is, as I've argued, primarily oral, unmediated by writing. Clifford has discussed the "complex and charged" relationship of the oral to the written in the Western tradition, one that "finds both rescue and irretrievable loss – a kind of death in life – in the making of texts from events and dialogues. Words and deeds are transient (and authentic), writing endures (as supplementarity and artifice)" (1986:115–16).[19] Elsewhere (Wogan and Sutton 2000) Wogan and I have argued that the appeal of Italian ethnicity as portrayed in popular culture rests on the romance of the oral in American culture. Focusing primarily on the film *The Godfather, Part 1,* we argue that a series of oppositions is set up between food, speech, authenticity and family on the one hand, and writing, money, individualism and alienation on the other. It is the shift from the oral contract, sealed by food and drink and guaranteed by a man's word of honor, to the written, legal contract, which marks the decline of the Corleone family as control passes from the honorable Don to his perfidious, college-educated, Americanized son Michael.

But there is a paradox presented by these nostalgia cookbooks, in that what is nostalgically longed for – the oral community and all the embodied knowledge that comes with it – is being preserved through writing, and in these cases through writing in its most commodified form: the mass-market cookbook.[20] Thus in examining these cookbooks I will be interested in looking at the different ways that they do or do not address this paradox. I will also chart what I suggest are several

19. It should be noted that Clifford, drawing on Derrida, is criticizing this particularly Western symbolism of writing. For an ethnographically grounded critique of the notion that writing has some universal, cross-cultural symbolism in relation to loss and memory, see Wogan 1998. Also it is not only in the oral/written opposition that this dialectic of memory and loss is played out. Kuchler notes a similar dynamic in Western public monuments, which attempt to salvage the past amidst fears of "sweeping cultural amnesia" (Kuchler 1999:53).

20. I do not deal with the topic of "community cookbooks" here, though others have begun to examine such cookbooks, not, for the most part, as sources of nostalgia, but rather of memory and women's history. This looks to be a very fruitful area of investigation, as indicated by the work of Ireland (1998) and the collection edited by Bower (1997).

distinct types of nostalgia exhibited to varying degrees by these cookbooks.

When I began to examine these cookbooks, I found that they fell into several distinguishable categories, or points on a continuum, ranging from cookbooks with brief anecdotes added to some recipes, to full-blown culinary memoirs, with recipes playing a small or supporting role. The first category resembles in most respects a standard cookbook, focused on a set of recipes arranged in course-by-course order, but containing some extra elements not found in the standard cookbook. *A Taste of Old Cuba*, by Lluriá de O'Higgins (1994), published by the major cookbook publisher Harper-Collins, contains the subtitle "More than 150 recipes for delicious, authentic and traditional dishes, highlighted with reflections and reminiscences." As we will see, the adjectives "authentic" and "traditional" play an important role in many ethnic cookbooks, as well as in the nostalgia cookbooks under investigation here. While this book is the least explicit of those under consideration here on questions of transmission and writing, I choose to discuss it because it provides a very clear example of one type of nostalgia to be found in cookbooks, what I call "nostalgia for a lost Eden."

The recipes are presented in typical fashion, divided into categories based on the conventional courses of a Western European meal, as well as on the basis of the main ingredient – seafood, chicken, beef, pork, rice, etc. The recipes are also laid out in standard cookbook format: a list of ingredients followed by fairly detailed instructions. But the book has two main additions/divergences. First, instead of pictures of the completed recipes that can be found in many cookbooks, there is a series of about 15 black-and-white photographs of the author and her family spaced out through the text, with descriptive captions, and no photograph larger than half a page. The photographs depict a well-dressed, wealthy family, family homes, beaches, clubs and "one of Cuba's most famous restaurants" where the author dined. Most cookbooks of course include a preface to many recipes, which may give some information concerning the ingredients or the origin of the recipe.[21] In this cookbook recipe prefaces also discuss the origins of

---

21. As in the following introduction to an Easter recipe from a Greek-American community cookbook: "The traditional Easter meal features a baby lamb cooked on a spit. In Greece, people go to the countryside. Here in the States, the tradition continues" (St Paul's Greek Orthodox Cathedral (1991:138)).

dishes, but discussions are interspersed with "reflections and reminiscences" concerning the author's family, their diverse Spanish origins, and anecdotes of their cooking practices in pre-revolutionary Cuba. Thus a recipe for codfish in garlic sauce is prefaced by "This dish, as Basque as jai-alai, was a favorite of my maternal grandmother, Maria Aguirregaviria y Aramberry," while on the following page a section on lobster recipes begins with several paragraphs of childhood memories:

> We raced home to call Papá, and he grabbed his heaviest fish net and ran back to the beach with us. He climbed into a rowboat he kept there, cast out his net and quickly snagged enough lobsters to fill the boat. In the meantime, we children would have the pleasure of catching langostas with our bare hands (1994:50–51).

These childhood memories of blissful family life are all implicitly contrasted to the present time of the author's "exile" in Miami. Fidel Castro is attacked in elliptical remarks throughout the reminiscences, such as a servant clearing the dinner table in 1959, who picks up a knife and states

> 'If there is going to be communism, I am going out in the street with this knife to fight against it!' Like so many others, she eventually fled Cuba for Miami. Serve this old-fashioned dish with white rice, fried plantains, and an avocado salad (1994:76).

The author's anti-Castroism leads to some strange culinary claims, such as "Alas, under Fidel Castro there are no more black beans in Cuba" (1994:144). The politics of the present stand in opposition to an imagined pre-political past, in which there was no social conflict.[22] The sugar boom of the early twentieth century is described simply as a period of "fabulous wealth" for the island (1994:223). Lluriá de O'Higgins is at pains to insist that despite her class position, she was not a snob, and her family, unlike some of their neighbors, ate humble dishes of Afro-Cuban origins (prepared by the family servants) with as much gusto as fancy cuisine (1994:19). Indeed, she stresses the African and Chinese influences on Cuban cuisine at various points, though her reminiscences are restricted to Afro-Cuban servants and Chinese

---

22. This can be compared with what Duruz (1999) describes for cookbooks that evoke 1950s nostalgia in Australia, a nostalgia for times perceived as conflict-free, pre-political, and childlike: "the fifties as a childhood for the nineties."

fruit and vegetable peddlers, and descriptions of certain recipes, for example, "This Afro-Cuban dish is like Afro-Cuban music: rich and sensuous" (1994:140).

It is easy to see how this cookbook might be classified in terms of what Appadurai terms "ersatz nostalgia," or nostalgia for things, such as the idealized 1950s nuclear family, which never in fact existed.[23] The recipes and reminiscences are meant to evoke a lost Eden, a time before the fall, with the stress not only on the extended family, but the harmonious community. It is interesting that she did not learn to cook as a child, as she notes that servants did most of the cooking in her household (1994:xiv). She did not learn cooking through apprenticeship to a mother, aunt or grandmother, but rather got a school education, and remembers childhood as a period of "so much time for playing" (1994:xiv). Thus her childhood memories are those of a consumer, unclouded by labor or responsibility, adding, perhaps to the sense of "lost Eden" represented by foods past (cf. Duruz 1999:233). As a literate woman, she can celebrate pre-Castro Cuban cuisine and life "like so many writers, artists and musicians" without any conflict over the commodification of practical knowledge. As we will see, this is not the case for our other cookbook writers.

Five customer reviews on Amazon.com all come from Cuban-Americans, stressing the authenticity of the recipes, and of her writing style. None of the reviewers mentions the politics of the book, but one states that "the reminiscences are true," while another claims that the book's anecdotes "bring alive a time and a place no longer available to us." The stress on authenticity is an interesting feature of current culinary discourse. As Warde emphasizes, it differs from a stress on the "traditional," in that authenticity does not *necessarily* suggest a long time perspective (1997:64–6). A dish can be authentically Chinese simply by being what Chinese eat, as opposed to adulterated *faux*-Chinese (Chow mein being a prototype of this). And it is this sense of "authentic" as opposed to traditional that tends to appeal to Western consumers of "exotic" cuisines: hence the appeal of restaurants where "X people actually go to eat." A specific appeal to "tradition" tends to evoke anti-modern sentiments, distrust of kitchen gadgetry or other short-cuts and a celebration of the labor-intensive cooking processes of past times. While this is expressed to some degree by Lluriá de

---

23. Appadurai (1996:76–77). On the "invention" of the nuclear family in the American imagination, see Coontz (1992). See also B. West (2000) on the nostalgic invention of the grandmother-cook in popular magazines in post-Socialist Hungary.

O'Higgins – who exhorts her readers to try making a soup stock at least once, but admits that bouillon cubes make an adequate substitute (1994:12) – it is not a major emphasis in her cookbook. It is this sense of "traditional," however, that forms a key tension in Carol Field's *In Nonna's Kitchen*. Field's book, along with Tropiano-Tucci and Scappin's *Cucina et Famiglia* discussed below, forms an intermediate category: while still resembling standard cookbooks in many ways, there is a much greater emphasis placed (in terms of textual space) on personal and social history as seen through the rubric of food. Thus *In Nonna's Kitchen* begins with a 23-page introduction on the changing cooking practices of "Italy's grandmothers." Throughout the recipe sections are long descriptive forays into Italian life, as well as a series of 3–5-page biographical sketches of the grandmothers who provided the author with the recipes for this book.

Carol Field does not focus on her own experience of Italy, nor does she mention her own background as justification for her project. This is not family history, as with the previous cookbook. Instead, Field frames her project in terms of what Clifford (1986) has called "salvage ethnography" – the description of customs on the verge of disappearing. As Field describes it, "They [the grandmothers] are the connection to a way of life that is gradually being lost in Italy, and when they are gone, that link will disappear with them" (1997:3). These *nonnas*, we are told, are the "keepers of memory" and "a link to an earlier time in the country's past" (1997:2). Their knowledge, which has been passed on from mother to daughter for generations, is now under threat from processes of modernization much like those described earlier in this chapter. Her ethnographic entry is facilitated by a young woman, Sofia Savelli, "fashionably thin in her chic miniskirt." Sofia works in an office in town, and admits that she neither knows how to cook, nor recognizes many of the dishes that Field is investigating. But she takes Field to meet a neighbor from her home village, one of the nonnas lionized in this book. Everywhere, Field finds change and loss. At certain moments she writes elegiacally, beginning subsequent paragraphs with the repeated phrase "Gone are the days when . . ." (1997:19–20). The *nonnas'* cooking, with its peasant 'simplicity' and attention to seasonality, is described in the past continuous tense, suggesting that these *nonnas* already belong to the past.

At first glance one might be tempted to describe Field's approach as what Rosaldo (1989:68–87) has called "imperialist nostalgia," that is, romantic nostalgia for worlds that "modern" peoples have destroyed in the processes of modernization, urbanization and industrialization.

Much has been written on this topic. In the Greek context, for example, Gefou-Madianou (1999) describes the historical shifts by which retsina wine-producing villagers went from being labelled as "backward peasants and drunkards" by elites in Athens, to being considered one of the bearers of an "authentic Greek folk tradition" in recent times, when cultural diversity offers both symbolic capital and valuable products for commodification and touristic consumption. In a country where whiskey had long been the drink of high status, retsina has "acquired a new cachet and has been identified as the characteristic Greek wine" (1999:417). What is elided in this folkloricization of village life and revalued consumption of village products, as Gefou-Madianou shows, is the complex history and relations of inequality between urban centers and rural villages that have gone into the creation of retsina as an "authentic" expression of Greek culture. Similarly Leitch, in her discussion of the Slow Food movement in Italy, describes the phenomenon of "Tuscanopia" – "in which Tuscan peasant cuisines . . . and picturesque rurality . . . seem to have become key fantasy spaces of modern urban alienation" (Leitch 2000; see also Duruz 1999:241). This post-modernist reclamation and celebration of the "multiculturalism" previously trampled by modernization and state-building processes has been recently dubbed the "cultures without people" approach to domination (Hill 1999).

Field skirts, but does not fall into this trap of imperialist nostalgia. This is because the "past" described by Field is in fact considerably more complex than what is portrayed in her opening paragraphs. In particular, she does not romanticize the past as a lost Eden, as does Lluriá de O'Higgins, nor does she portray it as a timeless bearer of tradition.[24] If there is nostalgia, it is primarily the nostalgia of her ethnographic subjects, mixed, as it is for the Kalymnians, with ambiguous and contradictory feelings about "modernity" and "tradition." Field describes the extreme poverty and scarcity that characterized life for many of the *nonna*s up until the 1960s, a poverty brought on by the sharecropping system, which left them "subject always to the whims of the seasons and the owners of the land" (1997:9). At the same time, people are nostalgic for the community that they saw as coming with such scarcity. Field recognizes the influence women wield through food

24. Indeed it would be difficult to portray present-day Italian villagers as the bearers of a timeless cooking tradition, given that, as Field notes (1997:6), many of the key ingredients such as corn, potatoes, peppers and tomatoes were introduced fairly recently to Italy.

preparation, while at the same time acknowledging the deference to men that was expected of them.

In describing food preparation itself, Field stresses the time investment involved – time that seems no longer available under contemporary conditions. One *nonna* contrasts the labor-intensive five-course meals of her youth to meals of today: "'We've had a revolution! We eat a lot less now . . . I'm happy to have lived the other life, but I don't have the spirit or desire to relive it. I prefer the life of today – it's so much more easygoing, more dynamic'" (1997:12). Thus the woman tells Field how she has found time-saving ways to prepare traditional dishes, such as buying puff pastry at the local shop instead of making it herself. Field describes in painstaking detail the techniques of the past, such as cooking poultry on sand-filled slabs inside a coal oven (1997:14). All of these techniques imparted special flavors that can no longer be reproduced with modern techniques. Yet not all techniques from the past are canonized. One *nonna* describes making flat breads on terracotta disks which have now been replaced by iron plates, confiding: "'Shall I admit it? Today's metal disks are really better than the terra-cotta ones we used to use'" (1997:18). The recipes that Field collects enact the tension between capturing the tastes of the past and dealing with contemporary time constraints, what Warde discusses as the antinomy between convenience and care characteristic of contemporary recipe advice: "The tension between viewing household cooking as an instrumental and technical activity [to be done as quickly as possible], as opposed to a labor of love" (1997:131). Field suggests that Italians are finding ways to have it all, to adapt traditional cuisine to modern demands, "looking backward as they look ahead" (1997:22). While far from a "time-saving" cookbook, Field's recipes suggest that compromises will be necessary at times. Thus in her recipe for oil-cured black olives (1997:51), she notes :

> When Nella Galletti's mother made this delicious antipasto, she started with large black uncured olives, washed them well, and then put them in a wood-burning oven at the lowest possible heat where they dried for 2 or 3 days until they were dry and deeply grooved with wrinkles. My approach is much easier: start with oil-cured black olives and toss them with flavors to make them spicy . . .

Field skirts the issue of writing and the commodification of recipes. On the one hand she reports that many of the *nonnas* found the idea of written recipes to be "absurd" (1997:27), as was the idea of any exact measurements. Yet elsewhere she documents the existence of family recipes that are part of the transmission process that has preserved local and sub-local variation in Italian cooking: "Some women are fortunate enough to possess the small kitchen notebooks kept by their grandmothers with old family recipes written in black ink in a spidery hand. They keep them carefully in a separate drawer, and some still use them, for they are the source of family dishes that pass from generation to generation" (1997:11). Further, as a seeming parallel to her project, she notes the role of school districts in Italy in attempting to preserve a culinary heritage by encouraging children to interview their grandparents for compiled cookbooks with titles such as *Lost Tastes* and *On the Path of Remembrances* (1997:21). Note that in each of these cases these recipes are not commodified cookbooks for sale in bookstores, but more along the line of family heirlooms, "inalienable possessions" (Weiner 1992), kept locked away in separate drawers to be given as gifts to future generations. Thus while Field bemoans the speed-ups of modern life represented, interestingly enough, by fax machines (1997:22), Field suggests that the reader of her book should not despair, that Italians can have their culinary heritage and eat it too, and Field can capture this culinary heritage in written form.

Another book that fits into a similar category to Field's, half cookbook, half *mémoire*, is *Cucina y Famiglia* by Tropiano Tucci and Scappin (1999). I wish to highlight some common themes and a few key differences between the two. If *In Nonna's Kitchen* highlights the threatened loss of tradition, *Cucina y Famiglia* tells an immigrant success story for a multicultural age, both at the level of people and of cuisine. This book is a collaboration in a number of ways. It is written primarily by an Italian-American woman with an Italian-born and trained New York chef. I say primarily, because there are several other authorial voices in the book, including Tropiano-Tucci's husband, Stan, and their son, the actor Stanley Tucci, as well as a writer/editor who is given front-page credit ("with Mimi Shanley Taft"). It contains many black-and-white family photographs, though, unlike Field, it also contains more typical cookbook fare: full-color plates of completed dishes. The book was inspired by the film *Big Night*, about an Italian restaurant in New York in the 1950s, which Stanley Tucci starred in, directed and co-wrote. The book also provides a recipe for the keynote dish in the film, *Timpáno*.

As with Field's book, *Cucina y Famiglia* begins with a long introduction, though here we are back to first-person narrative, and is broken up into sections written by Joan (Tropiano Tucci), Stan (her husband) and

Gianni (Scappin). Each section of the introduction ends with the signature of the corresponding author. These narratives display much less of a sense of loss than those collected by Field. Rather they are narratives of immigrant success, success both in terms of American society, and in keeping connected to the traditions of "home" (a trip to Italy for a year plays an important part in the narratives of Joan and Stan). What is stressed is the large extended family (including Italian neighbors, who become "fictive kin"), which has kept together, living nearby, through three generations. The family grow many ingredients in their own backyard garden, and Tropiano Tucci provides a number of detailed descriptions of the family activity of processing these base ingredients, such as bottling tomatoes (1999:41). The family gathers around mealtimes, the "kitchen and family" of the title, as in the following description of a meal, with obvious symbolism:

> Mary would place a huge oval board in the center of the table onto which she would pour cooked polenta. The polenta was then topped with a ragú sauce that included stewed meat and meatballs. Each person was given a fork and we ate toward the center, incorporating a little polenta in a little sauce for each bite. At the beginning of the meal one of the children would ask for a meatball, but Angelo would tell them they had to eat their way into the center before they could have one (1999:6).

No better evidence of this double success can be provided than the figure of Stanley Tucci, a successful actor who also keeps tradition alive by making the film *Big Night* and collaborating in making this cookbook. Here, however, there is an interesting tension between the cookbook and the film. *Big Night* is far less optimistic about the prospects for immigrant success without commodifying or creating ersatz tradition. Indeed, it is the chef Primo's refusal to compromise tradition and serve spaghetti and meatballs to his American customers that leads to the failure of the restaurant and his eventual return to Italy.

Scappin, as a first-generation migrant and co-author, gives his narrative a slightly different trajectory. He describes growing up in a "tiny village" in Italy, and the tradition of restaurant work in his family. He then narrates his culinary training, which takes him first to urban Italy and eventually to New York, where he begins to introduce Italian dishes such as *focaccia* and risotto to New York palates: "It is my belief that the energy and open-minded nature of New Yorkers allowed me to explore Italian cooking beyond the flavors and tastes of my own experiences. It was at Le Madri, in fact, that I developed a balance between sophistication and simplicity in cooking . . ." (1999:22–3). He returns to Italy to fulfil his dream of re-opening the family *trattoria*, only to find that his culinary style has "evolved" beyond the conservativeness of local palates: "The longer I remained in Italy, the more I missed America's ever-dynamic culinary community" (1999:24). Thus in 1998 he returned to New York, where he can enjoy "the best of both Italy and America," remaining faithful to Italian "traditions and simplicities," while at the same time continuing his "culinary growth" (1999:25). Thus, while Field opposed a traditional Italy to a modern Italy representing a lack of culinary knowledge, Scappin opposes Italy as a whole as repository of a static tradition to the United States, where culinary mixing and innovation renew tradition.

The issue of cooking time is not for the most part thematized in this book. Many of the recipes are involved and time-consuming, though shortcuts are suggested at various points, such as using a food processor and pasta machine to make fresh pasta (1999:119). The question of transforming oral into written recipes is captured in the issue of measurements. Scappin notes that in writing this cookbook he needed to be constantly reminded that recipes need to be exact for readers; but he shares the disdain for precise measurement noted earlier in this chapter. As he puts it, his own philosophy is "very Italian . . . 'a little of this and a little of that.' So my frequent use of the expression '*dipende*,' or 'it depends,' became an ongoing joke throughout this project" (1999:23). Here resistance to precise measurement is depicted as quaint, part of the traditional values that he hopes to modernize. But hesitation does not make it into the recipes themselves, except, perhaps, in the normalized form of "variations" on many of the recipes.

If the three cookbooks analyzed above retain the recipe form, and simply add other materials to the cookbook, my final example, Michael Lee West's *Consuming Passions* (1999) is more playful, challenging the concept of a standardized written recipe, and raising most directly the paradoxes of inscribing an oral tradition. *Consuming Passions* belongs to a separate category, the culinary memoir, in which text predominates and recipes play a supporting role, if they are included at all.[25] West's

---

25. The genre of culinary memoirs, though it has a long pedigree going back to the writings of M. F. K. Fisher, if not Brillat-Savarin, has shown an efflorescence of late. They tend to have an "ethnic" or regional focus, heightening their nostalgic appeal. Recent titles include Clarke (1999), Lang (1998), Lust (1998), Moore (1997) and Reichl (1998).

book describes her childhood and adulthood in the Louisiana Delta and Tennessee, and her extended family of relatives through the lens of what she refers to as "a food obsessed life" (the title of the first chapter). The book is divided up into chapters, organized around anecdotes, with titles such as "Uncle Bun's Barbecue," "Funeral Food," and "Bake Sales." Each chapter contains a few "family recipes" with names such as "Aunt Joyce's Biloxi Pot Roast." Home remedies and love medicines add to the folksy tone. Aunts, mothers and grand-mothers predominate among the cast of quirky characters, as a female line of transmission is celebrated (although West herself has two sons, who feature as cooks). In a play on biblical begats, West describes a recipe for her family's chocolate sheet cake as coming from her grandmother's grandmother: "Whenever I bake it, all of my forebears gather in my kitchen. Elizabeth taught Estelle to make this cake, and Estelle taught Mimi, and Mimi taught Ary Jean, and Ary Jean taught Michael Lee, and Michael Lee taught Trey and Tyler" (1999:169).

The emphasis in West's recipes is to capture some of the social life and indeterminacy that goes into cooking. Thus rather than providing "variations," recipe instructions contain digressions and multiple voices: "Sometimes I use white sugar, other times a blend of white and brown; honey is an admirable substitute. Don't be afraid to experiment. You have to work hard to hurt this recipe . . . Mimi [West's grandmother] added a handful of red-hot candies, stirring on low heat until the confection melted and the sauce turned a fierce shade of red. 'Children are extremely partial to candied applesauce,' she used to say" (1999:40). Recipes are sometimes integrated into the text, and not set off in separate boxes, which allows West to introduce more playful material: "Some cooks like to fry chicken while listening to Verdi – *La Forza del Destino* – but Bruce Springsteen will work, too . . . Some cooks let the chicken 'rest,' then they re-flour. (Oh, go on and use both hands. You can clean up later)" (1999:75).

If in this way West stresses a shared culinary inheritance within her extended family, she also emphasizes the extent to which cooking is a competitive activity among women, with secrets closely guarded. Just as Steinberg (1998:296) suggests of Bubbie's Challah that "perhaps it was right that the secret should remain hers, not to be simulated by some pretender," the women described by West believe that cooking knowledge equals power – not for nothing do they give their names to recipes! Of her mother, she writes "Just don't ask her for a recipe. She likes to be the family's sole source of perfect food" (1999:83). Her Aunt Tempe "baked cakes for a living in a small Louisiana town," so when neighbors asked for recipes "She'd pat her hearing aid and say: 'Sorry, my battery is on the blink'" (1999:93).[26] To family members, she would divulge pieces of recipes, but then change the subject, and if pressed, she would "wave her hand. 'It takes eight days to make that cake. And that's the easy part'" (1999:94). Interestingly, it is only when in the hospital, fearing that she has suffered a heart attack, that she gives out her secret. It is in this context that West makes explicit the relationship of transmission, writing and death. West begins and ends her book with funerals, which, she notes, are occasions for storytelling, but also for concern about possible breaks in continuity:

> At one funeral, Aunt Hettie pulled me aside and said 'This is a shame! What a loss!' I thought she was speaking of the relative we were about to bury . . . 'She's taken her gingerbread recipe to the grave,' Aunt Hettie moaned . . . And your own grandmother took her biscuits with her too.'
> 'No she didn't!' cried Mama. 'I know it by heart.'
> 'You'd better write it down,' warned Aunt Tempe. 'Young people don't know how to make scratch biscuits. They just pop open a can . . .'
> 'Food is a dying art,' said Tempe. 'At least in this family. We're burying our best recipes.' After the funeral, my mother drove me to her house, and in her sunny yellow kitchen, she taught me how to make my grandmother's biscuits' (1999:7).

This is followed by the recipe itself. Here writing serves as a mnemonic, saving tradition from being buried, but it is a last resort, to be used on the point of death, since the mother, whose life is not in question, still teaches her daughter orally and experientially how to make the biscuits. West though, writes the recipe, and those of her aunts, ensuring their wider "commodified" circulation (West's book is published by Harper-Collins as well), while at the same time fixing them and taking them

26. In his classic study of the restaurant industry, William Whyte (1948:29) notes a similar problem with the introduction of written recipes in taking skill out of the circuits of local knowledge and control:

> Operating without written recipes, the chef was king of the kitchen . . . If recipes were furnished, the manager could then supervise the chef much more closely. He could check to see that the recipes were being followed. He could bring in new recipes and revise old ones. Furthermore, this standardization would tend to take the skill out of the job and much of the prestige with it. It had taken the chef years to learn his craft, and now, in a small restaurant down the street, cooks were being trained through standardized recipes in a matter of weeks.

out of the local circulation of knowledge and secrets that she describes in her book. Perhaps realizing this, she attempts to subvert the written recipe by providing counter-discourses and voices within each recipe.

West is not the only one to use this connection between writing, death and the threat of loss implicit in transmission. In a Greek-American woman's account of her coming-of-age (Davidson 1998), writing recipes down has the power to kill: "a week after the recipes were written down, my grandmother was dead. As for my own mother, she refuses. If we want to know the recipes, we have to learn them . . . by heart, writing them with our bodies" (1998:259). As Clifford suggests, writing implies either distance, or death or both. Just as the embodied learning of recipes implies identity – the very identity that Steinberg and his siblings, in thinking about their grandmother's Challah, wished to avoid. Literacy, in Western symbolism, as noted above, represents the enduring, but unauthentic. By contrast, spoken words are transient and authentic, and I would suggest the same could be said of food (see Quigley 1997:50ff. on the romantic symbolism of the illiterate).

We have seen different types of nostalgia portrayed in these cookbooks, nostalgia for an imaginary lost Eden, nostalgia for that which was destroyed as part of modernization, and nostalgia for the immigrant/regional extended family at the table, at a time when everyday life seems increasingly fragmented and atomized. But the image of family, ethnic and regional identity mediated through cooking in an oral tradition comes out in all these cookbooks. The power of these symbols lies in their overwhelming association with the "real" and the "authentic" in US society. And overriding the different categories of nostalgia I have discussed is a "nostalgia for the real" in a society of increasingly mass-mediated experiences (see for example, Borgmann 1992).[27] As West

27. Borgmann notes the "receding of reality" from everyday experience in a number of domains, such as politics, scholarship, art, and labor processes. That experience of loss of reality to mediation is captured in the following quote from a pulp mill operator, which seems very much in line with the loss of *metis* and *techne* described by Scott (1998) as discussed above:

"With computerization I am further away from my job than I have ever been before. I used to listen to the sounds the boiler makes and know just how it was running. I could look at the fire in the furnace and tell by its color how it was burning. I knew what kinds of adjustments were needed by the shades of color I saw. A lot of the men also said that there were smells that told you different things about how it was running. I feel uncomfortable being away from these sights and smells. Now I only have numbers to go by" (cited in Borgmann 1992:165).

The popularity of "real TV," such as *Survivor*, at the time of this writing seems another indication of this nostalgia for the real.

(M.L. West 1999:258–9) sums up: "In every Southern family there's probably enough fodder for a dozen novels. Stories, recipes and secrets are passed down orally . . . Any curious Southerner can uproot buried truths – you just need to know where to dig." By using this metaphor of manual labor, West inscribes the contradictions of a project that uses writing to portray an authenticity that (in our ideology) writing has itself destroyed. But, as I noted in my discussion of Field, it is not writing itself that is problematic, it is writing that leaves the realm of family possession and becomes one more anonymous commodity in a sea of alienated products that threatens to remove cooking from the contexts of embodied knowledge and local transmission. Perhaps this is why a number of "customer reviews" of these books on Amazon.com note that they have given these books as gifts to family and friends ("Thank you Mrs O'Higgins, I now have something to pass on to my own daughter!"), thus reinscribing the commodity in the circuits of gift exchange (Carrier 1990). However, it seems that as long as we are offered frozen foods that "taste like homemade," and McDonald's comes up with even faster ways to deliver a quarter-pounder, as long as we associate food preparation with "love" and "family," while a capitalist economy continuously erodes the ties that bind, we will continue to reproduce these variations on nostalgia for the real, and one way that our longings will be inscribed is in the form of nostalgia cookbooks.

Coda: Kalymnian *Filla*

The careful reader will have noted that the predicament of cookbook writers and the predicament of anthropologists show numerous parallels. Anthropologists, too, often traffic in nostalgia, as the title of a collection on the history of anthropology, *Romantic Motives*, indicates (Stocking 1989). Anthropologists too, struggle with representing the dynamics of social life in static textual form, and work with various strategies – multivocality, evocation, indeterminacy – to subvert the limits of our genre. With that in mind I submit the following recipe elicited from a mother and daughter, Katerina Kardoulia and Katina Mixa, for *filla*, the Kalymnian "national" dish, also known as *dolmadhes*. Though in the past they had responded to my request for a recipe by simply showing me and my wife how *filla* were made, in this case I specifically asked for a recipe that I could write down. Thus I give no promises as to whether this recipe is actually usable, as my apprenticeship already includes, no doubt, many embodied assumptions.

FILLA

Eat this on Sundays. [Daughter speaking]: In Kos they eat it with much less meat, empty! And they go and buy grape leaves at the store instead of using all the grape leaves that they have in their own vineyards. Koans are difficult and twisted (*strifni*)! [Mother speaking]: The Koans learned from Kalymnians to use their grape leaves and not just feed them to their donkeys. Kalymnians opened their eyes!

Dried grape leaves, placed in hot water to soften
1 kilo ground meat
2 onions
2 spoons of butter
2 spoons of tomato sauce or paste
salt, to taste ("taste it!")
pepper
2 water glasses of rice
1–2 cups of water

Cook all the ingredients together until rice is done. Leave it for ½–1 hour (in order to take the smell out of the onion). Wrap in small packages of grape leaves, and cook in a little water till done [Note, this is the key step, but one that mother and daughter could not articulate to me in written instructions, and probably didn't feel that instructions were necessary, since they had shown me many times over the years. However, here is Davidson describing the process in her memoir *The Priest Fainted*:

> No one ever makes dolmades alone if she can help it. The lessons in patience are among the first a mother teaches her children: how to unroll the green leaves when young fingers make them too fat or too thin, how to select the right ones and cover up the tears or holes, how to use a teaspoon to measure the half-cooked rice. You must never lose your patience and overstuff your spoon. Never try to empty the bowl more quickly, because then the dolmades will be too fat and will burst in the heat of cooking. There are hundreds to be rolled (1998:64).]

Serve these with yoghurt or with *avgolemono*.

AVGOLEMONO

2 egg whites. Make into foam. Add the yolks and 2 lemons and a little juice from the *filla* so it's not too thick; then pour over the *filla* and shake the pot around to distribute. If you cook the *filla* with a stuffed pepper, the *filla* take the smell of the pepper. [Daughter speaking]: "My cousin in Athens made *filla*, but measured everything, counting how many *filla* she would buy, etc. But when she came with friends from Athens to visit they ate my *filla* and said 'Oh, I've never tasted anything like this before,' even though I had made them the night before and it wasn't a good batch. Also my neighbor with the goats doesn't have time to make them, because it takes so long to do all the folding, but one time when she made them recently her son ate them all day long, right out of the pot!"

Conclusion: The Repast Recaptured

I have argued in this book that food and memory taken together can shed new light on theoretical approaches and interests, from venerable issues such as ritual and exchange, to recent concerns with embodiment, structure and event, the senses, nostalgia and globalization. In Chapter 1 I argued that food memory helps us to understand some of the enduring aspects of ritual, while at the same time breaking down any hard-and-fast distinction between the ritual and the everyday. While elaborate rituals, such as the practices of reburial in Eastern Europe examined by Verdery (1999:115ff.), are ways of bringing *alternative temporalities into the present*, food and eating can index those different temporalities that make up the present on a daily basis, both in Seremetakis's moments of "stillness" over a cup of coffee, and in off-hand gestures such as a woman's giving her son a slice of watermelon to be eaten by hand "like in the old days." Both in moments of revitalization for Greek migrants, when the past becomes present, and in moments of prospective remembrance, when future merges with past, or even in nostalgia cooking, in which processed food is replaced by an imagined, "really real" meal, food offers some of the most quotidian points of entry into the blended temporalities of experience. But food does not simply work on the everyday level. Food memories work through the mutual reinforcement of the cosmic and the mundane, feeding the dead and feeding the living, the bread that is the staff and staple of everyday life and the *imitatio*, or resurrection of the sacred moment of Christ's passion.

Food memories also draw together the dead and the living in a concern for reputation and good name. Thus the topic of food generosity bridges the first two chapters and a consideration of the issue of exchange. Here, too, the special nature of food leads to interesting theoretical issues concerning memory and exchange. Food's perishability seems to be

Yiannis Roditis, Still Life with Prickly Pear Leaf, Figs and Koulora

its distinguishing characteristic, the fact that, as Visser (1999:122) recently notes of food gifts: "you eat them up, and the gift is gone. It doesn't hang around creating obligations, reminding you." Thus those interested in exchange and memory have tended to dismiss consideration of food for that of more solid objects. By contrast I argue that ritual feasting or mundane food exchanges can create lasting memory impressions, particularly when cultivated through narratives of past exchanges. Further, unlike solid objects, food *internalizes* debt, once again calling for verbal and non-verbal acts of remembrance and reciprocity. The repeated acts of food generosity that create friendships and memorable reputations on Kalymnos can be compared with the repeated acts of feeding that are part of the long-term process of creating kinship, or shared substance, between people in Ecuadorian society (Weismantel 1995; see also Carsten 1995). Furthermore, food exchanges, whether gift or theft, serve as a generalized reminder of a community life in which the roads of obligation are constantly open, not having been short-circuited by the specter of balanced reciprocity, buying food in a supermarket, which is really no reciprocity at all.

A concern running through the book has been the increased transnational flow of food and the people who eat it, and what globalization might mean for changing food memory practices. If one of the key questions in recent anthropological study is how globalization reconfigures identities and experiences, food memories give us numerous entry points into this topic. And they do so in a way that keeps these issues from flying off centripetally into the airy abstractions of cultural studies, and grounds questions of globalization processes in the everyday, quotidian experience of people and communities that is the hallmark of fieldwork-based anthropological study. In the context of examining the increasing commodification of staple foods, I am led to questions of the relationship of memory and imagination, and of the extent to which community food memories rely on memories specifically of food production. While those concerned with the increasingly centralized control of our food supply are, I suggest, correct about the threat to certain types of memories and meanings, the extent to which even commodified food can be transformed through active purchasing, processing, serving, exchanging and narrating suggests complex potentials for the reappropriation of the global through local meanings and practices. Thus local products become part of global circuits of exchange between a "home" and the lives of transnational migrants, while foreign products, such as Roquefort, are localized as part of Kalymnian specialities, and made part of local social relations, as when a man can use this commodity to enter a protest against the quality of his neighbor's locally-produced cheese.

An anthropology attentive to sensory experiences has, I argue in Chapter 3, much to tell us about the evocative power of food memory at the same time that it challenges a strict reliance on semiotic or symbolic interpretation. Memories of taste and smell by their very nature will tend to the idiosyncratic, the randomly associative, as opposed to symbols that may be more collectively cognized and debated (while still remaining "multivocal"). But this does not mean that memories of taste and smell are not illuminated by the associative fields, or taste- and smell-scapes, in which they are learned and experienced. Proust's *madeleine* memory took shape in a French *haut-bourgeois* social context in which children learned to be "delicate" (in the sense of "sickly" and contemplative, but also refined in their tastes). Whereas Kalymnian children are also taught the importance of attention to taste and smell, but in a very different context where men sniff basil and dream of a patriotic homeland, and young boys are taught that to smell a food and not at least get a small taste of it is a threat to their manhood.

While I separated questions of sense and structure for consideration in Chapters 3 and 4 respectively, clearly this is an analytic separation that does not stand up to experiential reality. For it is mundane repetition that gives sensory experiences their meaning over time. While Proust was one of our guides to sense memory, he was equally concerned with questions of meaning through repetition, witness the very structure of his work, as well as his long discourses on the structure of music and the power of the "little phrase" that continually returns in Vinteuil's *Sonata*. Each sensorily evoked memory of a past episode was a chance not just to reflect on the past, but on what had changed in between – similarity and difference again. Mary Douglas, who also relied on musical metaphors, was our guide in Chapter 4's consideration of structure. But she was also concerned with the sensual; food as an art form. She recognized the importance of the textures of food, even if she tended to put them into structural grids: rough-smooth:coarse–refined. Ethnographically, just as we seek to unite structure and event or the ritual and the everyday in a single (dialectic?) analysis, we must do the same for the structural and the sensual if we are to understand the power of memory to create meaning.

In Chapters 4 and 5 I take different perspectives on the recurring questions of sameness and difference, continuity and change, the oral and the literate, "tradition" and "modernity," in relation to meal structures and to processes of learning and doing cooking. In comparing and contrasting my Kalymnian ethnography with research done on the United States I have meant to suggest the productivity of the notion that there are many different possible ways that memory can be culturally structured in terms of food practices, reflecting a different historical consciousness. I have argued against using any simple dichotomy of "closed traditional communities" and "open, modern societies," most recently theoretically elaborated by Giddens (1991). Rather, along with Collier (1997) I have tried to show the extent to which "following tradition" involves choice, reflection, and variation. And also to show the extent to which "making one's own choices" is an imposed cultural prescription, with implications for the kind of food memories that will be reproduced in societies under the sway of an ideology of "modernity." I have suggested, however, that the differences between Kalymnos and an admittedly idealized "US popular culture" are good to think with about memories of the familiar and memories of the "new," or mundane and extraordinary meals. Even more productive might have been a three-way contrast: Greece, the US, and . . . or Kalymnos, Athens, New York, Carbondale. In other words, how do different national ideologies of the relationship of past and present play out similarly or differently in urban and rural contexts? As I have suggested throughout, there are some aspects of my discussion of Kalymnos that might apply to Greece more generally (for example, concern for the past, and its metaphorical exploration), and others that would not (lack of restaurants and cookbooks). The same can be said for my discussion of US popular food culture and the culture of food in Tidewater, North Carolina. Multiple contrasts seem the way to avoid stale truisms of the traditional and the modern, or other binarisms. This is the productivity that Boon suggests, that comes from moving beyond dividing the world into Zunis and Kwakiutls: "any culture's 'normality' is configured as a field of contradictions held together by reinforced replications of pattern, but also by bold opposition to alternatives implicitly resisted: Zuni/not-Apache, nor even Hopi; Dobu/not-Trobriand; Kwakiutl/not Salish nor Haidalike (although becoming more matrilineal)" (Boon 1999:29). The usefulness of these contrasts for thinking about food memories points to the fact that the equation of food, identity and memory – "you are what you ate" – is not enough. Rather, this equation can look very different from the point of view of a Greek island than it does at Oxford High Table or again at a trendy New York restaurant. These many cultural forms of remembering foods past require an ethnographic investigation that has been sorely lacking. And a sense of multiple possible types of food memories provides, I think, one possible way forward for those tired of what one colleague bemoaned as: "Please, not another study of food and identity!"

In the remainder of my conclusion I would like to give brief consideration to a few topics that I did not cover, or only touched upon, but which a few others have begun to work on. These promising new approaches suggest further possibilities for the kind of theoretically informed ethnographic exploration I have been arguing for throughout this book.

The Experience of Commodification

The first is a broader consideration of the "commodification of nostalgia" in a variety of food venues. Retro-style in food has been analyzed for food packaging and advertising, as in Visser's (1986:316ff.) discussion of the "invention" of old-fashioned ice cream, as well as for restaurants and coffeeshops (Duruz 2001; Kugelmass 1990). The commodification of tradition is explicitly part of the strategy of ethnic festivals, which often have an economic genesis. Magliocco (1998:153ff.)

perceptively analyzes the different uses of food in an Italian-American festival, from "display foods," the foods that non-Italians identify as markers of Italian ethnicity, to "re-christened foods," American foods such as ham-and-cheese sandwiches given Italian names (*pasticceto di prosciutto*) in the spirit of keeping the festival "authentic." Finally, there are "pseudo-foods," such as large wooden rounds meant to represent cheese in the cheese-rolling contest. As Magliocco (1998:157) notes, pseudo-food is the furthest removed from the tastes, smells and textures of Italian-Americans, and from the agricultural labor of the Italian immigrants:

> It is, then symbolic and highly abstract: food out of context, it is *meant* to be played with, created for use solely within the festival context . . . The substitution of pseudocheese for real cheese in the Clinton festival reflects the shift in the immigrants' economy (and thus also ethos) from subsistence to consumerism, from premarket to postmodern.

As with my discussion of cookbooks, the stress in these studies tends to be on "textual" analysis of symbolism, with some space given to discussion *within* the ethnic community whose traditions are being commodified. Thus Magliocco notes that a number of older Italian immigrants expressed resentment at the festival, not happy to celebrate and to market for mass consumption the same aspects of their culture that in earlier times had been used by the dominant community as a source of food-based stereotypes indicating Italian "backwardness" (1998:149). Rauch similarly notes that an Italian *festa* in Hartford Connecticut was transformed into an "Italian three day feast," so that Italian Americans, concerned over the downplaying of the religious significance of the *festa*, eventually decided to cancel it (Rauch 1988: 214ff.).

But the question of how such commodification is received by its intended audience remains. How do people eat at ethnic festivals and retro-restaurants? How do they choose between products at the supermarket offering the past, present or future in a can? And do people who read nostalgia cookbooks strictly follow the recipes, adapt and annotate them, or use them at all? How many of the readers of such books consider themselves to be members of the thematized groups reconnecting with "their own" identities, and how many are readers cruising for "other" identities? How much is the phenomenon of nostalgia cookbooks more accurately termed an "apodemialgia," a longing to get away from one's own home, part and parcel of tourist desire for commodified "experiences" (Valeri 2000; see also Long 1998)? And what of resistances to commodification? Duruz suggests that even within the structures of post-Fordian commodification there is room for De Certeauian reappropriations of "tradition" by the weak, for example in urban coffeeshops that appropriate public spaces and offer meanings of "home," while walking a fine line between gift and commodity transactions (Duruz 2000:20). Rauch also notes that *some* Italian food vendors during the *festa* felt that they were preserving their culinary heritage in America through making pizza "just like grandmother" (Rauch 1988:215). All of these venues offer the opportunity to study the experience of commodification, reinvention, or revitalization of the culinary past.

The Agronomy of Memory

In Chapter 3 I suggested that one of the main threats to food memories on Kalymnos is loss of knowledge of food production. Despite ecological anthropology's long tradition of studying agricultural production worldwide, functionalist and materialist emphases have meant that almost nothing has been written on the topic of production and memory. However with the increased emphasis in "new ecology" on local knowledges (Biersack 1999), perhaps this is soon to shift. A suggestive approach is provided by Dove (1999) in an essay entitled "The Agronomy of Memory and the Memory of Agronomy." In it he argues that certain crops may be cultivated long past their economic usefulness because they serve as "witnesses of the past." That is, these cultigens are retained as a small, ritualized part of production systems because they provide a history of the succession of staple crops in that region. This is mythically elaborated in the idea that certain crops in Southeast Asia – Job's tears and Italian millet – are the "parents" of rice, which succeeded them in historical time. It is also ritually elaborated in certain taboos that address the concern that the spirit of rice might fear that these archaic grains are "plotting" against it (1999:53ff.). While the history of grain succession is thus depicted as turbulent and political, Dove argues that this is quite different from Western development agriculture, which effects a "disappearance" of agricultural history, as each "scientific" improvement wipes out the need for previous production methods. While the memory of agronomy reveals the "contingency of contemporary agriculture," and leaves open the possibility of return to earlier methods, a "transcending of the present," development agriculture ensures its predominance through the erasure of the possibility of remembering alternatives (1999:60).

Dove suggests that these practices be seen as an *"in situ* conservation" of a historic heritage based on local ideologies and non-economic or non-ecological factors. He suggests that this is "not necessarily the same thing as conserving the biogenetic heritage from the past for the future, which is the typical reasoning of contemporary scientists and environmental activists" (1999:62). Nazarea (1998) sees a complementary role between gene-banking and what she calls "memory banking" of agricultural knowledge. She wishes to record the "pockets of memory" that exist in the minds of local farmers "on the margins" of the world system. Such memory banking, along with parallel *in situ* conservation practices, will help preserve knowledge of the options that have been sidelined by the Green Revolution, while maintaining local control over and benefit from this knowledge. Whether such knowledge can be formalized without being commodified, or, like the embodied knowledge of cooking, resists to some degree all formalization, are questions to be pursued.

It is also an open question for research whether organic farmers in the US and other countries are planting "heirloom seeds" for economic reasons, ecological reasons, or reasons of historical memory, and one would guess that a mixture of these reasons comes into play. The possibilities for study are not only rich ethnographically, but pose many of the same theoretical issues seen in contemporary debates over historical continuity and the "invention of tradition." For example, Clark Erickson's archaeological discoveries of ancient techniques of raised-field agriculture in the Lake Titicaca basin stimulated a successful reinvention, or perhaps an interrupted continuation, of this agricultural practice. They also suggest possibilities for resisting development policies and Green Revolution agriculture once again through reclaiming or remembering an interrupted agricultural heritage, whose traces were in this case not found in myth and ritual, but "embedded in and layered on" the physical features of the landscape (Erickson 1998:35; see also Kolata 1996). In all these respects, memories of food production should form a key aspect of both our ethnographic endeavors and our theoretical agendas.

Hunger Memories

Some Kalymnians suggested to me that they were so obsessed with food because of the hunger they had suffered during the Second World War. Recent work suggests that situations of extreme hunger provoke creative imaginative responses. In the case of Concentration Camp internees during the Second World War, remembrance of the past was seen as a way to "defy dehumanization and to dream of the past and of the future" (Berenbaum 1996:xvi). In many cases these defiances took the form of art: painting, performance, reading smuggled books or engaging in athletic activities (Berenbaum 1996:xiii). Jezernik (1999) argues that those inmates who defied hunger by upholding religious fasts or by forming bread into chess pieces were in many cases better able to survive, because they perceived themselves as not having been reduced to purely material beings: "Paradoxically those who subordinated themselves and were prepared to do anything to get a piece of bread, had an even smaller chance of survival than those who could voluntarily deprive themselves a part of or an entire meal, because the latter did not sacrifice their human dignity" (Jezernik 1999:27). At the same time, it is also clear that some "spiritual" pursuits and imaginative remembrances centered around food, as is witnessed by the cookbook compiled by the women of the Terezin Concentration Camp (De Silva 1996). This collection of recipes from home, written often on German propaganda leaflets, was the outgrowth of daily discussions – "even arguments" – about the correct preparation of dishes (De Silva 1996: xxviii). Called "cooking with the mouth," this discussion "'strengthened their resolution to survive, if only because it made more vivid, not what they sought to escape from, but what they sought to return to" (1996:xxxi).[1] As De Silva sums up: "It is to use as weapons not guns, nor bazookas, nor grenades, but the memory of dumplings" (De Silva 2000).

Hunger can also be the site for conflicting memories, as Caldwell (1999) illustrates. American food aid workers at a contemporary Russian soup kitchen assumed that generalized hunger was a condition of Russian political and social backwardness that they had come to alleviate. But for older Russian participants in the soup kitchen, "hunger" was associated with a specific time in the past: the Second World War. Caldwell finds people not only nostalgic for the "tastes of

---

1. Shephard (2000) and Thompson (2000) note a similar role of food memories and recipe collections both in the diaries and in the everyday discussions of Second World War POWS. As the POW Morris Lewis recalls "I spent a lot of time just writing out food and holiday menus to keep myself sane and focused . . . Imagine being asked by your soldiers to tell them what was going to be on the Christmas menu, all knowing that there never would be such a meal. But here we were, with each soldier coming to me and asking if they could put their dish on the menu. It did give us a sense of what we were remembering most and the will to go on another day" (Thompson 2000:7).

hunger" – wild sorrel, stinging nettle – but seeing their struggles with hunger during the war as part of their own participation in and contribution to these "historic" events. Thus the soup kitchen represented for them not a step from backwardness to progress, but an appropriate memorialization of their participation in history. As one soup kitchen volunteer told Caldwell, food programs are a means to let people, especially veterans and pensioners, know they are connected socially and that someone knows them and remembers them: "People work – their entire lives but then have no money and no one remembers them – Then they call me up and thank me [simply] for remembering them" (Caldwell 1999:8). Deprivation in the present creates, here, a space for the bubbling up of memories of hunger past, of another kind of history from below. For our purposes, deprivation of food can be seen as equally culturally inflected as abundance, and raises interesting questions: is "hunger" and the memories it provokes experienced as a challenge, a punishment, an injustice, a proper separation of the spiritual from the material (see for example, Walker-Bynum 1992), or something else? The hunger for memory (like the hunger for knowledge) becomes not merely a tired metaphor of processes of ingesting the past, but opens up the possibility of many oral histories of hunger that remain to be recaptured.

And Forgetting?

What might we learn by looking at the forgetting of foods as an active and purposeful process? I was brought abruptly to consider this question after a Greek man living in the UK reminisced to me about foods from home and then turned to his sister and asked if she had anything to add. "I don't miss Greece, I don't miss Greek food, I don't miss anything about Greece . . . except the sea," was her succinct reply. Surely such productive forgetting is as interesting as remembering. Forgetting has tended to be seen as the "enemy" in studies of nationalism, where the task of the analyst has often been seen as one of making silences "speak," of telling stories of oppression, or simply of difference, that have been edited out of the mainstream narratives of states and other dominant groups. The attempt by some to edit out the Turkish influences on Greek cuisine might be seen as one example of such hegemonic forgetting. Or the fact that in the past animal dung was sometimes used as fuel for roasting eggplants on Kalymnos – because of the distinct flavor it imparted – is similarly not seen as appropriate material for folklore collections, and will probably eventually be forgotten. Kravva's (2000) field research on food and memory among Jews in Thessaloniki focuses on the "shadows and silences" of what was once a thriving population, almost wiped out during the Second World War, and now nearly erased from everyday and state-sponsored memories of the city. Finally, my own earlier work on Kalymnos (Sutton 1998) was explicitly motivated by the wish to contrast a "historical consciousness" with what I perceived as the general disdain for "the past" in US popular culture. If in all these cases, then, forgetting is a problem, to be overcome by analysis, I raise the point again: can there be a productive role for forgetting foods past? When Renan speaks of the necessity for forgetting in constructing collective stories, I believe that he does not only mean to debunk such forgetting (Renan 1994 [1882]). And Western artists often view memory as a burden they must overcome in order to create (see Terdiman 1993:45ff.).

The idea that food might be used in creative forgetting was, in fact, raised in Chapter 2, in my discussion of Melanesian funeral feasting, in which food was used as a way of "killing" memories in order to create new spaces in the social structure. Perhaps more parallel to the deliberate forgetting by the sister of my Greek friend is the recounting of a number of feminist parables of the liberatory feeling for grandmothers, burdened by their culinary reputations, of forgetting how to cook (Babayan 1997; Yarbrough 1998). Yue draws on novelistic accounts, such as that of Sau-ling Wong, to get at the struggles of Chinese-American young women to come to terms with a culinary heritage. Wong's character Jade Snow contrasts her life with that of her friend Stella Green, the "ethnic" yet assimilated American:

Stella had grown up . . . developing a taste for roast beef, mashed potatoes, sweets, aspirin tablets and soda pop, and she looked upon her mother and father as friends. But it was very unlikely that she knew where her great-grandfather was born . . . Jade Snow had grown up . . . learning to embroider and cook rice, developing a taste for steamed fish and bean sprouts, tea and herbs . . . She not only knew where her ancestors were born but where they were buried, and how many chickens and roast pigs should be brought annually to their graves to feast their spirits (Wong, cited in Yue 1999:349).

There are paths to liberation, such fragments suggest, through forgetting the food of one's family, one's "culture," as well as through memory, or perhaps in balancing the two. But if the anthropology of memory is a young field, the anthropology of forgetting still waits to be born. A first stab has been made by Forty and Kuchler (1999), in a collection called *The Art of Forgetting*; but this is specifically focused on the relationship of forgetting to monumental architecture. However, Forty begins with Luria's *The Mind of a Mnemonist*, in which S. discovers the nightmare of having a perfect memory (something that we all casually aspire to): "With his capacity to remember everything, his greatest difficulty became the chaotic congestion of his mind with unwanted memories: he had to learn to forget what he no longer needed to remember" (Forty 1999:1). Interesting that one method he tried to use in forgetting was to write things down, "on the assumption that if this method enabled other people to remember what they did not want to forget, it might help him forget what he no longer wanted to remember." Eventually, when this failed, he tried burning the paper. Perhaps Jade Snow's individual dilemma could be solved through extra-individual means: the written recipes discussed in the last chapter. In other words, preserve the tradition as an alternative possibility, an archive that could always be referred to, while not making it an individual burden. However, some of the dilemmas of such an approach were highlighted in the last chapter as well: the sense that in preserving you are freezing, or even killing. And while S. used writing to forget semantic information he no longer found necessary, what of the "memory of the hands"? If we have begun to explore embodied memory, what of embodied forgetting? If we take Kapsalis's (1997) metaphor of "Yiayia's Hands" encrusted with stratigraphic layers of fossilized garlic and petrified olive oil, what happens if those layers get scraped away, and what is left underneath? If we begin to ask such questions, we might avert the problem of the never-ending cookbook, or, to twist a phrase from Marx, we might keep the specter of the tradition of past meals from weighing like a nightmare on the stomach of the living.

In sum, more ethnography, but ethnography that begins from the premise that food is not simply another topic that "symbolizes" identity, but one that challenges us to rethink our methods, assumptions and theories in new and productive ways.

I began this book with a provocation from an Oxford don after I had presented some first thoughts on my topic: "Why would anyone want to remember anything they had eaten?" I end with a feeling of having come full circle, nearly five years later, having just attended the Oxford Food Symposium, whose chosen topic for their yearly conference in September 2000 was "Memory." With titles ranging from "Food, Nostalgic Discourse and the Construction of Memory in

Postsocialist Hungary," to "Learning by Mouth: Edible Aids to Literacy," to "The Velveeta Chronicles," historians, anthropologists, psychologists, food writers and others finally came together to put this topic on the food map. While there were many productive discussions, and I have attempted to incorporate a number of the papers in the preceding chapters, there were a few doubters as well. At one panel an audience member posed the question: "Let me be provocative. Can we say anything beyond the fact that everyone has childhood memories of food to which they look back with fondness, and that mine are likely to be different from yours?" Indeed provocative, for if the answer was "no," than perhaps the topic of food memory deserves its relegation to analytic obscurity. Food memories could continue to be evoked, in poetic or hackneyed fashion by novelists and film-makers, but the rest would be best left for personal reflection.

I hope that I have shown that the answer to his question is a resounding "Yes!" That food memories raise some of the key questions that preoccupy not only anthropology, but the social sciences and humanities more generally. Indulge me in a final visualist metaphor (better than another food pun!): If we push beyond the anecdotal and mundane associations of food with memories of childhood, new vistas of investigation – ethnographically rich and theoretically trenchant – will open before us.

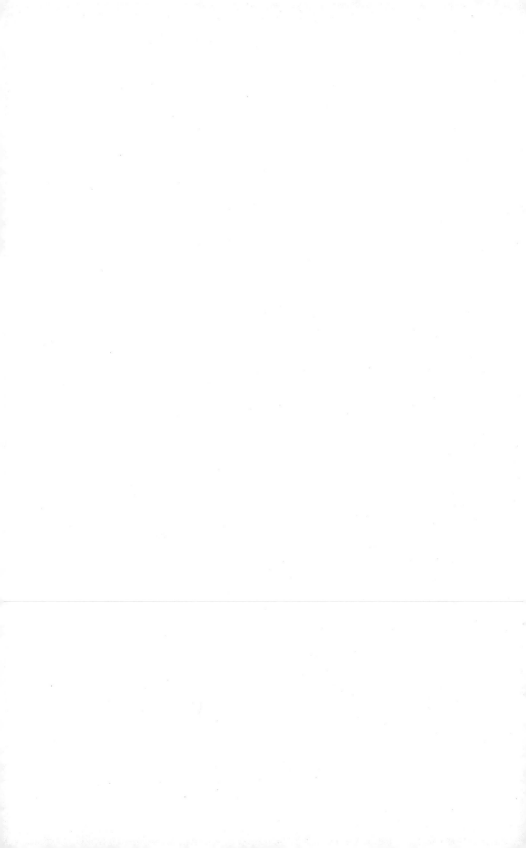

References

Abrahams, Roger
  1984 Equal Opportunity Eating: A Structural Excursus on Things of the Mouth. In *Ethnic and Regional Foodways in the United States: The Performance of Group Identity*, ed. L. Brown and K. Mussell, pp. 19–36. Knoxville, TN: University of Tennessee Press.

Acocella, Joan
  1999 American Pie: The Culinary Canon: From Ketchup to Cuisine Moralisée. *The New Yorker*. December 6:147-52.

Adams, Jane
  1994 *The Transformation of Rural Life: Southern Illinois 1890–1990*. Chapel Hill, NC: University of North Carolina Press.

Allison, Anne
  1991 Japanese Mothers and Obentos: The Lunch Box as Ideological State Apparatus. *Anthropological Quarterly* 64:195–208.

Anderson, Benedict
  1991 *Imagined Communities: Reflections on the Origin and Spread of Nationalism* (revised edn). London: Verso.

Appadurai, Arjun
  1996 *Modernity at Large: Cultural Dimensions of Globalization*. Minneapolis: University of Minnesota Press.

Arnott, Margaret
  1975 The Breads of Mani. In *Gastronomy: The Anthropology of Food and Food Habits*, ed. Margaret Arnott, pp. 297–304. The Hague: Mouton Publishers.

Babayan, Caroline
  1997 The Cook, the Maid, and the Lady. In *Through the Kitchen Window: Women Explore the Intimate Meanings of Food and Cooking*. ed. Arlene Voski Avakian, pp. 112–16. Boston: Beacon.

Bahloul, Joelle

1996 *The Architecture of Memory: A Jewish-Muslim Household in Colonial Algeria 1937–1962*, trans. Catherine de Peloux-Menage. Cambridge: Cambridge University Press.

Bardenstein, Carol

1999 Trees, Forests, and the Shaping of a Palestinian and Israeli Collective Memory. In *Acts of Memory: Cultural Recall in the Present*, ed. Mieke Bal, Jonathan Crewe and Leo Spitzer, pp. 148–68. Hanover, NH: University Press of New England.

Barthes, Roland

1986 The Reality Effect. In *The Rustle of Language*, trans. Richard Howard, pp. 141–8. New York: Hill and Wang.

Battaglia, Debbora

1990 *On the Bones of Serpents*. Chicago: University of Chicago Press.

Battistella, Edwin

1990 *Markedness: The Evaluative Superstructure of Language*. Albany, NY: SUNY Press.

Baumann, Zygmunt

1996 *Life in Fragments: Essays in Postmodern Morality*. Oxford: Blackwell.

Becker, A. L.

1994 Repetition and Otherness: An Essay. In *Repetition in Discourse: Interdisciplinary Perspectives, Volume Two*, ed. Barbara Johnstone, pp 162–75. Norwood, NJ: Ablex Publishing Co.

Beidelman, T.

1989 Agonistic Exchange; Homeric Reciprocity and the Legacy of Simmel and Mauss. *Cultural Anthropology* 4:227–59.

Bell, David, and Gil Valentine

1997 *Consuming Geographies: We Are Where We Eat*. London: Routledge.

Beoku-Betts, Josephine

1995 We Got Our Way of Cooking Things: Women, Food and Preservation of Cultural Identity among the Gullah. *Gender and Society* 9:535–55.

Berenbaum, Michael

1996 Forward. In *In Memory's Kitchen: A Legacy from the Women of Terezín*, ed. Cara De Silva, pp. ix–xvi. Northvale, NJ: Jason Aronson, Inc.

Bernasconi, Robert

1997 What Goes Around Comes Around: Derrida and Levinas on the Economy of the Gift and the Gift of Generosity. In *The Logic of the Gift: Toward an Ethic of Generosity*, ed. Alan Schrift, pp. 256–73. London: Routledge.

Berry, Wendell
   1998 The Pleasures of Eating. In *We Are What We Ate: 24 Memories of Food*, ed. Mark Winegardner, pp. 54–65. San Diego: Harcourt, Brace and Co.
Bertsch, Charlie
   1997 The Politics of the Microbrewery Revolution. Bad Subjects 16 (http://english-www.hss.cmu.edu/bs/16/Bertsch.html)
Biersack, Aletta (ed.)
   1999 Contemporary Issues Forum: Ecologies for Tomorrow: Reading Rappaport Today. *American Anthropologist* 101:5–112.
Billiri, Niki
   1982 *Our Kalymnos*. Athens (in Greek).
   1993 *The Customs Officer from Mira and Other Stories*. Athens: Ombros Publishers (in Greek).
Birdwell-Pheasant, Donna, and Daphne Lawrence-Zuniga
   1999 Introduction: Houses and Families in Europe. In *House Life: Space, Place and Family in Europe*, ed. D. Birdwell-Pheasant and D. Lawrence-Zuñiga, pp. 1–35. Oxford: Berg.
Boas, Franz
   1927 *Primitive Art*. Oslo.
Boon, James
   1999 *Verging on Extra-Vagance: Anthropology, History, Religion, Literature, Arts . . . Showbiz*. Princeton, NJ: Princeton University Press.
Booth, Sally
   1999 Reconstructing Sexual Geography: Gender and Space in Changing Sicilian Settlements. In *House Life: Space, Place and Family in Europe*, ed. D. Birdwell-Pheasant and D. Lawrence-Zuñiga, pp. 133–56. Oxford: Berg.
Borgmann, Albert
   1992 The Artificial and the Real: Reflections on Baudrillard's America. In *Jean Baudrillard: The Disappearance of Art and Politics*, ed. W. Stearns and W. Chaloupka, pp 160–76. New York: St. Martin's Press.
Bourdieu, Pierre
   1977 *Outline of a Theory of Practice*, trans. Richard Nice. Cambridge: Cambridge University Press.
   1982 *Distinction: A Social Critique of the Judgement of Taste*, trans. Richard Nice. Cambridge: Harvard University Press.
   1990 *The Logic of Practice*. Stanford, CA: Stanford University Press.
Bower, Anne (ed.)
   1997 *Recipes for Reading: Community Cookbooks, Stories, Histories*. Amherst, MA: University of Massachusetts Press.

Brown, Linda and Kay Mussell (eds)
    1984 *Ethnic and Regional Foodways in the United States: The Performance of Group Identity.* Knoxville, TN: University of Tennessee Press.
Bubant, Nils
    1998 The Odour of Things: Smell and the Cultural Elaboration of Disgust in Eastern Indonesia. *Ethnos* 63: 48–80.
Buxbaum, Edwin Clarence
    1967 The Greek-American Group of Tarpon Springs, Florida: A Study of Ethnic Identification and Acculturation. Ph.D. Dissertation, University of Pennsylvania, Department of Anthropology.
Caldwell, Melissa
    1999 Russia's Hungered Bodies: Imagined Temporalities in Post-socialist Moscow. Paper presented at the American Anthropological Association Meetings, panel on "History and the Politics of Desire: Nostalgic Futures Across the New Europe." Chicago, 19 November.
Campbell, Colin
    1983 Romanticism and the Consumer Ethic: Intimations of a Weber-style Thesis. *Sociological Analysis* 44:279–96.
Campbell, John
    1964 *Honor, Family and Patronage: A Study of Institutions and Moral Values in a Greek Mountain Community.* Oxford: Clarendon.
Caplan, Pat (ed.)
    1994 *Feasts, Fasts, Famine: Food For Thought.* Oxford: Berg.
Carr, David
    1986 *Time, Narrative and History.* Bloomington, IN: Indiana University Press.
Carrier, James
    1990 Gifts in a World of Commodities: The Ideology of the Perfect Gift in American Society. *Social Analysis* 29:19–37.
Carsten, Janet
    1995 The Substance of Kinship and the Heat of the Hearth: Feeding, Personhood, and Relatedness among Malays in Pulau Langkawi. *American Ethnologist* 22:223–41.
Chamberlain, Mary
    1995 Gender and Memory: Oral History and Women's History. In *Engendering History: Caribbean Women in Historical Perspective*, ed. V. Shepherd, B. Brereton and B. Bailey, pp. 94–110. Kingston, Jamaica: Ian Randle.
Clarke, Austin
    1999 *Pig Tails and Breadfruit: A Culinary Memoir.* New York: New Press.

Classen, Constance
1997 Foundations for an Anthropology of the Senses. *International Social Science Journal* 153:401–12.
Classen, Constance, David Howes and Anthony Synnott
1994 *Aroma: The Cultural History of Smell*. London: Routledge.
Clifford, James
1986 On Ethnographic Allegory. In *Writing Culture: The Poetics and Politics of Ethnography*, ed. J. Clifford and G. Marcus, pp. 98–121. Berkeley: University of California Press.
Cohen, Leah
1997 *Glass, Paper, Beans: Revelations on the Nature and Value of Ordinary Things*. New York: Doubleday.
Cole, Jennifer
1998 The Work of Memory in Madagascar. *American Ethnologist* 25:610–33.
Collier, Jane
1997 *From Duty to Desire: Remaking Families in a Spanish Village*. Princeton, NJ: Princeton University Press.
Comaroff, John, and Jean Comaroff
1992 *Ethnography and the Historical Imagination*. Boulder, CO: Westview Press.
1993 (eds). *Modernity and its Malcontents*. Chicago: University of Chicago Press.
Conklin, Beth
1995 "Thus are Our Bodies, Thus was Our Custom": Mortuary Cannibalism in an Amazonian Society. *American Ethnologist* 22:75–101.
Connerton, Paul
1989 *How Societies Remember*. Cambridge: Cambridge University Press.
Cook, Ian, and Philip Crang
1996 The World on a Plate: Culinary Culture, Displacement and Geographical Knowledges. *Journal of Material Culture* 1:131–53.
Coontz, Stephanie
1992 *The Way We Never Were: American Families and the Nostalgia Trap*. New York: Basic Books.
Corbin, Alain
1986 *The Foul and the Fragrant: Odour and the Social Imagination*. Oxford: Berg.
Counihan, Carole
1984 Bread as World: Food Habits and Social Relations in Modernizing Sardinia. *Anthropological Quarterly* 57:47–59.

Counihan, Carole
1999 *The Anthropology of Food and Body: Gender, Meaning and Power.* London: Routledge.
Cowan, Jane
1990 Dance and the Body Politic in Northern Greece. Princeton, NJ: Princeton University Press.
1991 Going out for Coffee? Contesting the Grounds of Gendered Pleasures in Everyday Sociability. In *Contested Identities: Gender and Kinship in Modern Greece,* ed. Peter Loizos and Evthimios Papataksiarchis, pp. 180–202. Princeton: Princeton University Press.
Csordas, Thomas
1994 Introduction: The Body as Representation and Being-in-the-World. In *Embodiment and Experience: The Existential Ground of Culture and Self,* ed. Thomas Csordas, pp.1–13. Cambridge: Cambridge University Press.
Cytowic, Richard
1993 *The Man Who Tasted Shapes.* London: Abacus.
Danforth, Loring
1982 *The Death Rituals of Rural Greece.* Princeton: Princeton University Press.
Davidson, Catherine Temma
1998 *The Priest Fainted.* New York: Henry Holt & Co.
Derrida, Jacques
1992 *Given Time, I: Counterfeit Money,* trans. Peggy Kamuf. Chicago: University of Chigago Press.
De Silva, Cara
1996 (ed.) *In Memory's Kitchen: A Legacy from the Women of Terezín,* trans. Bianca Steiner Brown. Northvale, NJ: Jason Aronson, Inc.
2000 Keynote Address. Oxford Symposium on Food and Cookery, St. Anthony's College, 9 September.
Devault, Marjorie
1997 Conflict and Defence. In *Food and Culture: A Reader,* ed. Carole Counihan and Penny Van Esterik, pp. 180–99. London: Routledge.
Dhositheos, Archimandrite
1995 *Cooks' Magic, Namely: Monks' Cookery Book.* Athens: Sacred Monastery Tatarnis (in Greek).
Douglas, Mary
1966 *Purity and Danger: An Analysis of the Concepts of Pollution and Taboo.* London: Routledge and Kegan Paul.
1971 Deciphering a Meal. In *Myth, Symbol and Culture,* ed. Clifford Geertz, pp. 61–82. New York: Norton.
1982 *In the Active Voice.* London: Routledge.

Douglas, Mary, and Jonathan Gross
    1981 Food and Culture: Measuring the Intricacy of Rule Systems. *Social Science Information* 20:1–35.
Doumanis, Nicholas
    1997 *Myth and Memory in the Mediterranean: Remembering Fascism's Empire.* London: Macmillan.
Dove, Michael
    1999 The Agronomy of Memory and the Memory of Agronomy: Ritual Conservation of Archaic Cultigens in Contemporary Farming Systems. In *Ethnoecology: Situated Knowledges/Located Lives,* ed. Virginia D. Nazarea, pp. 45–66. Tucson, AZ: University of Arizona Press.
Dragoumis, Ion
    1976 [1914] *Greek Civilization.* Athens (in Greek).
Dubisch, Jill
    1986 Culture Enters through the Kitchen: Women, Food and Social Boundaries in Rural Greece. In *Gender and Power in Rural Greece,* ed. Jill Dubisch, pp. 195–214. Princeton: Princeton University Press.
du Boulay, Juliet
    1974 *Portrait of a Greek Mountain Village.* Oxford: Clarendon Press.
du Boulay, Juliet, and Rory Williams
    1987 Amoral Familism and the Image of Limited Good: A Critique from a European Perspective. *Anthropological Quarterly* 60:12–24.
Duruz, Jean
    1999 Food as Nostalgia: Eating the Fifties and Sixties. *Australian Historical Studies* 113:231–50.
    2000 Home Cooking, Nostalgia and the Purchase of Tradition. *International Association for the Study of Traditional Environments Working Papers,* Vol. 139.
Elias, Norbert
    1978 [1939] *The Civilizing Process, Vol. 1: The History of Manners.* Oxford: Basil Blackwell.
Enloe, Cynthia
    1991 *Bananas, Beaches and Bases: Making Feminist Sense of International Politics.* Berkeley, CA: University of California Press.
Engen, Trygg
    1991 *Odor, Sensation and Memory.* New York: Praeger.
Erickson, Clark
    1998 Applied Archaeology and Rural Development: Archaeology's Potential Contribution to the Future. In *Crossing Currents: Continuity*

and Change in Latin America, ed. Michael B. Whiteford and Scott Whiteford, pp. 34–45. Upper Saddle River, NJ: Prentice Hall.

Evans-Pritchard, E. E.

1940 *The Nuer: A Description of the Modes of Livelihood and Political Institutions of a Nilotic People*. Oxford: Clarendon Press.

Eves, Richard

1998 *The Magical Body: Power, Fame and Meaning in a Melanesian Society*. Amsterdam: Harwood Academic Publishers.

Falk, Pasi

1994 *The Consuming Body*. London: Sage.

Farnell, Brenda

1994 Ethno-Graphics and the Moving Body. *Man* 29:929–74.

Feeley-Harnik, Gillian

1994 [1980] *The Lord's Table: The Meaning of Food in Early Judaism and Christianity*. Washington, DC: Smithsonian Institution Press.

Feld, Stephen

1982 *Sound and Sentiment: Weeping, Poetics and Song in Kaluli Expression*. Philadelphia: University of Pennsylvania Press.

Fernandez, James

1982 *Bwiti: An Ethnography of the Religious Imagination in Africa*. Princeton, NJ: Princeton University Press.

1986 *Persuasions and Performances: The Play of Tropes in Culture*. Bloomington, IN: Indiana University Press.

1988 Aesthetics, Synesthesia and Part-Whole Relations in Things Beautiful. Paper presented at the Society of Cultural Anthropology Meetings, May.

Field, Carol

1997 *In Nonna's Kitchen: Recipes and Traditions from Italy's Grandmothers*. New York: HarperCollins.

Fine, Gary Alan

1996 *Kitchens: The Culture of Restaurant Work*. Berkeley, CA: University of California Press.

Fischler, Claude

1988 Food, Self and Identity. *Social Science Information* 27:275–92.

Fog Olwig, Karen, and Kirsten Hastrup (eds)

1997 *Siting Culture: The Shifting Anthropological Object*. London: Routledge.

Forrest, John

1988 *"Lord I'm Coming Home." Everyday Aesthetics in Tidewater, North Carolina*. Ithaca, NY: Cornell University Press.

Forty, Adrian

1999 Introduction. In *The Art of Forgetting*, ed. Adrian Forty and Susanne Kuchler, pp. 1–18. Oxford: Berg.

Forty, Adrian, and Susanne Kuchler (eds)
1999 *The Art of Forgetting*. Oxford: Berg.

Foster, Robert
1990 Nurture and Force Feeding: Mortuary Feasting and the Construction of Collective Individuals in a New Ireland Society. *American Ethnologist* 17:431–48.

Fourlas, Dimitrios
1985 Cocoons and Figs in Neohori, Nafpaktia: Silk Cultivation and Food. *Laographia* 33:414–26 (in Greek).

Frantzis, George
1962 *Strangers at Ithaca: The Story of the Spongers of Tarpon Springs*. St Petersburg, FL: Great Outdoors Publishing Co.

Frenkel, Stephen
1998 A Pound of Kenya Please. In *The Taste of American Place: A Reader on Regional and Ethnic Foods*, ed. Barbara Shortridge and James Shortridge, pp. 57–63. Lanham, MD: Rowman & Littlefield.

Friedrich, Paul
1991 Polytropy. In *Beyond Metaphor: The Theory of Tropes in Anthropology*, ed. James W. Fernandez, pp. 17–55. Stanford, CA: Stanford University Press.

Fuster, Joaquin
1997 *The Prefrontal Cortex: Anatomy, Physiology and Neuropsychology of the Frontal Lobe*. Philadelphia: Lippincott-Raven.

Gavrielides, Nicholas
1974 Name Days and Feasting: Social and Ecological Implications of Visiting Patterns in a Greek Village of the Argolid. *Anthropological Quarterly* 47:48–70.

Gefou-Madianou, Dimitra
1999 Cultural Polyphony and Identity Formation: Negotiating Tradition in Attica. *American Ethnologist* 26:412–39.

Gell, Alfred
1977 Magic, Perfume, Dream . . . In *Symbols and Sentiments: Cross-Cultural Studies in Symbolism*, ed. Ioan Lewis, pp. 25–38. London: Academic Press.

Georges, Robert
1980 [1964] *Greek-American Folk Beliefs and Narratives: Survivals and Living Traditions*. New York: Arno Press.

Giard, Luce
1998 Part II: Doing-Cooking. In *The Practice of Everyday Life, Volume 2: Living and Cooking*, ed. Luce Giard, in association with Michel de Certeau and Pierre Mayol, trans. Timothy J. Tomasik, pp. 149–248. Minneapolis: University of Minnesota Press.

Giddens, Anthony
1991 *Modernity and Self-Identity: Self and Society in the Late Modern Age*. Stanford, CA: Stanford University Press.
Gilmore, David
1991 Commodity, Comity, Community: Male Exchange in Rural Andalusia. *Ethnology* 30:17–30.
Goddard, Victoria
1996 *Gender, Family and Work in Naples*. Oxford: Berg.
Gonzalez-Crussi, F.
1989 *The Five Senses*. New York: Vintage.
Goode, Judith, Janet Theophano and Karen Curtis
1984 A Framework for the Analysis of Continuity and Change in Shared Sociocultural Rules for Food Use: The Italian-American Pattern. In *Ethnic and Regional Foodways in the United States: The Performance of Group Identity*, ed. Linda Brown and Kay Mussell, pp. 66–88. Knoxville: Univ. of Tennessee Press.
Goody, Jack
1982 *Cooking, Cuisine and Class*. Cambridge: Cambridge University Press.
2000 *The Power of the Written Tradition*. Cambridge: Cambridge University Press.
Gottlieb, Alma
1998. Do Infants Have Religion? The Spiritual Lives of Beng Babies. *American Anthropologist* 100:122–35.
Graeber, David
1997 Manners, Deference, and Private Property in Early Modern Europe. *Comparative Studies in Society and History* 39:694–728.
Gregory, C. A.
1982 *Gifts and Commodities*. London: Academic Press.
Grignon, Claude, and Christine Grignon
1999 Long-term Trends in Food Consumption: A French Portrait. *Food and Foodways* 8:151–74.
Halbwachs, Maurice
1980 [1950] *The Collective Memory*. New York: Harper and Row.
Hamilakis, Yiannis
1998 Eating the Dead: Mortuary Feasting and the Politics of Memory in the Aegean Bronze Age. In *Cemetery and Society in the Aegean Bronze Age*, ed. Keith Branigan, 115–132. Sheffield: Academic Press.
Hannerz, Ulf
1996 *Transnational Connections*. London: Routledge.

Hanson, F. Allan
  1983 Syntagmatic Structures: How the Maoris Make Sense of History. *Semiotica* 46:287–307.
Hart, Laurie
  1992 *Time, Religion, and Social Experience in Rural Greece*. Lanham MD: Rowman & Littlefield.
Harvey, David
  1988 *The Condition of Postmodernity: An Enquiry into the Origins of Cultural Change*. Oxford: Blackwell.
Heldke, Lisa
  1992 Foodmaking as Thoughtful Practice. In *Cooking, Eating, Thinking: Transformative Philosophies of Food*, ed. Deane Curtin and Lisa Heldke, pp. 203–29. Bloomington, IN: Indiana University Press.
Heller, Steven
  1999 Appetite Appeal. *Social Research* 66:213–24.
Helms, Mary
  1993 *Craft and the Kingly Ideal: Art, Trade and Power*. Austin, TX: University of Texas Press.
Hendry, Joy
  1990 Food as Social Nutrition? The Japanese Case. In *Food For Humanity: Cross-Disciplinary Readings*, ed. Malcolm Chapman and Helen MacBeth, pp. 57–62. Oxford: Centre for the Sciences of Food and Nutrition.
Henze, Rosemary
  1992 *Informal Teaching and Learning: A Study of Everyday Cognition in a Greek Community*. Hillsdale, NJ: Lawrence Erlbaum Associates.
Herzfeld, Michael
  1985 *The Poetics of Manhood: Contest and Identity in a Cretan Mountain Village*. Princeton, NJ: Princeton University Press.
  1987a "As in Your Own House": Hospitality, Ethnography and the Stereotype of Mediterranean Society. In *Honor and Shame and the Unity of the Mediterranean*, ed. David D. Gilmore, pp. 75–89. AAA Special Publications 22. Washington DC: American Anthropological Association.
  1987b *Anthropology Through the Looking Glass*. Cambridge: Cambridge University Press.
  1990 Pride and Perjury: Time and the Oath in the Mountain Villages of Crete. *Man* 25:305–22.
  1991 *A Place in History*. Princeton, NJ: Princeton University Press.
  1992 Segmentation and Politics in the European Nation-State: Making Sense of Political Events. In *Other Histories*, ed. Kirsten Hastrup, pp. 62–81. London: Routledge.

Herzfeld, Michael

1995a Review of Classen. *Journal of the History of the Behavioral Sciences* 31:180–3.

1995b It Takes One to Know One: Collective Resentment and Mutual Recognition among Greeks in Local and Global Contexts. In *Counterworks: Managing the Diversity of Knowledge*, ed. Richard Fardon, pp. 124–42. London: Routledge.

Hill, Jonathan

1999 Nationalisme, Chamanisme et Histoirès Indigènes au Venezuela. *Ethnologie Française* 3:387–96.

Hirschon, Renée

1992 Greek Adults' Verbal Play, or, How to Train for Caution. *Journal of Modern Greek Studies* 10:35–56.

1998 *Heirs of the Greek Catastrophe*, 2nd Edition. Oxford: Berghan Press.

Hirst, William, David Manier and Ioana Apetroaia

1997 The Social Construction of the Remembered Self: Family Recounting. In *The Self Across Psychology: Self-Recognition, Self-Awareness and the Self Concept*, ed. Joan Snodgrass and Robert Thompson, pp. 162–79. New York: New York Academy of Sciences.

Hoffman, Susannah

n.d. The Olive and the Caper. New York: Workman, forthcoming.

Hoffman, Susannah, Richard Cowan and Paul Aratow

1974 *Kypseli: Women and Men Apart – A Divided Reality* (film). Distributed by the University Extension Media Center, University of California, Berkeley.

Hollander, John

1999 Writing of Food. *Social Research* 66:197–211.

Hoskins, Janet

1998 *Biographical Objects: How Things Tell the Story of People's Lives.* London: Routledge.

Howes, David (ed.)

1991 *The Varieties of Sensory Experience.* Toronto: University of Toronto Press.

Howes, David, and Marc Lalonde

1991 The History of Sensibilities. *Dialectical Anthropology* 16:125–35.

Hyde, Lewis

1979 *The Gift: Imagination and the Erotic Life of Property.* New York: Random House.

Ingold, Tim

1993 Tool-Use, Sociality and Intelligence. In *Tools, Language and*

Cognition in Human Evolution, ed. K. Gibson and T. Ingold, pp. 429–45. Cambridge: Cambridge University Press.

Iossafides, A. Marina
1992 Wine: Life's Blood and Spiritual Essence in a Greek Orthodox Convent. In *Alcohol Gender and Culture*, ed. Dimitra Gefou-Madianou, pp. 80–100. London: Routledge.

Ireland, Lynne
1998 The Compiled Cookbook as Foodways Autobiography. In *The Taste of American Place: A Reader on Ethnic and Regional Foods*, ed. Barbara Shortridge and James Shortridge, pp. 111–17. Lanham, MD: Rowman & Littlefield.

Jackson, Michael
1989 *Paths Toward a Clearing: Radical Empiricism and Ethnographic Inquiry*. Bloomington, IN: University of Indiana Press.

Jakobson, Roman, and Krystyna Pomorska
1983 *Dialogues*. Cambridge, MA: MIT Press.

James, Alice, and Loukas Kalisperis
1999 Use of House and Space: Public and Private Family Interaction on Chios, Greece. In *House Life: Space, Place and Family in Europe*, ed. D. Birdwell-Pheasant and D. Lawrence-Zuñiga, pp. 205–20. Oxford: Berg.

Jeanneret, Michael
1991 *A Feast of Words: Banquets and Table Talk in the Renaissance*. Chicago: University of Chicago Press.

Jezernik, Bozidar
1999 On Food and Morals in Extremis. *Food and Foodways* 8:1–32.

Jones, Harriet
1976 Synesthesia and its Role in Memory. Ph.D. Dissertation, Department of Psychology, University of Texas at Austin.

Kahn, Miriam
1994 *Always Hungry, Never Greedy: Food and the Expression of Gender in a Melanesian Society*. Prospect Heights, IL: Waveland Press.

Kalafatas, Michael
1998 The Bell Stone. *Brandeis Review* 18:20–27.

Kalcik, Susan
1984. Ethnic Foodways in America: Symbol and the Performance of Identity. In *Ethnic and Regional Foodways in the United States: The Performance of Group Identity*, ed. Linda Brown and Kay Mussell, pp. 37–65. Knoxville, TN: University of Tennessee Press.

Kapella, Themelina
1981 *Kalymnian Echoes*. Athens (in Greek).

Kapella, Themelina
    1987 *People and Things in Kalymnian Life.* "The Muses" literary publi-
    cation series #15. Athens (in Greek).
Kapsalis, Terri
    1997 Yiayia's Hands. In *Taste Nostalgia*, ed. Allen Weiss, pp. 27–32.
    New York: Lusitania Press.
Keller, Charles, and Janet Dixon Keller
    1996 *Cognition and Tool Use: The Blacksmith at Work.* Cambridge:
    Cambridge University Press.
    1999 Imagery in Cultural Tradition and Innovation. *Mind, Culture
    and Activity* 6:3–32.
Kelly, Traci Marie
    2001 "If I Were a Voodoo Priestess" Women's Culinary Autobio-
    graphies. In *Kitchen Culture in America: Popular Representations of
    Food, Gender and Race*, ed. Sherrie Inness, pp. 251–69. Philadelphia:
    University of Pennsylvania Press.
Kenna, Margaret
    1991 The Power of the Dead: Changes in the Construction and Care
    of Graves and Family Vaults on a Small Greek Island. *Journal of
    Mediterranean Studies* 1:101–19.
    1995 Saying 'No' in Greece: Some Preliminary Thoughts on Hospit-
    ality, Gender and the Evil Eye. In *Brothers and Others: Essays in
    Honour of John Peristiany*, ed. S. Damianakos *et al.*, pp. 133–46.
    Athens: EKKE.
    n.d. Why Does Incense Smell Religious? The Anthropology of Smell
    Meets Greek Orthodoxy. Manuscript. Department of Anthro-
    pology, University of Wales, Swansea.
Knight, John
    1998 Selling Mothers's Love? Mail Order Village Food in Japan. *Journal
    of Material Culture* 3:153–73.
Kolata, Alan
    1996 *The Valley of the Spirits: A Journey into the Lost Realm of the Aymara.*
    New York: John Wiley & Sons.
Kravva, Vasiliki
    2000 Food as a Vehicle for Remembering: The Case of Thessalonikan
    Jews. Paper Presented at the Oxford Symposium on Food and
    Cookery, St Anthony's College, 10 September.
Kremezi, Aglaia
    1999 *The Foods of Greece.* New York: Stewart, Tabori & Chang.
Kuchler, Susanne
    1987 Malangan: Art and Memory in a Melanesian Society. *Man*
    22:238–55.

1993 Landscape as Memory: The Mapping of Process and its Representation in Melanesian Society. In *Landscape: Politics and Perspectives*, ed. Barbara Bender, pp. 85–106. Oxford: Berg.

1999 The Place of Memory. In *The Art of Forgetting*, ed. Adrian Forty and Susanne Kuchler, pp. 53–72. Oxford: Berg.

Kugelmass, Jack

1990 Green Bagels: An Essay on Food, Nostalgia, and the Carnivalesque. *YIVO Annual* 19:57–80.

Kyriakidou-Nestoros, Alki

1975 *Folklore Studies*. Athens: Olkos (in Greek).

Lakoff, George, and Mark Johnson

1999 *Philosophy in the Flesh: The Embodied Mind and its Challenge to Western Thought*. New York: Basic Books.

Lambek, Michael

1998 The Past Imperfect: Remembering as Moral Practice. In *Tense Past: Cultural Essays in Trauma and Memory*, ed. Michael Lambek and Paul Antze, pp. 235–54. London: Routledge.

Lambek, Michael, and Paul Antze (eds)

1998 *Tense Past: Cultural Essays in Trauma and Memory*. London: Routledge.

Lang, George

1998 *Nobody Knows the Truffles I've Seen*. New York: Alfred A. Knopf.

Lave, Jean

1988 *Cognition in Practice: Mind, Mathematics and Culture in Everyday Life*. Cambridge: Cambridge University Press.

Lawless, Harry

1997 Olfactory Psychophysics. In *Tasting and Smelling*, ed. Gary Beauchamp and Linda Bartoshuk, pp. 125–174. San Diego: Academic Press.

Leach, Edmund

1965 *Political Systems of Highland Burma*. Boston: Beacon Press.

Leitch, Alison

2000 The Social Life of *Lardo*: Slow Food in Fast Times. *The Asia Pacific Journal of Anthropology* (formerly *Canberra Anthropology*) 1:103–18.

Lévi-Strauss, Claude

1970 *The Raw and the Cooked: Introduction to a Science of Mythology*. London: Jonathan Cape.

Leynse, Wendy

2000 "French" Food Versus "Malbouffe": Articulating National Identity in France. Paper Presented at the American Anthropological Association Meetings, San Francisco, 19 November.

Lluriá de O'Higgins, Maria Josefa
1994 *A Taste of Old Cuba: More Than 150 Recipes for Delicious Authentic and Traditional Dishes Highlighted with Reflections and Reminiscences*. New York: Harper Collins.

Long, Lucy (ed.)
1998 Special Issue: Culinary Tourism. *Southern Folklore* 53:179–252.

Lunt, P. K., and S. M. Livingstone
1992 *Mass Consumption and Personal Identity*. Buckingham: Open University Press.

Luria, A. R.
1968 *The Mind of a Mnemonist*. London: Avon.

Lust, Theresa
1998 *Pass the Polenta and Other Writings from the Kitchen, With Recipes*. South Royalton, VT: Steerforth Press.

MacClancy, Jeremy
1992 *Consuming Culture*. London: Chapmans.

McCorkle, Jill
1998 Her Chee-to Heart. In *We Are What We Ate: 24 Memories of Food*, ed. Mark Winegardner, pp. 146–55. San Diego: Harvest Original.

McGlone, Matthew
1996 Conceptual Metaphors and Figurative Language Interpretation: Food for Thought? *Journal of Memory and Language* 35:544–65.

McIntosh, William, and Mary Zey
1989 Women as Gatekeepers of Food Consumption: A Sociological Critique. *Food and Foodways* 3:317–32.

Magliocco, Sabina
1998 Playing with Food: The Negotiation of Identity in the Ethnic Display Event by Italian Americans in Clinton, Indiana. In *The Taste of American Place: A Reader on Regional and Ethnic Foods*, ed. Barbara Shortridge and James Shortridge, pp. 145–61. Lanham, MD: Rowman & Littlefield.

Marcus, Greil
1995 *The Dustbin of History*. Cambridge, MA: Harvard University Press.

Mars, Gerald, and Valerie Mars
2000 Food History and the Death of Memory. Paper Presented at the Oxford Symposium on Food and Cookery, St Anthony's College, 9 September.

Maschio, Thomas
1994 *To Remember the Faces of the Dead: The Plenitude of Memory in Southwestern New Britain*. Madison, WI: University of Wisconsin Press.

Mayol, Pierre
  1998 Bread and Wine. In *The Practice of Everyday Life, Volume 2: Living and Cooking*, ed. Luce Giard, in association with Michel de Certeau and Pierre Mayol, trans. Timothy J. Tomasik, pp. 85–100. Minneapolis: University of Minnesota Press.
Megas, George
  1982 [1963] *Greek Calendar Customs*. Athens: Rhodis.
Meigs, Anna
  1988 Food as a Cultural Construction. *Food and Foodways* 2:341–57.
  1992 Food Rules and the Traditional Sexual Ideology. In *Cooking, Eating, Thinking: Transformative Philosophies of Food*, ed. D. Curtin and L. Heldke, pp. 109–18. Bloomington: Indiana University Press.
Mennell, Stephen
  1995 *All Manners of Food*. Urbana, IL: University of Illinois Press.
  1996 Sociogenetic Connections Between Food and Timing. *Food and Foodways* 6:195–204.
Miller, Daniel
  1995 (ed.) *Acknowledging Consumption: A Review of New Studies*. London: Routledge.
  1998 *A Theory of Shopping*. Ithaca, NY: Cornell University Press.
Mintz, Sidney
  1979 Time, Sugar and Sweetness. *Marxist Perspectives* 2:56–73.
  1985 *Sweetness and Power: The Place of Sugar in Modern History*. New York: Penguin.
  1996 *Tasting Food, Tasting Freedom*. Boston: Beacon Press.
Moore, Judith
  1997 *Never Eat Your Heart Out*. New York: Farrar, Straus & Giroux.
Moran, Warren
  1993 Rural Space as Intellectual Property. *Political Geography* 12:263–77.
Morgan, Lewis Henry
  1950 [1876] *Montezuma's Dinner: An Essay on the Tribal Society of the North American Indians*. New York: New York Labor News Co.
Munn, Nancy
  1986 *The Fame of Gawa: A Symbolic Study of Value Transformation in a Massim (Papua New Guinea) Society*. Cambridge: Cambridge University Press.
Murcott, Anne
  1983 'It's a Pleasure to Cook for Him': Food, Mealtimes and Gender in Some South Wales Households. In Eva Garmarnikow *et al.* (eds), *The Public and the Private*, pp. 78–90. London: Heinemann.

Murcott, Anne
    1997 Family Meals – A Thing of the Past? In *Food, Health and Nutrition*, ed. Pat Caplan, pp. 32–49. London: Routledge.
Murphy, John
    1986 The Voice of Memory: History, Autobiography and Oral Memory. *Historical Studies* 22:157–75.
Narayan, Uma
    1995 Eating Cultures: Incorporation, Identity and Indian Food. *Social Identities* 1:63–86.
Nazarea, Virginia
    1998 *Cultural Memory and Biodiversity*. Tucson, AZ: University of Arizona Press.
Nelson, Michelle, and Jacqueline Hitchon
    1995 Theory of Synesthesia Applied to Persuasion in Print Advertising Headlines. *Journalism and Mass Communication Quarterly* 72:346–60.
Nora, Pierre
    1989 Between Memory and History: *Les Lieux de Mémoire*. *Representations* 26:7–25.
Nordstrom, Carolyn
    1995 War on the Front Lines. In *Fieldwork Under Fire*, ed. C. Nordstrom and A. Robben, pp. 129–53. Berkeley, CA: University of California Press.
Noyes, Dorothy, and Roger D. Abrahams
    1999 From Calendar Customs to National Memory: European Commonplaces. In *Cultural Memory and the Construction of Identity*, ed. Dan Ben-Amos and Liliane Weissberg, pp. 77–98. Detroit, MI: Wayne State University Press.
Obeyesekere, Gananath
    1995 Western Mythmaking in the Understanding of the Other. In *The Conditions of Reciprocal Understanding*, ed. James W. Fernandez and Milton B. Singer, pp. 165–89. Chicago: Center For International Studies.
Ohnuki-Tierney, Emiko
    1990 (ed.) *Culture Through Time: Anthropological Perspectives*. Stanford, CA: Stanford University Press.
    1992 *Rice as Self: Japanese Identities Through Time*. Princeton, NJ: Princeton University Press.
Ong, Walter
    1977 *Interfaces of the Word: Studies in the Evolution of Consciousness and Culture*. Ithaca, NY: Cornell University Press.

Orlove, Benjamin, and Arnold Bauer

1997 Giving Importance to Imports. In *The Allure of the Foreign*, ed. Benjamin Orlove and Arnold Bauer, pp. 1–29. Ann Arbor, MI: University of Michigan Press.

Ormondroyd, Joan

1997 A Beet Recipe. In *Through the Kitchen Window: Women Explore the Intimate Meanings of Food and Cooking*, ed. Arlene Voski Avakian, pp. 24–9. Boston: Beacon.

Osborne, Peter

1995 *The Politics of Time: Modernity and the Avant-Garde*. London: Verso.

Pallson, Gisli

1994 Enskillment at Sea. *Man* 29:901–27.

Palmer, Catherine

1998 From Theory to Practice: Experiencing the Nation in Everyday Life. *Journal of Material Culture* 3:175–99.

Panourgia, Neni

1995 *Fragments of Death, Fables of Identity: An Athenian Anthropography*. Madison, WI: University of Wisconsin Press.

Papanikolaos, Vasilios

1989 *O Ayios Savvas, O Neos, O En Kalymnou*. Kalymnos: Ieras Monis (in Greek).

Papanikolas, Helen

1987 *Amalia-Yeiorgos*. Salt Lake City: University of Utah Press.

Parkin, David

1992 Ritual as Spatial Direction and Bodily Division. In *Understanding Ritual*, ed. Daniel de Coppet, pp. 11–25. London: Routledge.

Parmentier, Richard

1987 *The Sacred Remains: Myth, History and Polity in Belau*. Chicago: University of Chicago Press.

Pavlides, Eleftherios, and Jana Hesser

1986 Women's Roles and House Form and Decoration in Eressos, Greece. In *Gender and Power in Rural Greece*, ed. Jill Dubisch, pp. 68–96. Princeton: Princeton University Press.

Pels, Peter

1998 The Spirit of Matter: On Fetish, Rarity, Fact, and Fancy. In *Border Fetishisms: Material Objects in Unstable Spaces*, ed. Patricia Spyer, pp. 91–121. London: Routledge.

Peterson, Yen, and Laura D. Birg

1988 Top Hat: The Chef as Creative Occupation. *Free Inquiry in Creative Sociology* 16:67–72.

Petridou, Elia
 2001 Milk Ties: A Commodity Chain Approach to Greek Culture. Doctoral Thesis, Department of Anthropology, University College, London.
 n.d. The Taste of Home. In *Home Possessions: Material Culture Behind Closed Doors*, ed. Daniel Miller. Oxford: Berg, forthcoming.
Pettis, Joyce
 1995 *Toward Wholeness in Paule Marshall's Fiction*. Charlottesville, VA: University of Virginia Press.
Pillsbury, Richard
 1998 *No Foreign Food: The American Diet in Time and Place*. Boulder, CO: Westview Press.
Proust, Marcel
 1982 *Remembrance of Things Past*, Vol. 1, trans. C. K. Scott Moncrieff and Terence Kilmartin. New York: Vintage.
Quigley, B. Allan
 1997 *Rethinking Literary Education*. San Francisco: Jossey-Bass.
Radcliffe-Brown, A. R.
 1948 [1922] *The Andaman Islanders*. Glencoe, IL: Free Press.
Rappaport, Joanne
 1994 *Cumbe Reborn*. Chicago: University of Chicago Press.
Rasmussen, Susan
 1996 Matters of Taste in Tuareg Society. *Journal of Anthropological Research* 52:61–83.
 1999 Making Better 'Scents' in Anthropology: Aroma in Tuareg Sociocultural Systems and the Shaping of Ethnography. *Anthropological Quarterly* 72:55–73.
Raspa, Richard
 1984 Exotic Foods among Italian-Americans in Mormon Utah: Food as Nostalgic Enactment of Identity. In *Ethnic and Regional Foodways in the United States: The Performance of Group Identity*, ed. Linda Brown and Kay Mussell, pp. 184–95. Knoxville, TN: University of Tennessee Press.
Rauch, Anthony
 1988 *Festa Italiana* in Hartford, Connecticut: The Pastries, the Pizza, and the People Who 'Parla Italiano.' In *'We Gather Together': Food and Festival in American Life*, ed. Theodore Humphrey and Lin Humphrey, pp. 205–217. Ann Arbor, MI: UMI Research Press.
Reichl, Ruth
 1998 *Tender at the Bone: Growing Up at the Table*. New York: Random House.

Renan, Ernest
  1994 [1882] What is a Nation? In *Nationalism,* ed. John Hutchinson and Anthony Smith, pp 17–18. Oxford: Oxford University Press.
Reyna, Stephen
  1997 Theory in Anthropology in the Nineties. *Cultural Dynamics* 9:325–50.
  n.d. Making Connections, Desire, Force and Hermeneutics in a New Social Anthropology. London: Routledge, forthcoming.
Richards, Audrey
  1939 *Land, Labor and Diet in Northern Rhodesia.* London: Oxford University Press.
Rosaldo, Renato
  1989 *Culture and Truth: The Remaking of Social Analysis.* Boston: Beacon.
Roseberry, William
  1996 The Rise of Yuppie Coffees and the Reimagination of Class in the United States. *American Anthropologist* 98:762–75.
Rosman, Abraham, and Paula Rubel
  1971 *Feasting With Mine Enemy: Rank and Exchange Among Northwest Coast Societies.* New York: Columbia University Press.
Rozin, Elizabeth, and Paul Rozin
  1981 Culinary Themes and Variations. *Natural History* 90:7–10.
Sacks, Oliver
  1995 The Landscape of His Dreams. In *An Anthropologist On Mars,* pp. 153–87. New York: Alfred A. Knopf.
Sahlins, Marshall
  1972 *Stone Age Economics.* Chicago: Aldine.
  1976 *Culture and Practical Reason.* Chicago: University of Chicago Press.
  1981 *Historical Metaphors and Mythical Realities: Structure in the Early History of the Sandwich Islands Kingdom.* Association for the Study of Anthropology in Oceania, Special Publication No. 1. Ann Arbor, MI: University of Michigan Press.
  1985 *Islands of History.* Chicago: University of Chicago Press.
Sartori, Allesandra
  2000 Cecina de Leon: Identity and Cultural Representation of a Spanish Traditional Food in a Global Economy. Paper Presented at the American Anthropological Association Meetings, San Francisco, 19 November.
St Paul's Greek Orthodox Cathedral
  1991 *The Complete Book of Greek Cooking.* New York: Harper Collins.

Schieffelin, Bambi
1990 *The Give and Take of Everyday Life: Language Socialization of Kaluli Children*. Cambridge: Cambridge University Press.

Schieffelin, Edward
1976 *The Sorrow of the Lonely and the Burning of the Dancers*. New York: St Martin's Press.

Schlanger, Nathan
1990 The Making of a Soufflé: Practical Knowledge and Social Senses. *Techniques et Culture* 15:29–52.

Scott, James
1998 *Seeing Like a State: How Certain Schemes to Improve the Human Condition Have Failed*. New Haven, CT: Yale University Press.

Sederocanellis, Ann
1995 *Spanning a Century: A Greek-American Odyssey*. New York: Vantage Press.

Seremetakis, C. N.
1991 *The Last Word: Women, Death and Divination in Inner Mani*. Chicago: University of Chicago Press.
1994 The Memory of the Senses: Pts. 1&2. In *The Senses Still: Perception and Memory as Material Culture in Modernity*, ed. C. N. Seremetakis, pp. 1–43. Boulder: Westview Press.

Shephard, Sue
2000 'A Slice of the Moon.' Paper Presented at the Oxford Symposium on Food and Cookery, St Anthony's College, 9 September.

Shiva, Vandana
1999 *Stolen Harvest: The Hijacking of the Global Food Supply*. Cambridge, MA: South End Press.

Shore, Brad
1996 *Culture in Mind*. Oxford: Oxford University Press.

Sperber, Dan
1975 *Rethinking Symbolism*. Cambridge: Cambridge University Press.

Stallybrass, Peter
1998 Marx's Coat. In *Border Fetishisms: Material Objects in Unstable Spaces*, ed. Patricia Spyer, pp. 183–207. London: Routledge.

Steinberg, Stephen
1998 Bubbie's Challah. In *Eating Culture*, ed. Ron Scapp and Brian Seitz, pp. 295–7. Albany, NY: SUNY Press.

Steingarten, Jeffrey
1997 *The Man Who Ate Everything; And Other Gastronomic Feats, Disputes and Pleasurable Pursuits*. New York: Vintage.

Stewart, Charles

1989 Hegemony or Rationality? The Position of the Supernatural in Modern Greece. *Journal of Modern Greek Studies* 7:77–104.

1997 Fields in Dreams: Anxiety, Experience, and the Limits of Social Constructionism in Modern Greek Dream Narratives. *American Ethnologist* 24:877–94.

Stocking, George (ed.)

1989 *Romantic Motives: Essays on Anthropological Sensibility*. Madison, WI: University of Wisconsin Press.

Stoler, Ann, and Karen Strassler

2000 Castings for the Colonial: Memory Work in 'New Order' Java. *Comparative Studies in Society and History* 42:4–48.

Stoller, Paul

1989 *The Taste of Ethnographic Things: The Senses in Anthropology*. Philadelphia: University of Pennsylvania Press.

1995 *Embodying Colonial Memories: Spirit Possession, Power and the Hauka in West Africa*. New York: Routledge.

Strathern, Andrew

1996 *Body Thoughts*. Ann Arbor, MI: University of Michigan Press.

Sultan, Nancy

1999 *Exile and the Poetics of Loss in the Greek Tradition*. Lanham, MD: Rowman & Littlefield.

Sutton, David

1997 The Vegetarian Anthropologist. *Anthropology Today* 13:5–8.

1998 *Memories Cast in Stone: The Relevance of the Past in Everyday Life*. Oxford: Berg.

Tannen, Deborah

1989 *Talking Voices: Repetition, Dialogue and Imagery in Conversational Discourse*. Cambridge: Cambridge University Press.

Taylor, Ann Christine

1993 Remembering to Forget: Identity, Memory, and Mourning among the Jivaro. *Man* 28:653–78.

Terdiman, Richard

1993 *Past Present: Modernity and the Memory Crisis*. Ithaca, NY: Cornell University Press.

Terrio, Susan

1996 Crafting *Grand Cru* Chocolates in Contemporary France. *American Anthropologist* 98:67–79.

Terrio, Susan

2000 *Crafting the Culture and History of French Chocolate*. Berkeley: University of California Press.

Theodossopoulos, Dimitrios
    1999 The Pace of the Work and the Logic of the Harvest: Women, Labour and the Olive Harvest in a Greek Island Community. *Journal of the Royal Anthropological Institute* (NS) 5:611–26.
Thomassen, Bjørn
    1996 Border Studies in Europe: Symbolic and Political Boundaries, Anthropological Perspectives. *Europaea* 2:37–48.
Thompson, Jan
    2000 Prisoners of the Rising Sun: Food Memories of American POWs in the Far East During WWII. Paper Presented at the Oxford Symposium on Food and Cookery, St Anthony's College, 10 September.
Tilley, Christopher
    1999 *Metaphor and Material Culture*. Oxford: Basil Blackwell.
Tomlinson, Graham
    1986 Thought for Food: A Study of Written Instructions. *Symbolic Interaction* 9:201–16.
Tonkin, Elizabeth
    1992 *Narrating Our Pasts: The Social Construction of Oral History*. Cambridge: Cambridge University Press.
Toren, Christina
    1993 Making History: The Significance of Childhood Cognition for a Comparative Anthropology of Mind. *Man* 28:461–78.
Tratsa, Maxi
    1998 The Memory of Taste: Review of Bozi, *Cappadokia, Ionia, Pontos: Tastes and Traditions*. *To Vima*, 19 April (in Greek).
Tropiano Tucci, Joan, and Gianni Scappin
    1999 *Cucina y Famiglia: Two Italian Families Share Their Stories, Recipes and Traditions*. New York: William Morrow.
Turner, James
    1984 "True Food" and First Fruits: Rituals of Increase in Fiji. *Ethnology* 23:133–42.
Turner, Terence
    1989 A Commentary. *Cultural Anthropology* 4:260–4.
Turner, Victor
    1969 *The Ritual Process: Structure and Anti-Structure*. Ithaca, NY: Cornell University Press.
Urban, Greg
    1991 *A Discourse-Centered Approach to Culture: Native South American Myths and Rituals*. Austin, TX: University of Texas Press.
    1994 Repetition and Cultural Replication: Three Examples From Shokleng. In *Repetition in Discourse: Interdisciplinary Perspectives*,

Volume Two, ed. Barbara Johnstone, pp 145–61. Norwood, NJ: Ablex Publishing Co.

Valeri, Renée
2000 Between Their Memories and Mine: Comfit Revisited. Paper Presented at the Oxford Symposium on Food and Cookery, St Anthony's College, 10 September.

Valeri, Valerio
1990 Constitutive History: Genealogy and Narrative in the Legitimation of Hawaiian Kingship. In *Culture Through Time: Anthropological Perspectives*, ed. E. Ohnuki-Tierney, pp. 154–92. Stanford, CA: Stanford University Press.

Verdery, Katherine
1999 *The Political Lives of Dead Bodies: Reburial and Postsocialist Change*. New York: Columbia University Press.

Visser, Margaret
1986 *Much Depends on Dinner: The Extraordinary History and Mythology, Allure and Obsessions, Perils and Taboos, of an Ordinary Meal*. New York: Grove Press.
1999 Food and Culture: Interconnections. *Social Research* 66:117–30.

Vroon, Piet
1997 *Smell, The Secret Seducer*, trans. Paul Vincent. New York: Farrar, Straus & Giroux.

Walker-Bynum, Caroline
1992 *Fragmentation and Redemption: Essays on Gender and the Human Body in Medieval Religion*. New York: Zone Books.

Warde, Alan
1997 *Consumption, Food and Taste: Culinary Antinomies and Commodity Culture*. London: Sage.

Ware, Fr. Kallistos
1979 *The Orthodox Way*. Crestwood, NY: St Vladimir's Seminary Press.

Watson, James (ed.)
1997 *Golden Arches East: McDonald's in East Asia*. Stanford, CA: Stanford University Press.

Weiner, Annette
1992 *Inalienable Possessions: The Paradox of Keeping-While-Giving*. Berkeley, CA: University of California Press.

Weismantel, Mary
1995 Making Kin: Kinship Theory and Zumbagua Adoptions. *American Ethnologist* 22:685–703.

West, Barbara
2000 "If there's sugar, flour and lard in the pantry then there's no problem" Food, nostalgic discourse, and the construction of

memory in postsocialist Hungary. Paper Presented at the Oxford Symposium on Food and Cookery, St Anthony's College, 10 September.

West, Michael Lee
1999 *Consuming Passions: A Food-Obsessed Life*. New York: Harper-Collins.

Whyte, William
1948 *Human Relations in the Restaurant Industry*. New York: McGraw Hill.

Wilk, Richard
1999 "Real Belizian Food": Building Local Identities in the Transnational Caribbean. *American Anthropologist* 101:244–55.

Williams, Brett
1984 Why Migrant Women Feed their Husbands Tamales: Foodways as a Basis for a Revisionist View of Tejano Family Life. In *Ethnic and Regional Foodways in the United States: The Performance of Group Identity*, ed. Linda Brown and Kay Mussell, pp. 113–26. Knoxville: Univ. of Tennessee Press.

Winegardner, Mark (ed.)
1997 *We Are What We Ate: 24 Memories of Food*. San Diego: Harvest Original.

Wogan, Peter
1998 Magical Literacy: Encountering a Witch's Book in Ecuador. *Anthropological Quarterly* 71:186–202.
n.d. *Imagined Communities* Reconsidered: Is Print Capitalism What We Think it is? *Anthropological Theory 1*: forthcoming.

Wogan, Peter, and David Sutton
2000 A Dinner He Can't Refuse: Food and Orality in *The Godfather, Part I*. Paper presented at the Southwestern Popular Culture Association meetings, Albuquerque, NM, 10 February.

Wood, Roy
1994 *The Sociology of the Meal*. Edinburgh: Edinburgh University Press.

Yarbrough, Steve
1998 Grandma's Table. In *We Are What We Ate: 24 Memories of Food*, ed. Mark Winegardner, pp. 205–20. San Diego: Harvest Original.

Yiakoumaki, Vassiliki
2000 On the Visibility of the Landscape of Ethnicity Through the Lens of the Cultural Politics of Food in Modern Greece. Paper Presented at the American Anthropological Association Meetings, San Francisco, November 19.

Young, Michael
  1971 *Fighting With Food*. Cambridge: Cambridge University Press.
Yue, Gang
  1999 *The Mouth That Begs: Hunger, Cannibalism and the Politics of Eating in Modern China*. Durham, NC: Duke University Press.
Zairi, Maria
  1989 The Kolliva. *Kalymnian Chronicles* 8:247–53 (in Greek).
Zinoviev, Sofka
  1991 Hunters and Hunted: *Kamaki* and the Ambiguities of Sexual Predation in a Greek Town. In *Contested Identities: Gender and Kinship in Modern Greece*, ed. Peter Loizos and Evthimios Papataksiarchis, pp. 203–20. Princeton, NJ: Princeton University Press.
Zonabend, Françoise
  1984 *The Enduring Memory: Time and History in a French Village*, trans. Anthony Foster. Manchester: Manchester University Press.

Author Index

Subject Index

The italicized *n* after a page number refers to a footnote on that page. Italicized page numbers refer to illustrations.